Ius Gentium: Comparative Perspectives on Law and Justice

Volume 134

Ius Gentium is a book series which discusses the central questions of law and justice from a comparative perspective. The books in this series collect the contrasting and overlapping perspectives of lawyers, judges, philosophers and scholars of law from the world's many different jurisdictions for the purposes of comparison, harmonisation, and the progressive development of law and legal institutions. Each volume makes a new comparative study of an important area of law. This book series continues the work of the well-known journal of the same name and provides the basis for a better understanding of all areas of legal science.

The *Ius Gentium* series provides a valuable resource for lawyers, judges, legislators, scholars, and both graduate students and researchers in globalisation, comparative law, legal theory and legal practice. The series has a special focus on the development of international legal standards and transnational legal cooperation.

Nuhu Yidana

Consumer Law and Policy on Faulty Goods

A Comparative Analysis of the Law in Ghana and the UK

Springer

Nuhu Yidana
College of Law
SOAS University of London
London, UK

ISSN 1534-6781 ISSN 2214-9902 (electronic)
Ius Gentium: Comparative Perspectives on Law and Justice
ISBN 978-3-032-08699-0 ISBN 978-3-032-08700-3 (eBook)
https://doi.org/10.1007/978-3-032-08700-3

This Springer imprint is published by the registered company Springer Nature Switzerland AG.
The registered company address is: Gewerbestrasse 11, 6330 Cham, Switzerland

I fully dedicate this book to my late parents—Alhaji Yakubu Tia (Kparipirana—Chief of Kparipiri) and Hajia Fati Yakubu.

Preface

In today's fast-paced world, the fabric of every known aspect of human life is continuously being reshaped by the growing forces of technology, including the production of a wide range of astonishing collections of goods that cater to the insatiable diverse needs of consumers around the globe. While the benefit of the overwhelming options of goods to consumers is far beyond any possible imagination, the obvious concern of consumers at the time of purchase of these goods is the certainty of the quality of the goods. This concern of consumers raises critical questions about the existing law's readiness to effectively guarantee consumers' right to receive goods of the right quality in their contractual agreements. Against this backdrop, this book evaluates the adequacy of the existing law for the protection of consumers when they are supplied faulty goods in Ghana. The analysis of the law in Ghana is compared with the law in England and Wales. Specifically, the analysis offers a comparative diagnosis of the requirements for the quality of goods with respect to the obligations of traders of goods, remedies for consumers, and mechanisms of redress in Ghana and the UK as influenced by EU law. The book first dissects the prevailing requirements of the law in Ghana and then examines the identified gaps in the light of the UK law whilst being mindful of the unique circumstances in the domestic setting in Ghana. The book first discovered that the existing law on the requirements for the quality obligations of traders of goods, remedies for consumers, and means of redress in Ghana are inadequate in affording consumers the needed protection when they are supplied with faulty goods. The comparative discussion further found that whereas the UK law and the reforms motivated by EU law contained important lessons from which Ghana could take guidance, some modifications of the relevant English laws are necessary to better reflect the domestic realities of consumer issues in Ghana. Drawing on the comparative analysis, this book proffers possible solutions and recommendations for legislative and judicial consideration in resolving the present deficiencies of the requirements for the quality of goods with respect to traders' obligations, remedies for consumers, and means of redress in Ghana. Overall, this book significantly provides a valuable contribution to the ongoing debate for the development of consumer law in developing countries such as Ghana, with a particular focus on the quality duties of traders, remedies for consumers, and mechanisms for the settlement of consumer disputes. The book highlights the shortfalls of the law and the measures countries like Ghana need to take to strengthen the law for the protection of consumers in Ghana.

London, UK Nuhu Yidana

Acknowledgements

With profound humility and gratitude, I give thanks to the Almighty Allah, the source of all possibilities. His divine grace, unceasing mercy, and sustaining power have carried me through every challenge triumphantly in the milestones of my academic journey. By His will, what once seemed unreachable has become reality.

This book is a revised and updated version of my doctoral thesis, which I submitted earlier to the University of Hull for my doctoral award. This book would not have been possible without the support, sacrifice, and encouragement of many.

I am particularly grateful to Dr Mike Varney and Diana Wallis, who stepped forward to supervise my doctoral thesis in my final year when my initial supervisors could no longer continue with me due to circumstances beyond their control. Their insightful feedback, clarity, wisdom, and belief in my work helped steer it to its full potential and made the transition to this published volume possible. To Professor Christian Twigg-Flesner and Professor Mike Whitehouse, I remain sincerely grateful for the solid intellectual foundation they helped nurture during the first three years of my doctoral studies. Their mentorship during the uncertain beginnings of my doctoral journey undoubtedly laid the groundwork for what eventually become this book.

I acknowledge with profound thanks to Ghana Education Trust Fund (GETFund), whose generous sponsorship allowed me to fully dedicate myself to my research and completed on record time. A special tribute goes to the Late Sir Dr. Edward N. Gyader, whose foresight and confidence in my proposal secured that vital support. May his legacy continue to inspire others as it has on me.

The revision of my doctoral thesis into the present book form took shape as part of my SOAS-sponsored research leave, for which I am immensely grateful to SOAS and the School of Law. My gratitude to all colleagues in the School of Law, SOAS University of London for their unwavering support and inspiration throughout this process. I especially thank my Head of Department for approving my sponsored research leave, which was crucial in allowing me to complete this book. I also thank Professor Emilia Onyema for her encouragement towards the publication of this work and Professor Egosa Ekhator of the University of Darby for consistently challenging and inspiring me to revise my thesis for publication. To all those who play diverse roles, I say thank you.

My debt of gratitude to Springer and the editorial team for their diligent follow-ups, encouragement, and patience throughout the revision process. Your dedication has been invaluable in bringing this book to completion.

Above all, my deepest thanks to my lovely wife (Samiratu Ahmed Wuni) and children (Sugru Mohammed-Mubarak, Unaamzuaya Haroon, Tipe-Awuni Aisha, Zilinsungu Ma'suum, and Naa-Silinsungu Yaqoub-Ali) for their understanding, patience, and enduring my insufficient attention during the time I dedicated to complete this book. Your love and support made this journey possible. My final debt of gratitude goes to my late parents, Alhaji Yakubu Tia (Kparipirana—Chief of Kparipiri) and Hajia Fati Yakubu, whose prayers, sacrifices, and enduring faith shaped my journey and made this work possible. May Almighty Allah grant you eternal rest in Jannatul Firdaus. This book is more than an academic milestone—it is a story of resilience, faith, and extraordinary power of belief. May it serve as a reminder that with purpose, support, and divine grace, no goal is beyond reach.

Competing Interests The author has no competing interests to declare that are relevant to the content of this manuscript.

Contents

Abbreviations

ADR	Alternative Dispute Resolution, Ghana
B2B	Business to Business Contracts
B2C	Business to Consumer Contracts
C2C	Consumer to Consumer Contracts
CEO	Chief Executive Officer
CJEU	Court of Justice of the European Union
CPA	Consumer Protection Authority, Ghana
CPP	Consumer Protection Policy, Ghana
CPR	Civil Procedure Rules, UK
CRA	Consumer Rights Act, UK
DRO	Dispute Resolution Ombudsman, UK
EU	European Union
FDA	Food and Drugs Authority, Ghana
FSO	Financial Service Ombudsman, UK
GDP	Gross Domestic Product
GSA	Ghana Standards Authority, Ghana
HPA	Hire-purchase Act/Decree, Ghana
MCOL	Money Claim Online, UK
NCCE	National Commission for Civic Education, Ghana
NRSC	National Road Safety Commission, Ghana
OS	Ombudsman Service, UK
SGA	Sale of Goods Act, Ghana and UK
SGSA	Supply of Goods and Services Act, UK
SSGA	Sale and Supply of Goods Act, UK
TFO	The Furniture Ombudsman, UK
UCTA	Unfair Contract Terms Act, UK
UK	United Kingdom

Chapter 1
Introduction

1.1 Introduction

Thanks to the rapid advancements in technology, businesses of all industries are now able to operate with unprecedented efficiency, and manufacturing is certainly no exception. The evolving technological innovations are continuously empowering manufacturers to optimise their production processes, innovate at an accelerated pace and deliver a wide range of consumer goods of varied descriptions. Given its outstanding versatility and user-friendliness, technology is now being widely implemented in various facets of manufacturing, making it a key driver in the industry's evolution. Undoubtedly, technology will continue to transform the manufacturing landscape in the foreseeable future. The unrelenting influence of technology in manufacturing has led to explosions of homogeneous consumer goods worldwide.[1] The growing phenomenon of homogeneity of consumer goods the world over continues to evolve at an overwhelming speed. The astonishing technology-oriented manufacturing, coupled with the rapid pace of globalisation, momentous trade liberalisation and the ever-increasing volume of international trade, have all contributed to an unprecedented proliferation of standardised consumer goods across the world.[2] This is further boosted by interconnected global supply chains spearheaded by multinational enterprises and the rise in e-commerce platforms ushering in distance selling across borders.[3] The increasing global character of standardised consumer goods has made it possible for consumers around the globe to have access to identical products[4] thereby transforming not only the way we live, work, and

[1] Herrero et al. (2023); Harbour and Koslove (2009).

[2] Tyson et al. (2023).

[3] UNCTAD (2019).

[4] Yidana (2023).

N. Yidana, *Consumer Law and Policy on Faulty Goods*, Ius Gentium: Comparative Perspectives on Law and Justice 134,
https://doi.org/10.1007/978-3-032-08700-3_1

interact with the world around us but also creating a convergence of what is consumed globally, especially in recent years.

As consumers around the world have access to and consume identical goods, it is undeniable that they may face uniform or common problems regarding the quality of their purchases. This unification of potential quality issues suggests that similar mechanisms should be implemented to safeguard consumers when they are supplied with goods that do not work. This is crucial to create a fair and just marketplace that benefits both consumers and businesses alike. The overwhelming need to have comparable laws for the protection of consumers of these identical goods in various jurisdictions is hugely emboldened by the growing prevalence of substandard goods with increasing potential for the supply of faulty goods to consumers in their contractual dispensation.[5] In 1985, the United Nations General Assembly recognised the challenges that consumers face by adopting the UN Guidelines for Consumer Protection, which have since been expanded and revised.[6] In particular, the United Nations (UN) Guidelines for Consumer Protection are broadly a valuable resource that can help in the formulation of national legislation, especially in developing countries, to ensure that consumers are protected and treated fairly, regardless of where they live.[7] Although the UN Guidelines encapsulate a broad array of consumer protection aspects, these include consumers' protection regarding the quality of goods they buy.

Despite the existence of the UN Guidelines for almost three decades, certain countries, Ghana included, have failed to enact legislation that integrates these guidelines for the safeguarding of their consumers.[8] This is in contrast to the

---

[5] Šostar and Oniku (2024); Gaikeviča (2022); Nottage and Paterson (2019); Chatterjee and Sahoo (2011); Donoghue and De Klerk (2009).

[6] Although the General Assembly first adopted the Guidelines in resolution 39/248 of 16 April 1985, they were later expanded by the Economic and Social Council in resolution 1999/7 of 26 July 1999 and have now been revised and adopted by the General Assembly in resolution 70/186 of 22 December 2015. It is instructive to mention that the UN Guidelines for Consumer Protection are the product of Consumer International's vigorous campaigns. The predecessor of Consumer International, formed in 1960 under the name 'International Organisation of Consumer Unions, ' spearheaded the campaign then. For details, see the United Nations guidelines for consumer protection, available online at <https://unctad.org/topic/competition-and-consumer-protection/un-guidelines-for-consumer-protection> accessed on 19/07/2025.; see also Harland (1987).

[7] On the heels of the UN Guidelines for Consumer Protection lies EU Directives on consumer protection which member countries implemented to boost their domestic laws for the protection of consumers. The European Union, for example, has been at the forefront with Directives on consumer protection initiatives to boost member countries' consumer protection laws. For instance, Council Directive 85/374/EEC of 25 July 1985 on the approximation of the laws, regulations and administrative provisions of the Member States concerning liability for defective products, as amended by Directive 99/34/EC; Directive 92/59/EEC of 29 June 1992 on general product safety as amended by DIRECTIVE 2001/95/EC OF THE EUROPEAN PARLIAMENT AND OF THE COUNCIL of 3 December 2001.

[8] Admittedly, there is presently an ongoing effort by the government to enact a law on consumer protection. It is hoped the arguments advanced in this book will greatly contribute to the formulation of a robust consumer protection law for the defence of consumer rights in Ghana.

numerous other countries that have been inspired by the UN Guidelines to formulate consumer laws for the protection of consumers. Consequently, consumers in Ghana are left with only the Sale of Goods Act 1962 and the Hire Purchase Act 1974, which are derived from the English Sale of Goods Act 1893, as their primary legal recourse for addressing concerns regarding the quality of goods they purchase. As the primary legislation predates the UN Guidelines, the crucial question is whether the existing law adequately provides for the protection of consumers when supplied with faulty goods.

The increasing urgency to address this crucial question is particularly amplified by the alarming reality that the Ghanaian market is not only inundated with technologically oriented standardised products, akin to many other countries, but also grappling with a substantial surge in the influx of substandard goods in the marketplace.

The burgeoning need to address this crucial question is particularly heightened, by the fact that the Ghanaian market is not only inundated with technology-oriented standardised products like many other jurisdictions but also faces a substantial influx of substandard goods in the marketplace.[9] In August 2018, for example, the Ghana Standards Authority discovered a staggering 197 substandard electrical materials out of a sample of 204 and a paltry 7 quality-compliant footwear out of 127 sampled in a market surveillance.[10] Considering the distressing statistics, the then Director General of the Ghana Standards Authority boldly characterised the overwhelming prevalence of substandard goods in the Ghanaian marketplace as a national crisis.[11] Evaluating the flood of substandard goods in the market space, Dowuona-Hammond rightly argues that the situation exposes Ghanaian consumers to poor-quality goods, among others.[12]

The major concern about the prevalence of substandard goods in the Ghanaian market is that every consumer is being exposed to buying them with potential breakdowns shortly after being put to use. It has especially been observed that 'dodgy products are like bad air; they affect everybody. Every bad product is like bad air; nobody can say they can escape from it ....'[13] So, in effect, every consumer in Ghana is a potential buyer of these substandard quality products, with the possibility that the goods will fail to function as required. This, therefore, raises critical questions of both academic and practical importance as to whether there is sufficient protection under the existing law in Ghana for consumers who are supplied with faulty goods. This is particularly in respect of whether there are: 1. adequate obligations placed on sellers to supply quality goods to consumers; 2. sufficient remedies for consumers who are supplied with faulty goods; and 3. effective means through

---

[9] Ghana Standards Authority (6th November 2018); Dodoo (2017); Gyimah (20th May 2010); See also, Aborchie-Nyahe (2014); Boateng (2014).

[10] Ghana Standards Authority (6th November 2018); Dodoo (6 November 2017); Ekuful (2018).

[11] Ghana Standards Authority (6th November 2018); Alhassan (25th October 2015).

[12] Dowuona-Hammond (2018); Yidana (2023); Yidana (2021).

[13] Prof. Alex Dodoo, the CEO of the GSA, bemoaned the canker of substandard goods in the Ghanaian market. For details, see Dodoo (2017).

which consumers may seek redress where the seller fails to remedy the faulty goods they are supplied.

The extent to which the prevailing obligations of sellers, remedies for consumers and means of redress are adequate to guarantee the protection of consumers when they are supplied with faulty goods in Ghana is presently uncertain. In particular, in her conference presentation on the state of consumer protection in Ghana, the Director of the Consumer Advocacy Centre and Government Consultant of the Ghana Consumer Protection Policy, Irene Aborchie-Nyahe, asserted that about 95% of respondents in a survey they conducted revealed that they had had problems with various goods they bought, but never took any action due to their lack of confidence in the regime.[14] This reinforces the uncertainty about the adequacy of the existing law for the protection of consumers in Ghana, with a particular focus on the trader's obligations, consumer remedies and redress mechanisms.

The present book, therefore, conducts a comprehensive analysis of the requirements for the quality of goods, remedies for consumers, and mechanisms for redress of disputes arising out of a seller's supply of goods which are not of the right quality under the law in Ghana. Given that the law in Ghana was inspired by the then English law, which has evolved over the years on account of its interaction with the European Union Law as a former member of the EU, it is significant to analyse the law in Ghana in comparison with the English law. In particular, it would be useful to help resolve any potential deficiencies in the law in Ghana. The book first dissects the prevailing requirements of the law in Ghana and then examines the identified gaps in the light of UK law and its EU experiences while being mindful of the unique circumstances in the domestic setting in Ghana as there is no 'one size fits all' solution to all problems.[15]

The book examines the current legal frameworks for consumer protection in Ghana, with a particular emphasis on the quality requirements of goods, remedies for consumers, and mechanisms of redress in Ghana. It highlights the gaps in the quality requirements for consumer protection in Ghana and compares them with those of the UK, which arguably has one of the most comprehensive consumer protection frameworks in the common law world.

Drawing on the comparative analysis of Ghana and the UK, the book proposes specific measures that Ghana can take to strengthen its consumer protection framework. These measures include both legislative intervention and judicial activism directed towards the protection of disadvantaged consumers. Overall, this book makes an important contribution to the ongoing debate and calls for the formulation of consumer-tailored legislation in Ghana. It highlights the need for a more comprehensive and proactive approach to consumer protection and provides valuable insights into how countries like Ghana can develop effective consumer frameworks that can adequately safeguard the rights of consumers in Ghana.

---

[14] Aborchie-Nyahe (2014), p. 12.

[15] See the underlining rationale for the need to draw guidance from existing solutions to similar problems from other jurisdictions under the 'the rationale for use of English law for the comparative analysis' later in this Chapter below (para 1.4).

Before the substantive analysis of the law in Ghana and the UK in the later part of this book, it is imperative to provide an outline of the specific laws that are central to the present analysis under both jurisdictions. This is out below.

1.2 Brief Overview of the Requirements of the Law in Ghana and the UK

As noted above, the central focus of this book is to examine the adequacy of the requirements for the quality of goods, associated remedies for consumers and the means of enforcement of consumer rights in Ghana. As also pointed out, the analysis will be carried out in light of English law for possible guidance in resolving any concerns that arise in the Ghanaian regime. This subsection, therefore, provides a brief background to the prevailing system with a focus on the tripartite requirements for the quality of goods, consumer remedies, and mechanisms of redress for consumers in both regimes.

Specifically, the requirements for the quality of goods and associated remedies in Ghana are contained under the Sale of Goods Act (SGA)[16] and the Hire Purchase Decree (HPA).[17] These requirements are mainly a legacy of the 19th-century English Sale of Goods Act 1893. This was the result of Ghana being a former colony of the British, with the English law having equal force in Ghana as in the UK at that time.[18] Following independence, however, Ghana took steps to develop its domestic laws, which included the 1962 SGA, under which the present requirements for the quality of goods (with some modifications)[19] and remedies for consumers are based.[20] It is important to note that the SGA, 1962, initially regulated both contracts of sale and hire purchase as well as conditional sales transactions. However, in 1974, hire purchase and conditional sales agreements were detached from the Sale of Goods Act.[21]

---

[16] Sale of Goods Act 1962 [Act 137] section 13.

[17] Hire-purchase Decree 1974 [NRCD 292] Sections 13 and 14.

[18] It is worth stating that from 1876 to 1957, the English common law, the doctrines of equity and the statutes of general application as the system of laws in Britain equally had similar force of law in Ghana (formerly, the Gold Coast colony) then. It is also important to state that the Gold Coast at the beginning was made up of the coastal areas of the present day Ghana and Lagos - part of the present day Nigeria. This was subsequently expended to include the Ashanti protectorate (1902) and the British Togoland (the northern territories) in 1916/22 and were later merged to the Gold Coast before independence in 1957. For details, see Amissah (1976). [1–31].

[19] The standard term for the quality of goods was especially modified from the then English law principle of merchantable quality to 'free from defects which are not declared'—section 13 (1) (a) of the Sale of Goods Act 1962, Act 137.

[20] This remained 'the main source of our law as far as contracts for Sale of Goods are concerned ….', The Supreme Court in *Andreas Bschor GMBH & Co. KG v. 1.Birim Wood Complex Ltd & 2. Birim Timbers Ltd*, [2015] SC (CA) No. J4/9/2015, [4].

[21] The Ghana Law Commission had found that the fusion of the hire purchase and conditional sales arrangement with the sale of goods law were engendering difficulties in terms of key definitional

The current requirements for the quality of goods and remedies for consumers are therefore expressed in both the SGA and the HPA.

In terms of enforcement, the main route is the court where the practices and procedures are similarly drawn from the foundations of the English law judicial practices and procedures. The required procedures for a case to be brought before a court of law in Ghana are found under the District Court Rules[22] and High Court (Civil Procedure) Rules.[23] There are also Alternative Dispute Resolution (ADR) mechanisms through which the courts may refer a matter which has been filed before them to have the matter determined without it going through the court trial process.[24]

It is important to state that the present regime, as indicated above, governs matters of consumer and non-consumer nature. However, following years of campaigns for a more tailored regime to be introduced to specifically deal with consumer matters, the Government of Ghana adopted a Consumer Protection Policy in 2014.[25] The adopted policy is currently being drafted into a bill for legislative consideration.[26]

In the case of the UK, the requirements for the quality of goods and remedies for consumer were initially drawn from the general Sale of Goods Act 1893[27] which itself was a codification of the common law authorities on the implied quality and fitness doctrines.[28] The requirements were, however, amended first in 1973 and consolidated as the Sale of Goods Act 1979 in respect of contract of sales.[29] This was

issues as reported in the attached Memorandum to the Hire Purchase Decree 1974, NRCD 292.

[22] (2009) C.I. 59.

[23] (2004) C.I. 47.

[24] Section 72 of the Courts Act 1993, Act 459 and Order 58 of the High Court (Civil Procedure) Rules 2004 requires the Courts to encourage parties to have their disputes resolved through negotiated settlement and mediation. This has been enhanced by the Judiciary's adoption of a Court-connected ADR Manual in 2010 that mainly echoed the need for Courts to first require parties in civil disputes to have their matter resolved through ADR processes with only room for litigation where this fails to resolve the dispute.

[25] , The Ministry of Trade and Industry, Draft Consumer Protection Policy, (2014), The Government of Ghana; See also, GNA, Cabinet Approves Law on Consumer Protection (undated), available online at http://ghana.gov.gh/index.php/media-center/news/233-cabinet-passes-law-on-consumer-protection, last accessed on 15/06/2025.

[26] Follow-ups to the Legal Drafting Department of the Ministry of Justice and Attorney General reveals that the adopted Policy Document is still in the drafting process and not yet available for public consumption as at 12/06/2025.

[27] Section 14 and 53, the Sale of Goods Act, 1893.

[28] This has been made clear per Lord Morris of Borth-y-Gest in *Henry Kendall & Sons (a firm) v. William Lillico & Sons Ltd and Others* [1969] 2 AC 31, 91H; per Lord Diplock in *Ashington Piggeries Ltd and Another v Christopher Hill Ltd* [1972] AC 441, 501; Lord Justice Rimer in *BSS Group Plc v Makers (UK) Limited (t/a Allied Services)* [2011] EWCA Civ 809; [2011] WLR 2747641; See also, Bridge (2017), para. 11-046; Twigg-Flesner et al. (2016), p6; See also, Howells and Weatherill (2005), p168; Bradgate and Twigg-Flesner (2003), p. 46.

[29] Section 14, Sale and Supply of Goods Act 1994, c. 35 amending subsection 2, Sale of Goods Act, 1979, c. 54.

subsequently amended in 1994.[30] The requirements under the SGA 1979 were again amended with the UK implementation of the EU Sales Directive in 2002.[31] It is important, however, to note that the 1973 Act was still the applicable law in relation to hire purchase contracts.[32] Moreover, the quality requirements for contracts of hire and other supply transactions in matters of consumer sales were governed by the SGSA 1982.[33] The overall provisions of the 1973, 1979 (as amended) and 1982 Acts, as stated above, are now expressed under the Consumer Rights Act 2015, albeit with some modifications mainly governing consumer-trader relationships.[34]

In terms of seeking redress under English law, the traditional civil court system has been the main mechanism through which a consumer may bring an action for the redress of a consumer dispute since the emergence of consumer claims. In particular, a claim may first be made at the County Court with leave to appeal to the High Court and then to the Court of Appeal and finally to the Supreme Court. In 1973, however, the County Court small claims scheme was established to handle small claims, including consumer disputes.[35] This was later revised first, in 1981 and 1991 with further reforms in response to the 1996 Woolf Report.[36] The present required procedure is contained under Part 27 of the Civil Procedure Rules (CPR) where consumer claims which are not more than £10,000 are allocated to the Small Claims Track of the County Court.[37] This can be made online in case of a claim for a fixed sum.[38] In addition to the use of the small claims track, Ombudsmen services also exist in various sectors through which a consumer may file a complaint to obtain an impartial redress on a dispute. These are voluntary initiatives by trade associations that seek to impartially resolve conflicts between their members and consumers. In 2015, the UK introduced Alternative Dispute Resolution for Consumer Disputes[39] implementing the EU Directive on ADR for Consumer

[30] Section 14, Sale and Supply of Goods Act, 1994, c. 35 amending subsection 2, Sale of Goods Act, 1979, c. 54.

[31] The Sale and Supply of Goods to Consumers Regulation 2002 implemented the EC Directive 1999/44/EC on Certain Aspect of the Sale of Consumer Goods and Associated Guarantees, (25th May, 1999), The European Parliament and of the Council into Section 14 and Part 5 of the Sale of Goods Act, 1979.

[32] Section 10, Supply of Goods (Implied Terms) Act 1973, c. 13.

[33] Sections 4 and 9, Supply of Goods and Services Act 1982, c. 29.

[34] This is clearly specified under the Explanatory Notes to the CRA, 2015, Note 24 under the title, 'Impact on Existing Legislation', at p7; See also, Barry et al. (2016)., para. 3.07.

[35] Bridge (2017), para. 14-250.

[36] Bridge (2017), para. 14-250.

[37] The applicable procedure under the small claims track is contained in Part 27, Civil Procedure Rules, available online at https://www.justice.gov.uk/courts/procedure-rules/civil/rules/part27 accessed on 15/05/2025.

[38] This is available online at https://www.gov.uk/make-court-claim-for-money accessed on 15/05/2025.

[39] Regulations 2015 S.I. 2015/542.

Disputes.[40] The ADR Regulations reinforces the operation of the Ombudsmen services by requiring traders to inform consumers about the Ombudsman services through which they may seek redress regarding a dispute the trader is unable to resolve internally.[41] The 2015 ADR Regulation further requires the establishment of Ombudsmen services in sectors where there are none for the purpose of dealing with consumer disputes. Under the English law, consumers may also be able to seek free legal advice on a matter of dispute from the Citizens Advice Bureau and Law Centres to empower him to be able to make a decision regarding the matter.

In summary, it can be seen that the regime in Ghana on the requirements for the quality of goods, associated remedies, and means of redress largely draws upon the then English law driven by the colonial ties albeit with some modifications since the 1962 SGA and the 1974 HPA. Similarly, English law has had the benefit of a series of reforms over the years, mainly responding to shortfalls that are found to beset the law, evidenced in reported reviews of the prevailing law predating each given reform[42] or the UK implementation of its EU obligations.[43] It is worth noting that if the present effort to leave the EU materialises, the UK will have no obligation to implement subsequent EU Law. However, the UK will continue to apply the inherited EU laws and the courts may still follow the CJEU in respect of decisions on laws the UK has inherited until parliament decides otherwise.[44]

For the present purpose, however, the main question, as noted earlier, is, can the present regime in Ghana afford consumers adequate protection when they are supplied with faulty goods? In the same vein, to what extent can the English regime, which is a hybrid of its response to domestic concerns and implementation of its EU obligations, provide measures that can assist in resolving possible defects of the law

[40] Directive 2013/11/EU on Alternative Dispute Resolution for Consumer Disputes implemented by the UK through the Alternative Dispute Resolution for Consumer Disputes (Competent Authorities and Information) Regulations 2015 S.I. 2015/542.

[41] Regulation 19 of the Alternative Dispute Resolution for Consumer Disputes (Competent Authorities and Information) Regulations 2015 S.I. 2015/542 implementing Directive 2013/11/EU on Alternative Dispute Resolution for Consumer Disputes.

[42] Howells and Twigg-Flesner (2010); See also, The Law Commission, Consumer Remedies for Faulty Goods, (2009), the Law Com No 317 and SCOT Law Com No 216; The Davidson Review, Implementation of EU Legislation (2006), Davidson Review Final Report; The Law Commission, Sale and Supply of Goods, (1987), Law Com No. 160; The Law Commission, Consultation Memorandum No. 58, Sale and Supply of Goods, (1983), Working Paper No. 85 and The Scot Law Com; The Law Commission, Implied Terms in Contracts for the Supply of Goods, (1979), the Law Com. No. 95; The Law Commission, Exemption Clauses in Contract, First Report Amendments to the Sale of Goods Act 1893, (1969), Law Com. No. 24, Scott. Law Com. No. 12.

[43] The Sale and Supply of Goods to Consumers Regulations 2002 implementing DIRECTIVE 1999/44/EC of the European Parliament and of The Council of 25 May 1999 on certain aspects of the sale of consumer goods and associated guarantees; see also, The Alternative Dispute Resolution for Consumer Disputes Regulations 2015, Regulations 2015 S.I. 2015/542 implementing Council Directive 2013/11/EU of the European Parliament and of the Council of 21 May 2013 on Alternative Dispute Resolution for Consumer Disputes and amending Regulation (EC) No 2006/2004 and Directive 2009/22/EC.

[44] See, the UK, EU (Withdrawal) Act 2018, s 6(2).

in Ghana while bearing in mind the peculiar local circumstances in Ghana? These are the main critical questions this book seeks to address, which are further divided into manageable questions below.

1.2.1 Research Questions

In light of the above, the book addresses the following six research questions as follows:

1. To what extent can the current requirements for the quality obligations of traders of goods afford consumers a sufficient degree of protection with respect to faulty goods in Ghana?
2. To what extent can the English law and its EU experiences with respect to the requirements for the quality obligations of traders of goods assist in resolving any identified deficiencies in the regime in Ghana within the domestic context?
3. Does the present regime provide sufficient remedies for consumers when they are supplied with faulty goods?
4. Will the English law and its EU-motivated remedies for faulty goods be useful in contributing towards addressing limitations of the law in Ghana, taking the local circumstances into account?
5. Are the prevailing mechanisms for the redress of disputes adequate and suitable for the enforcement of consumer rights in Ghana?
6. To what degree can the English law and its EU experience regarding the approach to the enforcement of consumer rights be helpful in assisting to address shortfalls of the redress schemes in Ghana, taking into consideration the domestic circumstances?

1.3 Contribution of the Book

The book holds much value to the projection of consumer goals in Ghana in several respects. First, a limited body of research has been conducted broadly in the field of consumer protection in Ghana.[45] The limited body of literature has largely focused only on the broad need for a comprehensive consumer protection regime in Ghana. Divergent reasons, some of which have outlived their usefulness, informed calls for

[45] Ansa-Asare (1980); Ansa-Asare (1981); Dowuona-Hammond (1995); Dowuona-Hammond and Atuguba (2006); Dowuona-Hammond (2007), p. 337; Aborchie-Nyanahene et al. (2014); Nkansah (2015); Dowuona-Hammond (2018); Yidana (2020); Yidana (2021, 2023, 2024).

a comprehensive consumer protection regime.[46] Whilst the studies have done a great deal to canvass for the need to devise increased measures for the protection of consumers, they have not specifically dealt with the key issues addressed in this book. In particular, none of the studies is known to have exclusively been devoted to measuring the adequacy and appropriateness of the quality requirements of goods, the associated remedies, and redress mechanisms in Ghana.

It is fair, however, to indicate that some of the commentators have briefly mentioned the seller's obligation regarding quality products. Nevertheless, the various passing comments do not sufficiently address the substantive issues that affect consumers regarding the growing concerns about the quality of goods in the Ghanaian market. The issues of the quality requirements of goods, associated remedies, and redress mechanisms are undoubtedly important as they have, over the years, most especially in recent times, been at the centre stage of many seller-consumer disputes in Ghana.[47] Unfortunately, the unresolved questions surrounding the requirements of the quality obligations of traders, associated remedies, and means of redress have not been addressed. This clearly is not helpful to the cause of consumers in Ghana. The present book, therefore, contributes to filling this gap. This book first identifies the various loopholes and then searched for potential remedies that will fit the pitfalls from a comparative angle.

The second most significant potential value of this book is the possible opportunity for the results to be incorporated into the framing of the comprehensive regime to safeguard consumers in Ghana. As noted earlier, the government is presently taking steps, as evidenced in the cabinet's approval of a policy document, for the protection of consumers in Ghana.[48] This essentially renders this book timely for its findings will be a useful reference material to key stakeholders who will help shape the frame of the law. In particular, it will be a useful document to lawmakers, consumer consultants, and policy activists among others, in dictating the outcome of the law on consumer protection in Ghana.

The book will equally be valuable in providing useful guidance in the determination of matters relating to the quality requirements of goods, the associated consumer remedies, and redress mechanisms. In particular, the results of this study will possibly be a reference document for the courts on matters that are put before them especially if the recommendations of this book are implemented in the planned consumer protection law Ghana is seeking to formulate.

---

[46] In the specific case of the works of Kwaku Ansa-Asare, the main challenge at the time was the shortage of consumer goods. This brought about traders hoarding goods and only selling to consumers who were prepared to pay higher prices. This mainly constituted the central basis of his thesis, calling for a comprehensive consumer protection regime that would confer more effective rights to purchasers. This basis has outlived its usefulness in contemporary times demonstrated by the massive influx of varied kinds of goods into the country.

[47] *Rockson v Armah* (1975) 2 GLR 116 p119; *Yirenkyi v Tormekpey* (1987-88) 1 GLR 533; *G. A. Sarpong & Co. v Silver Star Auto Ltd* (2010) HCGLR; *Continental Plastics Engineering Co. Ltd. v IMC Industries – Technik GMBH* (2009) SCGLR 298; *Georgia Hotel Ltd v Silver Star* (2012) 2 SCGLR.

[48] Ministry of Trade and Industry, 'Draft Consumer Protection Policy' (2014).

In addition, the main object of this research, as already mentioned, is to contribute towards enhancing the requirements of the law with respect to the quality of goods, remedies for consumers and means of redress to better afford consumers with more effective protection in matters of faulty goods in Ghana. The results of this research would actively support key stakeholders in their educational campaign effort to champion consumer goals in Ghana. In particular, consumer activists, consumer lawyers and their clients would find useful guidance from the outcome of this book. Moreover, the research findings would sensitise and create increased awareness regarding the clarity of the various issues with respect to the requirements for the quality of goods, related remedies, and means of redress, especially if the results of this book are implemented by the legislature and the judiciary respectively.

More so, as noted previously, there is presently a dearth of academic literature on consumer law in Ghana. This book would, therefore, bolster the literature on consumer law in Ghana. The book would add to the body of reference materials on the subject, which would inform the direction of future research and development of consumer law in Ghana. In sum, this book would be valuable material that would help in shaping the agenda of consumer law development in Ghana on account of the itemised contributions.

1.4 Rationale for the Use of English Law for the Comparative Analysis

The premise of this book, as clearly indicated earlier, is rooted in the argument that the adequacy of the present law in Ghana to sufficiently afford consumers the required protection when supplied with faulty goods is uncertain. The central task of this book is, therefore, to ascertain the degree of protection available with a particular focus on aspects that need enhancement to effectively afford consumers the needed protection when supplied with faulty goods by traders. The analysis of law in Ghana (which will be carried out in Chaps. 2, 4 and 6) will be directed at discovering the exact limitations of the present law in Ghana. The various identified deficiencies under the law in Ghana will then be subjected to comparative analysis with the English law and its EU experience respectively (in Chaps. 3, 5 and 7). The discussion will essentially focus on identifying viable solutions to the shortfalls of the law in Ghana whilst being mindful of circumstances in the domestic setting in Ghana to guarantee effective reform outcomes. There is, therefore, the need to clearly provide highlights of the underlying justification for the use of English law for the comparative analysis in this book, as earlier noted.

To start with, it is important to first note that it might be argued that the choice of the regime to be compared with should be one that expresses similar socio-economic and cultural conditions as the domestic regime in Ghana so as to produce useful results. While admitting that such an ideal regime will surely make a meaningful comparison, it undoubtedly remains the case that the range of socio-economic and cultural factors across countries of the world differ so much that it is practically very rare to find such commonalities. Moreover, it is a common practice for inspirational guidance to be drawn from foreign jurisdictions in the framing of domestic response to problems of a common kind although the societies may have no connection in terms of socio-economic and cultural relations.[49] What is required is to better appreciate the existing distinctions and advance the relevant argument for the comparison which itself must be useful as a starting point.[50] It has therefore been advised further that recourse to foreign law for inspiration should be based on pragmatism, relevance, accessibility, affinity among others, instead of random selection of the regime(s) simply to bolster narrow or personal views.[51] In effect whilst the choice of the regime for the comparative discourse is not premised on the similarities of socio-economic and cultural conditions which are rare to find as noted above, it will nevertheless be based on pragmatic considerations, relevance, accessibility and affinity. As will be shown clearly below, the English regime and its EU experience satisfies all these criteria.

It has been suggested that the choice of a legal system for the purposes of comparison is basically dependent on the specific research questions that the researcher seeks to address in the comparative study.[52] Taking into consideration the research questions as set out earlier, the English law and its EU experience is chosen for the comparative discourse as stated above. The choice of a regime(s) for comparative analysis is expected to always be justifiably backed by a rationale underlying its suitability in order to reflect the acceptable practice from the point of view of legal scholarship.[53]

In line with the above observation, the first premise that accounts for the selection of the English law is grounded on its response to similar problems presently confronting consumers in Ghana. As indicated above, the substantive object of the book is to address questions about the adequacy of the quality obligations of traders of goods, consumer remedies and redress mechanisms under the regime to afford effective protection to consumers in matters of faulty goods. These are matters the English law has dealt with.[54] As noted above, it is a settled practice within the domain of comparative law to have recourse to foreign regimes that resolve similar problems confronting the domestic regime for guidance towards addressing the local problems.[55] In particular, it has been noted that: 'legal systems are compared by considering their various judicial responses to similar situations.'[56] Goode *et' al*

---

[49] Watson (2001), p. 4.

[50] Smits (2012), p. 170.

[51] Markesinis and Fedtke (2012), p. 167; See also, Hoecke (2015).

[52] Orucu (2006), p. 442; Hoecke (2015), p. 1.

[53] Hoecke (2015), p. 1; Jansen (2006), p. 306.

[54] See a brief outline of the present English regime earlier in para. 1.2. The detailed analysis will be carried out in Chaps. 3, 5 and 7 of this book.

[55] For further supporters of this scholarship, see Smits (2006), p. 514; Zweigert and Kötz (1998), p. 46; Koopmans (1996).

[56] Michaels (2006), p. 340.

further stressed that: 'if other jurisdictions have found better solutions to a common problem … then why not adopt them' in resolving matters of a similar nature.[57] The adoption of foreign solutions to commonly shared problems in a domestic setting will nevertheless need to be evaluated carefully within the local context so as not to allow intellectual curiosity to lead to imitation that circumvents the normative harmony of the local law.[58] The choice of the English law for the comparison will therefore enable Ghana to draw possible guidance from its found solutions to resolve the deficiencies of the regime in Ghana.

The second underlying reason for the choice of the English law for the comparison is premised on the basis that the regime on the quality requirements of goods, associated remedies, and redress mechanisms in Ghana historically has a shared relationship with the English law prior to many of its recent reforms engineered by its EU influence.[59] The reforms of the quality requirements, remedies and redress mechanisms of the English law over the years seems to respond to many of the shortfalls of its earlier regime on which basis the regime in Ghana was formulated with minor modifications as noted earlier.[60] In seeking to resolve similar limitations of the law in Ghana of which the English law has taken the lead, it is appropriate to examine the solutions devised by the English law especially within the context of Ghana to ascertain whether or not those solutions will be suitable to fill the gaps in Ghana. Watson particularly made the observation that historical ties and habits of legal thoughts constitute an important starting point for a useful comparison that could possibly resolve problems in a domestic regime.[61] Recourse to legal families with shared roots has also been observed to have the tendency of offering the best fit solutions to the domestic concerns.[62] Smits has similarly contended that 'a common legal history is *a* very helpful' basis upon which comparison could be made in seeking solutions to domestic problems.[63] Moreover, it has further been stressed that in dealing with a subject matter which is commonly shared with another country, it is that country that should be the first port of call for the purpose of comparison under normal conditions, with very rare 'need to go outside this "closed" circle of systems'.[64] Using the historical heritage as the basis for the comparison has also been observed as offering a viable setting for a meaningful comparison to easily triumph.[65] The commonalities Ghana shared with the English law therefore makes the choice of the English law a good option for the comparative discourse.

---

[57] Goode et al. (2015), para. 4.29, p. 128.

[58] Barak (2005), pp. 169–170; Goode et al. (2015), para.4.27, pp. 127–128.

[59] See the brief outline earlier at para. 1.2. The rest of the book will engage the detailed discussions.

[60] See 'Brief review of the requirements of the law in Ghana and the UK' at para. 2.1 earlier in this Chapter.

[61] Watson (1993).

[62] Du Plessis (2006), p. 478; Bell (2006), p. 1261.

[63] Smits (2006), p. 514, emphasis added.

[64] Markesinis and Fedtke (2012), p. 167.

[65] Markesinis and Fedtke (2012), p. 167; Watson (1993).

The next important rationale for the selection of English law for the comparative discussion rests on English law being one of the leading well-matured regimes and equally having a widely rich pool of academic commentary from which Ghana could benefit on account of the comparison. Moreover, the present English regime has also implemented the EU Directives on the various aspects of consumer sales, as noted previously, which Ghana could draw from in the conduct of this comparative analysis. Recourse to particular jurisdiction for a comparative study on the basis of the regime's settled maturity and the broad availability of literature has been highly encouraged by leading commentators in comparative law. For example, Watson has observed that a legal 'system may be chosen because of the general respect in which it is held'.[66] It has also been submitted that a comparison with a more experienced regime could likely be efficient in helping to address domestic problems much easier and should not be sidestepped.[67] It has similarly been contended that 'the richness or maturity of a legal system and its related literature' is a favourable determinant in the selection of a particular regime for comparison.[68] This underlines one of the reasons why the English regime is predominantly the right choice in the limelight for the comparative discourse.

Other considerations which do not warrant detailed consideration are the fact that both regimes use the English language as the official medium of expression and are from the same legal family of common law. These factors are highlighted by leading comparatists as a basis upon which comparison could be carried out.[69] The knowledge of the language of the legal system being studied is particularly seen to be a significant and crucial entry into the universe of thought and world vision of the foreign regime. The language ability is especially argued to enhance the imaginative capacities of the legal comparatists to better understand the respective regimes' differences and equivalences and 'the likelihood that newness and difference will have unexpected locations and provenance in another system.'[70] Moreover, drawing from the same legal family consequently makes the comparative engagement quite easy in most instances on account of familiarity with the concepts in both regimes that are being compared.[71] The commonalities of language and legal systems are not, therefore, excluded as added benefits to the use of English law for the comparison in this book.

Another important rationale in favour of the English regime as the appropriate choice for the comparative analysis lies in the persuasive impact of its judicial decisions on the courts in Ghana. Essentially, the courts in Ghana, in most instances, rely on the judicial authorities of the English courts for persuasive purposes in the

---

[66] Watson (1993), p. 98.

[67] Smits (2006), p. 514.

[68] Markesinis and Fedtke (2012), p. 167.

[69] Hoecke (2015), p. 1; Goode (2015), para. 4.63, p. 153; Curran (2006), p. 676; Bell (2006), p. 1261.

[70] Curran (2006).

[71] Hoecke (2015), p. 1; Bell (2006), p. 1261.

determination of many cases that are placed before them and that the law in Ghana has not fully been developed to tackle. For instance, the Supreme Court in Ghana recently observed that: 'in considering our judgment, we did not come across a Ghanaian case in which the provision was construed, so we shall consider some English authorities for their persuasive effect.'[72] Moreover, lawyers most often rely on English law authorities to advance their arguments before the courts in Ghana with the hope of persuading the courts to draw guidance from the authorities in making determinations in their favour.[73] The existing favourable use of English jurisprudence for persuasive effect by actors in the legal field places English law on a good pedestal for a meaningful outcome that may easily influence the needed reform in Ghana. It has particularly been observed that recourse to a chosen regime will likely produce useful comparative dividends where legal actors in the domestic regime already have an active interest in resorting to the regime for persuasion.[74] This is because the yielded results could easily receive a strong push essentially from the legal actors and the ruling elite.[75] This, therefore, underscores the practical utility of using the English jurisdiction for the comparative analysis.

It is anticipated that the English regime and its EU experience will provide very crucial guidance in finding answers to the research questions. This will form useful grounds for this book to put forward recommendations for legislative consideration in Ghana, as previously underscored.

1.5 The Scope and Limitations of the Book

The main focus of the study is to evaluate the adequacy of the present regime with respect to the requirements for the quality of goods, associated remedies, and means of redress for the protection of consumers in Ghana. The principal agenda is to identify possible inadequacies of the requirements of the law, which might leave the

[72] *Andreas Bschor GMBH & Co. KG v Birim Wood Complex Limited* [2015] CA. No J4/9/2015 [9]; There are countless instances in which the Courts have relied on English authorities for persuasive guidance. To mention, but few in relation to matters of the quality requirements of goods are: *PYNE & ASSOCIATES v AFRICAN MOTORS* [2017] CA NO. J4/38/2013; see also, *G. A. Sarpong v Silver Star Auto Limited* [2014] GHASC 121, J4/43/2013; See also, *Georgia Hotel Limited v Silver Star* [2012] 2 SCGLR; See also, *Continental Plastics Engineering Co. Ltd. v IMC Industries – Technik GMBH* [2009] SCGLR 298; See also, *G. A. Sarpong & Co. v Silver Star Auto Ltd* [2010] HCGLR; *Yirenkyi v Tormekpey* [1987–1988] 1 GLR 533; *Rockson v Armah* [1975] 2 GLR 116 [119] among others.

[73] This is a common practice in most cases that are put before the courts in Ghana. For example, See, *Pyne & Associates v African Motors* [2017] C.A. No. J4/38/2013; See also, *G. A. Sarpong v Silver Star Auto Limited* [2014] GHASC 121, J4/43/2013; See also, *Georgia Hotel Ltd v Silver Star* [2012] 2 SCGLR; See also, *Continental Plastics Engineering Co. Ltd. v IMC Industries – Technik GMBH* [2009] SCGLR 298; See also, *Rockson v Armah* [1975] 2 GLR 116.

[74] Smits (2006), p. 514.

[75] Orugu (2003), p. 467.

Ghanaian law in a deficient state to effectively afford consumers the required protection against the incidence of faulty goods. The spotlight of the examination of the law will first focus on the quality requirements of goods for consumers in respect of the obligations of traders in Ghana. This will be carried out in Chap. 2 of this book. The various shortfalls that might undercut the law's adequacy to appropriately safeguard consumers with respect to faulty goods will be pointed out in evaluating the law.

The second task will be to scrutinise the prescribed remedies for consumers, especially when they are supplied with faulty goods in breach of the quality obligations of the seller. Similar to the first task above, the embedded limitations and uncertainties of the law to offer viable solutions to disgruntled consumers who are sold faulty goods will also be highlighted. This will be carried out in Chap. 4 of this book. Chapter 6 will further consider the available mechanisms for the redress of consumer disputes in Ghana. The discussion will centre on the medium through which dissatisfied consumers may resort to redress after suffering unduly with the purchase of faulty goods. The limitations regarding the redress mechanisms will be indicated as well. The review of the law will dwell on the coverage of the law relating to the imposed quality obligations of traders, the defined remedies, and the means of redress for consumers when they are supplied with faulty goods.

As pointed out earlier, the examination of the regime in Ghana will help identify possible limitations and uncertainties that are inimical to the effective protection of consumers in relation to faulty goods. The essence of this important endeavour is solely to contribute towards addressing the gaps from a comparative discourse. The identified shortfalls of the law in Ghana will particularly be discussed in light of the English law and its EU experience while being mindful of the local circumstances in Ghana, as noted earlier.

As highlighted previously, the issue of substandard quality of goods, which is the substantive problem of consumers, may likely cause physical injury or harm or damage to the consumer. This may lead to tortious liability arising from sellers' supply of substandard quality of goods to consumers. However, the reach of this present book does not extend to cover issues arising in relation to tortious actions. This is a specialist field that requires comprehensive treatment, particularly regarding instances in which injury, harm or damage is caused as a result of substandard quality of goods being supplied to a consumer. The present book is, however, confined to the quality obligations of sellers of goods, the remedies for consumers in respect of faulty goods, and the mechanisms of redress of consumer disputes over faulty goods, as previously noted.

A further crucial aspect which will not be addressed in the book is the regulatory responsibility of designated institutions for the policing of the market through premarket and post-market surveillance activities directed at getting rid of substandard quality products from the market. As earlier pointed out, the essence of the highlights of the exacerbating situation of substandard goods in Ghana is in respect of where the goods break down vis-à-vis the obligation of sellers to supply goods which are free from defects, the remedies for consumers when they are supplied with faulty goods, and means of seeking redress. The domain of regulatory mandate as regards substandard products will, therefore, be excluded from the limits of this book.

Another important element that this book will exclude is sales by description, as provided in section 11 of the SGA 1962. The provision particularly states that: 'in a contract for the sale of goods by description whether or not the sale is by sample as well as by description, there is an implied condition that the goods shall correspond exactly with the description'.[76] The courts have stated that the primary obligation of the trader under this provision '…is to deliver those goods, the specific goods … which substantially correspond to the description or sample by which those goods were sold to the buyer."[77] It has been stated that whilst goods supplied by a trader may correspond to their contract description, they may not have the quality attributes expected of the particular kind of goods.[78] Conversely, goods may meet their quality requirements but fail to correspond to their description.[79] It has, therefore, been submitted that the object of sale by description is concerned with the identity of the goods and not the quality requirements of the goods.[80] On account of this, sale by description as an implied term of a contract, which is concerned more with the identity of the goods, will not be explored further in this book. As highlighted previously, the focus of this book is on the quality requirements in respect of the obligations of traders of goods.

1.6 Outline of the Book Chapters

This book is divided into eight chapters, including this introductory chapter. This chapter provides the background setting of the book. This highlights the abundance of innovative goods on account of the growing influence of technology and the alarming influx of substandard goods menace in the Ghanaian market, which intensifies consumers' exposure to the potential of buying faulty goods, raising crucial questions on whether the law is adequate to protect consumers. As this book addresses the question from a comparative perspective of the law in Ghana and the UK, this chapter proceeded to provide a brief highlight of the relevant laws in Ghana and the UK. The chapter also provides the contribution of the book and its value to the generality of the subject of consumer protection in Ghana. This chapter also sets out the rationale for the choice of English law for the comparative analysis. The

[76] Sale of Goods Act 1962, Act 137.

[77] *G. A. Sarpong v Silver Star Auto Ltd* [2014] SCGHA, p6 of judgement; See also, *Robin Hood Mill Ltd v Farah* [1963] 2 GLR 149.

[78] *Arcos Ltd v E.A. Ronaasen & Son* [1933] AC 470; See also Goode and McKendrick (2020), para 11:41; Goode and McKendrick (2016), pp. 317–319; Scott and Black (2000), pp. 156–157.

[79] *Arcos Ltd v E.A. Ronaasen & Son* [1933] AC 470; Goode and McKendrick (2020), para 11:41; Goode and McKendrick (2016), pp. 317–319.

[80] Goode and McKendrick (2016), pp. 317–319; Goode and McKendrick (2020) para 11. 41–43.

chapter equally delineated the explicit scope of the book and its limitations. Also included in this chapter is this outline of the various chapters of the entire book.

Chapters 2, 4, and 6 provide a detailed review of Ghanaian law regarding the quality requirements of goods, consumer remedies, and redress mechanisms. The discussion in these three chapters highlights the deficiencies of the law that leave the regime unhelpful for the protection of consumers in matters of faulty goods in Ghana. Chapter 2 dissects the quality obligations of traders of goods in Ghana and specifically sets out the limitations and uncertainties of the quality requirements of goods in Ghana. Chapter 3 focuses on resolving the deficiencies of the requirements for the quality of goods under the law in Ghana. The analysis is considered in light of English law but within the context of Ghana.

Chapter 4 further examines the remedies for consumers under the law in Ghana with highlights of the embedded limitations and uncertainties. Similarly, Chap. 5 addresses the identified deficiencies of the remedies for consumers in Ghana drawing guidance from the English law as influenced by EU law but in the context of Ghana. Chapter 6 reviews the mechanisms for the redress of consumer disputes in Ghana. The analysis sets out the shortfalls that need to be addressed to better afford consumers with a sufficient degree of protection. Chapter 7 further analysis the shortfalls of the dispute settlement mechanisms in Ghana through the lens of English law as influenced by EU law in resolving the concerns within the local context in Ghana. The analysis of the chapters points out the improvements that are crucial to enhancing the potency of the law in Ghana. Chapter 8 provides a conclusion to the book by highlighting the central questions of the book and a brief summary of the key arguments and recommendations. Chapter 2 below is devoted to analysing the quality requirements of goods under the law in Ghana with a highlight of aspect of the law that need improvement to effectively enhance the degree of protection for consumers in Ghana.

References

Aborchie-Nyahe I (2014) The state of consumer protection in Ghana', COMESA, FTC – USA and CFTC. In: The Sixth Annual African Dialogue Consumer Protection Conference, Lilongwe, Malawi, 8–12 September, 2014

Alhassan BS (2015, 25th October) The "Murder" on Ghana Roads. Whose Fault? Part III. <https://www.modernghana.com/news/651494/1/the-murder-on-ghana-roads-whose-fault-part-iii.html>, Accessed 6 July 2025

Amissah ANE (1976) The supreme court, a hundred years ago' In: Daniels EWC, Woodman GR (eds) Essays in Ghanaian law. Ghana Publishing Corporation, pp 1–31

Ansa-Asare K (1980) Consumer protection. Rev Ghana Law 12:176

Ansa-Asare K (1981) The case for a comprehensive framework of consumer protection in Ghana. Rev Ghana Law 13(14):73

Barak A (2005) Purposive interpretation in law. Princeton University Press, pp 169–170

Barry D et al (2016) Blackstone's Guide to the Consumer Rights Act 2015. Oxford University Press

Bell JS (2006) Comparative administrative law. The Oxford Handbook of Comparative Law, p 1261
Boateng I (2014) Counterfeit mobile phones: the situation in Ghana. In: ITU Workshop on "Combating Counterfeit & Substandard ICT Devices" Geneva (17th–18th November 2014)
Bradgate R, Twigg-Flesner C (2003) Blackstone's guide to consumer guarantees: a guide to the new provisions of consumer sales law. Oxford University Press, p 46
Bridge MG (2017) Benjamin's sale of goods, 10th edn. Sweet & Maxwell, para. 11–046
Chatterjee A, Sahoo S (2011) Consumer protection: problems and prospects. Postmod Open 7(9):157–182
Curran VG (2006) Comparative law and language. In: Zimmermann R, Reimann M (eds) The Oxford handbook of comparative law. Oxford University Press, p 676
Dodoo A (2017) Substandard Electrical Cables Flooding Market - Standards Authority Cautions. <https://www.myjoyonline.com/news/2017/november-6th/substandard-electrical-cables-flooding-market-standards-authority-cautions.php,>, Accessed 4 June 2025
Donoghue S, De Klerk HM (2009) The right to be heard and to be understood: a conceptual framework for consumer protection in emerging economies. Int J Consum Stud 33(4):456–467
Dowuona-Hammond C (1995) Protecting the purchaser of goods under Ghanaian law. Rev Ghana Law 19:105
Dowuona-Hammond C (2007) Evolution of consumer protection law in ghana - developments from independence to date. In: Josiah-Aryeh NA, Mensa-Bonsu AFH, Henrietta JAN, Dowuona-Hammond C, Appiagyei-Atua K (eds) Ghana law since independence: history, development and prospects. Black Mask Ltd, p 337
Dowuona-Hammond C (2018) Consumer law and policy in Ghana. J Consum Policy 41(4):333–354
Dowuona-hammond C, Atuguba R (2006) The policy and legal framework for consumer protection in Ghana. Friedrich Ebert Foundation (FES)
Du Plessis J (2006) Comparative law and the study of mixed legal systems. In: Zimmermann R, Reimann M (eds) The Oxford handbook of comparative law. Oxford University Press, p 478
Ekuful C (2018) Empower GSA to Destroy Sub-Standard Products – Prof. Dodoo. <https://www.gsa.gov.gh/2018/12/empower-gsa-to-destroy-sub-standard-products-prof-dodoo/>. Accessed 13 June 2025
Gaikeviča D (2022) Consumer protection in cases of unfair commercial practices, misleading advertisements, and defective products
Ghana Standards Authority (2018) 197 Out of 204 Electrical Items Substandard – Standards Authority. <https://www.gsa.gov.gh/2018/09/197-out-of-204-electrical-items-substandard-standards-authority/>. Accessed 05 June 2025
GNA, Cabinet Approves Law on Consumer Protection (undated) Available online at http://ghana.gov.gh/index.php/media-center/news/233-cabinet-passes-law-on-consumer-protection, Accessed 15 June 2025
Goode R, McKendrick E (2016) Goode on commercial law, 5th edn. Penguin
Goode R, McKendrick E (2020) Goode and McKendrick on commercial law. Penguin UK
Goode R, Kronke H, McKendrick E (2015) Transnational commercial law: text, cases, and materials, 2nd edn. Oxford University Press
Gyimah A (20th May 2010) Menace of Fake, Substandard Imported Goods' <http://www.ghanaweb.com/GhanaHomePage/NewsArchive/Menace-of-Fake-Substandard-Imported-Goods-182332> Accessed 05 July 2025
Harbour PJ, Koslove TI (2009) Section 2 in a Web 2.0 World: an expanded vision of relevant product markets. Antitrust Law J 76:769
Harland D (1987) The United Nations guidelines for consumer protection. J Consum Policy 10(3):245–266
Herrero AG, Czapnik B, Chen L, Shrestha R, Verico K, Dash P, Hawke G (2023) In: Prakash A (ed) Regional integration in Indo-Pacific: connectivity, cooperation, and new supply-chain linkages. Economic Research Institute for ASEAN and East Asia
Hoecke V (2015) Methodology of comparative legal research, Law and Method 1

Howells G, Twigg-Flesner C (2010) Consolidation and simplification of UK consumer law. BIS
Howells G, Weatherill S (2005) Consumer protection law, 2nd edn. Ashgate, p 168
Jansen N (2006) Comparative law and comparative knowledge. In: Zimmermann R, Reimann M (eds) The Oxford handbook of comparative law. Oxford University Press, p 306
Koopmans T (1996) Comparative law and the courts. Int Comp Law Quart 453
Markesinis B, Fedtke J (2012) Judicial recourse to foreign law: a new source of inspiration? Routledge-Cavendish, p 167
Michaels R (2006) The functional method of comparative law. In: Zimmermann R, Reiman M (eds) The Oxford handbook of comparative law. Oxford University Press, p 340
Nkansah LA (2015) Consumer protection in Ghana: an appraisal of the law. Joseph Ayo Babalola Univ Law J 2(1):185–200
Nottage LR, Paterson JM (2019) Consumer contracts and product safety law in Southeast Asia: Partly trading up?
Orucu E (2006) Methodology of comparative law. In: Smits JM (ed) Encyclopaedia of comparative law. Edward Elgar Publishing, p 442
Orugu E (2003) Comparatist and extraordinary places. In: Legrand P, Munday R (eds) Comparative legal studies: traditions and transitions. Cambridge University Press, p 467
Scott C, Black J (2000) Cranston's consumer and the law, 3th edn. Butterworths, pp 156–157
Smits JM (2006) Comparative law and its influence on national legal systems. In: Zimmermann R, Reimann M (eds) The Oxford handbook of comparative law. Oxford University Press, p 514
Smits JM (2012) Rethinking methods in European private law. In: Adams M, Bomhoff J (eds) Practice and theory in comparative law. Cambridge University Press, p 170
Šostar M, Oniku A (2024) A cross-country analysis of consumer rights awareness and complain frequency. In: 9th International Conference Vallis Aurea: Sustainable Development and Innovation. Josip Juraj Strossmayer University of Osijek, Faculty of Tourism and Rural Development in Pozega, pp 341–352
The Davidson Review (2006) Implementation of EU Legislation, Davidson Review Final Report
The Law Commission (1969) Exemption Clauses in Contract, First Report Amendments to the Sale of Goods Act 1893, Law Com. No. 24, Scott. Law Com. No. 12
The Law Commission (1979) Implied Terms in Contracts for the Supply of Goods, the Law Com. No. 95
The Law Commission (1983) Consultation Memorandum No. 58, Sale and Supply of Goods, Working Paper No. 85 and The Scot Law Com
The Law Commission (1987) Sale and Supply of Goods, Law Com No. 160
The Law Commission (2009) Consumer Remedies for Faulty Goods, the Law Com No 317 and SCOT Law Com No 216
The Ministry of Trade and Industry (2014) Draft Consumer Protection Policy. The Government of Ghana
Twigg-Flesner C et al (2016) Atiyah and Adams' sale of goods, 13th edn. Pearson, p 173
Tyson LDA, Zysman J, Judge B (2023) The new logic of globalization: uncertainty, volatility, and the digital economy. University of California, Berkeley Roundtable on the International Economy, Berkeley
UNCTAD (2019) Key Statistics and Trends in International Trade 2019. United Nations Publications
United Nations guidelines for consumer protection, Available online at <https://unctad.org/topic/competition-and-consumer-protection/un-guidelines-for-consumer-protection> Accessed 19 July 2025
Watson A (1993) Legal transplants, 2nd edn. University of Georgia Press
Watson A (2001) Society and legal change, 2nd edn. Temple University Press, p 4
Yidana N (2020) Enacting a consumer protection law in Ghana: possible lessons from the UK Consumer Rights Act 2015. Law Res Rev Quart 6(4):323–342

Yidana N (2021) Consumer Protection in Ghana: Oversight, Enforcement and Recommendations. Commercial Law Research Network Nigeria (CLRNN)

Yidana N (2023) Regulatory remedies in the enforcement of product quality and safety standards in Ghana: a case for reform from a comparative analysis. Bus Law Rev 44(1)

Yidana N, Nkansah LA (2024) Consumer Law in Ghana. In Are Legal Systems Converging or Diverging? Lessons from Contemporary Crises (pp. 101–125). Cham: Springer International Publishing.

Zweigert K, Kötz H (1998) In: Weir T (ed) An introduction to comparative law, vol 3, 3rd edn. Clarendon Press, Oxford, p 46

Chapter 2
Quality Requirements of Goods Under Ghana Law

2.1 Introduction

The present Chapter examines the requirements for the quality of goods regarding the obligations of traders in Ghana. The analysis of the law will endeavour to ascertain whether the quality requirements of goods are sufficient to afford the necessary protection to consumers when they purchase faulty goods in Ghana. The findings in the analysis will provide the basis for subsequent comparative analysis with the English law in Chap. 3 of this book to contribute towards addressing any unresolved issues within the Ghanaian context to ensure that consumers are better protected.

Before the substantive discussion, however, it is important to restate, as noted previously in Chap. 1, that the present laws for the quality requirements of goods are found under the SGA 1962[1] and the HPA 1974.[2] These pieces of legislation govern transactions of both consumer and non-consumer matters, as indicated in the previous Chapter. It is also worth restating, as mentioned in Chap. 1 earlier, that the government of Ghana has adopted a more tailored Consumer Protection Policy since 2014. However, this is before the Drafting Department of the Attorney General and Minister of Justice to be drafted into a Bill for parliament consideration. In effect, the analysis in this Chapter is confined to provisions of the SGA and the HPA, as noted above. Whilst it is proper to use consumer case law for the conduct of the analysis in relying on the provisions of the SGA and HPA for the purpose of this present discourse, it is worth noting that there is presently limited case law purely on consumer matters pertaining to the requirements for the quality obligations of traders of goods in Ghana. The discussion will, therefore, draw upon non-consumer case law in which the courts have made determinations on the quality

[1] Act 137.

[2] NRCD 292.

N. Yidana, *Consumer Law and Policy on Faulty Goods*, Ius Gentium: Comparative Perspectives on Law and Justice 134,
https://doi.org/10.1007/978-3-032-08700-3_2

requirements for guidance in appreciating the text of the law. It is, however, significant to mention that this will be done with caution as the courts' determination of consumer matters might differ from non-consumer case law. It is also necessary to indicate that the use of non-consumer case law will be made clear in the case citation. In short, the analysis of the quality obligations of traders will draw guidance from both consumer and non-consumer case law to deepen the substance of the discussion but with caution in drawing conclusions in non-consumer case law where necessary.

The chapter is organised into five main sections. This first part introduces the chapter by highlighting the specific question being addressed. The second section discusses the issues in relation to the standard term for the quality expression of goods in Ghana. The third part discusses the seller's statutory obligation regarding the fitness of goods. This part especially reviews the rules concerning the need for the buyer to make known the purpose for which he/she is buying the goods. The fourth part provides the instances where the standard requirement for the quality of goods and the requirement for the fitness of goods may not apply. This focuses on sales in the ordinary course of the seller's business and instances where the parties may introduce exemption clauses into their contractual transaction or agreement. The fifth part provides a conclusion which mainly highlights the issues identified in this Chapter that need to be addressed to better enhance the law for the protection of consumers in Ghana. The requirement for the quality obligations of traders of goods to consumers is discussed below.

2.2 Highlights of the Requirements for the Quality of Goods in Ghana

As already noted above, the requirements for the quality of goods in respect of the obligations of traders are expressed under the SGA and the HPA. The quality obligations of sellers are specifically stipulated under section 13 (1) of the Sale of Goods Act[3] and section 14 of the Hire Purchase Decree.[4] The primary focus of this present section of this chapter is to examine the adequacy of the standard requirements for the quality of goods in Ghana in respect of the duties of traders. The standard requirement for the quality of goods which a trader is expected to supply to consumers in a contract is that the goods should be free from defects which are not disclosed in the case of sales contracts and merchantable quality in respect of hire purchase or conditional sales agreement.[5] The critical question therefore, is to what extent can these defined standards of quality requirements afford consumers with a guaranteed degree of protection when they are supplied with faulty goods? The

[3] Act 137, 1962.

[4] NRCD 292, 1974.

[5] Section 13(1)(a), SGA, 1962, Act 137; Section 14(1), NRCD 292.

analysis below seeks to address this important question. The discussion seeks to ascertain the extent to which the obligations of traders to supply goods to consumers which are free from defects in sales contracts, or goods of merchantable quality in hire purchase or conditional sales, offer the required protection to consumers in Ghana. The issues regarding the standard term for the quality of goods is first discussed below.

2.2.1 Standard for Quality of Goods: Definitional Issues

The standard for the quality of goods that are supplied in a contract is that the goods should be free from defects as regards sales contracts and merchantable quality in the case of hire purchase or conditional sales agreements. Taking the standard that the goods should be free from defects in a contract of sale first, for example, the law applies equally to both new and second-hand goods in Ghana.[6] For instance, the Supreme Court has submitted concisely that: "… a seller of either first or second-hand goods is …liable for all defects in them.'[7] In a similar expression, the Court maintained that 'the duty imposed by the Ghana law is the same for sellers of both new and second-hand goods.'[8] Whilst the above observations are specifically in reference to non-consumer matters, the same determination seems to be expected in consumer matters.

The seller's obligation to supply the buyer with goods which are free from defects is specifically confined to the time of delivery of the goods. In the non-consumer case of *G. A. Sarpong & Co v Silver Start Auto Ltd* before the High Court, it was stated that the statutory requirement for the goods to be free from defects 'hinges on whether or not at the time of the sales contract, there were defects, latent or otherwise in the goods complained of.'[9] In a further non-consumer case of *Continental Plastics Engineering Co. Ltd. v. IMC Industries – Technik GMBH,*[10] the Supreme Court stated that the buyers' had failed to prove the existence of the defects in the machine at the time of the contract, or time of delivery and could not therefore benefit from the statutory duty that is imposed on the seller to supply goods that are free from defects. The Court particularly stated that the law 'can only be prayed in aid of

[6] *Georgia Hotel Ltd v Silver Star* [2012] 2 SCGLR; *G. A. Sarpong & Co. v Silver Star Auto Ltd* [2010] HCGLR; *Continental Plastics Engineering Co. Ltd. v IMC Industries – Technik GMBH* [2009] SCGLR 298.

[7] See the non-consumer case of *Continental Plastics Engineering Co. Ltd. v IMC Industries – Technik GMBH* [2009] SCGLR 298, p304; *Georgia Hotel Ltd v Silver Star* [2012] 2 SCGLR; *G. A. Sarpong & Co. v Silver Star Auto Ltd* [2010] HCGLR; Similarly observations had been made by commentators. For example, See also, Mills (1978).

[8] *G. A. Sarpong & Co. v Silver Star Auto Ltd* [2014] SCGLR, p9 of ruling; ibid. J. E. A. MILLS, [172].

[9] This was stated in the non-consumer case of *G. A. Sarpong & Co. v Silver Star Auto Ltd* [2010] HCGLR, [4].

[10] [2009] SCGLR 298.

buyers who succeed in establishing the existence of defects in goods bought at the time the contract is concluded.'[11] In the case of *G. A. Sarpong & Co. v Silver Star Auto Ltd*[12] before the Supreme Court on appeal, the defects in the vehicle were held to have existed at the time of the car's delivery to the buyers and only manifested subsequently rendering the defects beyond repair. The Court therefore stated that the sellers essentially delivered an inferior vehicle to the buyers and the vehicle could not be said to be free from defects at the time of the delivery of the vehicle. Although the observations in the above case law were made in relation to non-consumer matters, similar or stricter determination is possibly expected in matters of purely consumer cases especially as consumers may be seen to be more vulnerable.

It is important to further note that the implied duty imposed on sellers to supply assured quality of goods which are free from defects is especially in reference to latent defects. Latent defects in goods was construed in the non-consumer case of *A. G. Sarpong & Co v. Silver Star Auto Ltd*[13] to mean defects which originate from the point of manufacture or production of the goods which are largely not discoverable by either the seller or the buyer at the material time of the formation of the contract. In other words, 'the defect is a manufacturing defect, which must exist at the time of production and delivery of the product. By being a hidden or latent defect both the seller, and most importantly, the buyer, could not detect, or be aware of the defect upon reasonable examination at the time of conveyance.'[14]

It is significant to point out that the duty of the seller to supply goods which are free from defects in the case of a contract of sale or merchantable quality as regards hire purchase or conditional sales under the law in Ghana is an implied condition.[15] In light of the duty being an implied condition of the contract, the Court in the non-consumer case of *Georgia Hotel Ltd v. Silver Star Auto Ltd* made the following observation that: '[i]t does follow that if there were defects, particularly latent defects, which are not discoverable …, the seller cannot escape liability for the breach of an essential condition of the contract."[16]

By far, it can be seen that the standard of quality that the goods should be free from defects applies equally to both new and second-hand goods with the liability of sellers being centred on whether the defects, latent or otherwise, existed at the time of the contract or delivery of the goods. In considering this spectrum of

---

[11] [2009] SCGLR 298, p. 304.

[12] [2014] SCGLR.

[13] *G. A. Sarpong & Co. v Silver Star Auto Ltd* [2014] 72 G.M.J.

[14] Per Sophia Adinyira JSC in *Georgia Hotel Ltd v Silver Star* [2012] 2 SCGLR.

[15] *Georgia Hotel Ltd v Silver Star* [2012] 2 SCGLR; *G. A. Sarpong & Co. v Silver Star Auto Ltd* [2010] HCGLR; *Continental Plastics Engineering Co. Ltd. v IMC Industries – Technik GMBH* [2009] SCGLR 298.

[16] *Continental Plastics Engineering Co. Ltd. v IMC Industries – Technik GMBH* [2009] SCGLR 298, [304].

liability on sellers as regards the supply of goods with defects in a contract, the Supreme Court concluded that the duty on sellers is a heavy one.[17]

While the liability of sellers for defects in goods, as observed above, is directly relevant to dealing with the problem of consumers as regards faulty goods, there remain unresolved concerns pertaining to the expected standard of quality of goods. First, the statute has not defined the phrase 'free from defect' as a standard term for the quality of goods. It is, however, important to note that the court has provided some guidance with respect to what amounts to a defect. In particular, while relying *on the 8th edition of the Black's Law Dictionary* in the non-consumer case of *G. A. Sarpong & Co. v. Silver Star Auto Ltd*,[18] the High Court submitted that a defect is a shortcoming or an imperfection in a part of the goods, which is especially vital to the operation or safety of the goods. The crucial concern, however, is that this definition does not seem to offer sufficient guidance that will help in the determination of the standard of quality of goods with respect to the goods being free from defects. Essentially, the shortcoming or imperfection that may affect the functionality of goods a seller supplies was precisely what was noted to confront consumers who are uncertain of the extent of protection available under the law in Ghana, as highlighted earlier in Chap. 1.

In this regard, what may seem important to better serve the needs of consumers is a definition of the implied standard of quality of goods being free from defects that could vividly set out a very clear criteria through which the quality of goods may be assessed.[19] It is, however, important to state that section 81 of the SGA provides that the quality of goods includes the state or condition of the goods.[20] Nevertheless, this does not seem to completely address the issue regarding providing a clearer criterion as a yardstick for the determination of the quality of goods. The clarity of the law as regards the essential criterion through which faults or defects in goods may be tested in light of the implied standard of quality will be significant in clearing the doubts of consumers about the extent to which they may be protected when they buy defective or substandard goods. The present law as noted does not however appear to sufficiently provide such a clear outline that will offer the needed guidance in dealing with matters where consumers are sold goods which are defective in Ghana.

Moreover, the implied condition of merchantable quality as the standard for the quality of goods sold in the case of hire purchase or conditional sales agreement noted earlier has equally not been defined under the Hire Purchase statute. The court in addressing an issue pertaining to second hand goods nevertheless provided some guidance as to what merchantable quality might mean. Especially while relying on

[17] *G. A. Sarpong & Co. v Silver Star Auto Ltd* (2014) 72 G.M.J.

[18] (2010), unreported judgement of the High Court, [4].

[19] Yidana (2020).

[20] 1962, Act 137.

the then-English case of *Bartlett v. Sidney Marcus Ltd*[21] in *Rockson v. Armah*,[22] the Court of Appeal stated that the second-hand car in dispute was merchantable if it was in a usable condition, even though it was not perfect.

Taking merchantable quality as the standard of quality from the perspective of goods being in a usable condition even when not perfect, however, seems not to be comprehensive in addressing the problems of consumers with respect to when they purchased faulty goods. In the first place, many of the examples cited with respect to the problems of consumers in the market in Ghana were in relation to new goods. However, the observation of the Court regarding viewing merchantable quality through the lens of the usable condition of the goods, even when not perfect, as clearly indicated above, was in reference to second-hand goods and may not be suitable in the case of new goods. In addition, the view of merchantable quality, as noted above, may turn to create the impression that it is normal for defects to be present in goods which traders supplied, provided the goods are usable.[23] This largely does not portend well for the protection of consumers in the market especially where a consumer is trapped with faulty goods. As similarly noted earlier about the implied standard in contracts of sale, what might be appropriate to help in responding to the problem of faulty goods when supplied to consumers is a defined standard that provides clear criteria through which the quality of goods may be tested. Unfortunately, the SGA and the HPA do not expressly provide an explicit criterion for guidance in serving the needs of consumers. This is largely not helpful in affording clear guidance for assessing the quality of goods with respect to consumer protection in Ghana.

In sum, whilst the Court's explanation of the standards of quality in both sales contracts and hire purchase or conditional sales agreements are significant in creating some level of understanding, they nevertheless appeared inadequate to appropriately offer clearer guidance to the test of the quality of goods in response to the problems of consumers in Ghana. Addressing this deficiency of the standard requirement for the quality of goods is important in ensuring that a reliable criterion is appropriately set out to guide the assessment of the quality of goods in Ghana. This is especially important to better serve the needs of consumers when they are supplied with faulty goods in Ghana.

Another closely linked issue is the lack of a uniformly expressed standard term for the quality of goods under the regime in Ghana. As shown in the discussion above, the standard term for the quality of goods in contracts of sale differs from the standard term regarding hire purchase or conditional sale contracts. The question to ask, however, is whether the variation of standard terms is suitable for safeguarding the interest of consumers in Ghana if a consumer buys faulty goods. In Chap. 1, it was noted that consumers' distrust in the regime was mainly on account of the uncertainties they have regarding the extent to which they may be protected under

[21] [1965] 1 WLR 1013.

[22] [1975] 2 GLR 116, p. 120.

[23] Nuhu Yidana (2020).

the prevailing law. The operational effect of the two standard terms may, therefore, possibly heighten the worry of consumers, particularly as to whether the implied duty of the goods being free from defects or the implied merchantable quality is the standard they should rely on for protection. This uncertainty may nevertheless be removed where a broadly effective standard that has the tendency of reflecting the goals of consumers whether goods are acquired in a contract of sale, hire purchase or under conditional sales. Presently as seen however, this does not exist under the regime. Addressing this potential source of confusion is important in ensuring that consumers can confidently have a reliable express standard term of quality to rely on, which they could decide whether they are acquiring their goods under a contract of sale or hire purchase.

2.2.2 The Litmus Test/Assessment Criterion for the Quality of Goods

As earlier noted, the seller has an obligation under the law in Ghana to supply goods which are free from defects in the case of sales contracts and merchantable quality in hire purchase or conditional sales agreements. With respect to the discussion on the seller's duty to supply goods which are free from defects, it is clear that the implied duty is to the effect that the goods should be free from latent defects. In particular, in the non-consumer case of *Pyne & Associates v. African Motors*,[24] the plaintiffs detected a series of defects ranging from noise in the dashboard, malfunctioning of the four-wheel drive system and the CD-player being scratchy in a newly acquired Suzuki Vitara XL- 7 vehicle, which the defendants repaired pursuant to the vehicle's one-year sales warranty. The plaintiffs, however, sought to repudiate the contract in a subsequent complaint of alleged vibration of the vehicle's body and front panel eleven (11) months into the contract. It was maintained by the Supreme Court that: '… even though the vehicle appeared to have been riddled with some defects, these cannot legitimately be deemed as latent, or hidden …'.The defects were deemed not latent or hidden for the buyers to be able to exercise their right after a period of 11 months. The crux of the determination was centred on the argument that the buyers, in keeping the vehicle after becoming aware of the defects meant that they were satisfied with the repairs and that a curious examination or inspection should have revealed the defects.

In a similar non-consumer case of *Continental Plastics Engineering Co. Ltd v IMC Industries-Techninik GMBH*,[25] the Supreme Court held that the liability which the seller cannot always escape is that of latent defects but not patent defects which the buyer ought to discover on examination. In the instant case, the plaintiff brought an action to recover the cost of a plastic machine he had sold to the buyers. The

[24] (2017) SC, [14].

[25] [2009] SCGLR, p. 304.

argument of the buyers that the plastic machine they were supplied with had a series of defects was rejected by the court on the basis that the defects were not latent defects. More significantly, in *Rockson v Armah*,[26] it was held that the discovery of latent defect meant that the goods were inferior which fundamentally altered what had been bargained for and therefore, the consumer could not be said to have opted for it in that state.

While emphasis appeared to be placed heavily on latent defects the goods were expected to be free from, it seems that the goods' durability, safety, aesthetic features, fitness for all their known purposes among others did not appear to come under the implied standard for the quality requirements of goods. It is important to indicate that the High Court in disposing of the matter in the non-consumer case of *G. A. Sarpong & Co Ltd. v Silver Star Auto Ltd*,[27] made reference to the values attached to ease of handling, reliability, comfort and pride in the appearance in respect of high classes of goods consumer purchases while relying on the then English case of *Rogers and Another v Parish (Scarborough) Ltd.*[28] Nevertheless, the Supreme Court in dealing with the case on appeal from the Court of Appeal stated that the quality characteristics were only peculiar to the then English law. The Court went further to stress that the regime in Ghana is more centred on latent defects in the goods which is completely different from what is available under the English law.[29] This observation by the Supreme Court unequivocally clear all doubts regarding the exclusion of aesthetic appearance, reliability, and ease of handling characteristics from the reading of the implied duty. This appeared to also echo succinctly the Court's earlier verdict in the *Continental Plastics Engineering Co. Ltd*[30] case noted above, that the seller's liability reflects latent defects and not patent defects.

The discussion also seems to show that the determination of the quality of goods may not equally be extended to cover technical regulatory standards which goods are often expected to meet. It is important to state that a number of technical regulatory standards make it an offence for manufacturers and traders to supply substandard goods into the market.[31] In effect, a trader may be guilty of the offence of supplying substandard goods into the market if the goods he trades in are not in conformity with the technical regulatory requirements.[32] It is, however, unclear if a consumer who has been supplied with the goods which a regulatory authority found

---

[26] [1975] 2 GLR 116, p. 119.

[27] [2010], unreported. This judgement of the High Court went on an appeal first to the Court of Appeal and later to the Supreme Court.

[28] [1987] QB 933.

[29] [2014] SC [8–9].

[30] [2009] SCGLR [304].

[31] See for example, section 21 of the Standards Authority Act 1973, NRCD 173; See also, Regulation 23 of the Energy Efficiency Standards and Labelling (Household Refrigerating Appliances) Regulations, (2009) LI 1958; See also, Regulation 2, Energy Efficiency Standards and Labelling (Non-Ducted Air Conditioners And Self-Ballasted Fluorescent Lamps) *Regulations*, (2005), LI 1815 among others.

[32] Yidana and Nkansah (2024). pp. 101–125).; Yidana (2020).

to be substandard can rely on the non-conformity of the goods to the technical standards to seek a remedy. In particular, the question as to whether the assessment of the quality of the goods will include the non-conformity is unresolved.

It can be seen that whereas the criterion for the quality of goods is concerned with latent defects, there remain unresolved questions with respect to a consumer who is confronted with issues of the goods' durability, safety, appearance and finish, general fitness, and conformity of the goods to their technical standards. Essentially, the non-express inclusion of these factors in testing the quality of goods does not seem helpful to the practical concerns of consumers. In particular, in a market survey to identify and prioritise segments of the consumer market for maximum results in the purchase of 'technology-driven clean cooking stoves', for example,[33] it was discovered that consumers were broadly more concerned about the durability, aesthetic, safety, and functional reliability of the goods, among others, in making their purchasing decisions for various products in the market.[34] Other consumer science studies on consumer preferences have also favoured aesthetics, durability, efficiency and conformity to quality standards as being central to consumer purchasing decisions.[35] Clearly, consumers' primary quest is to have goods which are safe, durable, reliable, efficient, and functional with aesthetic features. This may be argued as not being limited to only cooking stoves but similarly inclusive of the wide range of goods in the Ghanaian market. The exclusion of those aspects from the remits of the quality of goods that reflect the expectations of consumers does not portend well for the protection of consumers in the Ghanaian market. This is especially problematic, taking into consideration the possibility of a consumer being supplied with substandard goods that may start to betray defects. Addressing the concerns of the limited reflection of the current regime to the main problems of consumers will, therefore, be very helpful in ensuring that the regime better serves the needs of consumers in Ghana.

2.3 Circumstances in which the Obligations of Sellers' to Supply Quality Goods to Consumers' Do Not Apply

The implied duty of the seller to supply goods that are free from defects or merchantable quality is not an absolute requirement in all circumstances. The quality of goods the seller is expected to supply will not particularly apply in certain instances. These mainly include a defect which the seller disclosed before or at the time of the contract and where the buyer examined the goods prior to the formation of the

[33] Charcoal and fire wood are widely the main sources of energy for cooking in most homes in Ghana. The use of cooking stoves is therefore considered to be technology driven means of cooking energy.

[34] Pascaud and Thivillon (2014), [7–8].

[35] Ackah et al. (2021).

contract. Other instances are where the sale is not carried out in the course of the seller's business and where the seller has excluded himself from the liability of the particular defect through express provision in the agreement which s/he had brought to the attention of the buyer at the time of the contract. While the former will be discussed in this section, the latter will be examined later in this chapter after the review of implied duty of fitness following this section. This has become necessary on account of the fact the latter exclusionary situations as will be seen subsequently equally applies to the implied obligation of fitness of goods which is to be examined afterwards as indicated. The focused of this section as noted, is on where the seller has declared a particular defect and where the buyer has examined the goods to which the seller's liability for the defects in the goods will be excluded. The seller's liability exclusions in these circumstances, though limited, may serve as avenues through which a consumer could be deprived of the benefits of the defined protection under the law. The discussion at this point seeks to assess the extent to which the exclusionary situations may be applied without unduly undermining the interest of the consumer. The discussion below reflects the various circumstances in which the implied obligations of the seller will not apply in respect of the goods being free from defects or merchantable quality respectively in contract of sale and hire purchase agreements.

2.3.1 Where the Seller Is Excluded from Liability for Disclosed Defects

As indicated earlier, the seller has an implied obligation to supply goods that are free from defects or goods of a merchantable quality depending on whether it is a contract of sale or a hire purchase or conditional sale. The seller will therefore be liable where there is a breach of his obligation to supply goods that are free from defects or merchantable quality. However, the seller will not be liable for defects in the goods which he clearly discloses to the buyer prior to the contract which the buyer subsequently complained of.[36] For instance, in the non-consumer case of *Continental Plastics Engineering Co. Ltd. v. IMC Industries—Technik GMBH,*[37] the Supreme Court succinctly construed the seller's liability of exclusion for declared defects by stating that: '[b]ased on what we believe is pure common sense, the seller is … not liable for defects which he fully discloses or declares to the buyer at the time of the contract of sale.' In the *G. A. Sarpong and Co's* case, the Court again reaffirmed its construction of the provision that the seller is not liable for those

[36] The Statutes stipulate that the seller will be excluded from liability for defects in the goods which he has clearly made known to the buyer prior to the contract particularly in section 13(1) (a) of the Sale of Goods Act, 1962, Act 137 and section 14 (4)–(5), of the Hire Purchase Decree, 1973, NRCD 173

[37] Continental Plastics Engineering Co. Ltd. v. IMC Industries—Technik GMBH (2009) SCGLR 298, p. 304.

defects which he has clearly made known or declares to the buyer before or at the time of the contract.[38]

Nevertheless, where the seller is aware of any defects in the goods but fails to disclose them, he will be liable to the buyer for the defects. It was particularly noted in *Silver Star v. Georgia Hotel Ltd*[39] that where it is shown that the seller knew or was aware of the defects in the goods but deliberately or negligently failed to disclose the defects to the buyer before or at the time of the contract, the seller cannot escape liability.

However, as observed above, where the seller discloses the defects he was aware of before the contract, liability for the defects shifts to the buyer. The exclusion of the seller from liability for declared defects seems to imply that the buyer should have equal level of knowledge about the defects similar to the seller after being told by the seller and should be bound by his decision to buy the goods. In particular, in *Rockson v. Armah,*[40] shortly after delivery of the contract vehicle, some defects started to manifest and the buyer eventually detected that the vehicle had been involved in an accident. The buyer nevertheless went on with the contract after the seller accepted the occurrence of the accident and carried out repairs of the defects through a wayside fitter. Although it was not the seller who disclosed the defect, the fact that the buyer became aware of the defects and went on with the contract, it was held by the Court of Appeal that the buyer acted on his own volition after being fully aware of the defects and should be bound by his election.

As noted above, the essence of excluding the seller from liability for disclosed defects is premised on the likely effect of the buyer gaining equal level of knowledge similar to the seller about the particular state of the goods. This particularly reflects the argument that the primary object of information disclosure is to address the imbalances that might exist between the seller and the consumer in relation to quality information of the goods.[41] Generally, consumers are mostly observed to have insufficient knowledge about the state of the goods at the time of purchase compared to sellers of the goods.[42] This mirrors the express observation that: 'consumers may often lack adequate information on the reliability, durability, and running costs of products, whilst sellers will generally have superior information on these matters.'[43] The information asymmetry in many instances results in consumers making purchasing decisions without adequate knowledge of the reliability of the goods, and the defects may only become manifest when the goods are in use.[44] It has particularly been contended that consumers with problems of goods they buy often

---

[38] G. A. Sarpong& Co. v. Silver Star Auto Ltd. (2014) 72 G.M.J, p80; See also, J. E. A. Mills, Rockson v. Armah: A Case of Caveat Emptor, Caveat Venditor or Neither?, (1978–1981) 15 UGLJ, 168 at p. 172.

[39] (2010–2012) 1 GLR 449, p. 467.

[40] Rockson v. Armah (1975) 2 GLR 116, p. 121.

[41] Howells (2005), pp. 349–370, pp. 354–355; Twigg-Flesner (2004).

[42] Twigg-Flesner (2004); Miller et al. (1998); Ziegel (1973), p. 190.

[43] Ramsay (2012).

[44] Cartwright (2004); Twigg-Flesner (2004).

exhibit among others, considerable amount of knowledge disparity regarding the attributes and technical components of the goods.[45] Primarily, the seller's disclosure of known defects will in effect seek to correct the deficiency of the consumer product knowledge. This will enable the consumer to act based on an informed knowledge about the state of the goods in making a purchasing decision.[46] In light of this, the seller's liability exclusion as noted above is grounded on the theory that the consumer acted after having been duly informed about the said defects.

The important question that remains unsettled however is the extent to which the consumer processes the disclosed defects in making a purchasing decision. This is especially with respect to the consumer's capacity to properly understand the extent of the defect and appreciate the wider implication of the disclosed information in making a sound decision at the material time of the purchase. As rightly argued, the benefit of information in guiding the consumer is anchored on it being properly understood and acted upon.[47] However, consumers are mostly observed to exhibit poor attitude towards disclosed information especially at the contractual stage of buying the goods.[48] This is often attributed to the effect of overloads of information that preoccupied most consumers in their daily lives, thereby making it practically difficult for a consumer to properly decode the declared information about the quality defects of the goods.[49]

Moreover, the nature of the information the seller discloses has also been highlighted to sometimes contribute in worsening the plight of the consumer in fully understanding the import of the information about the exact quality of the goods. In particular, it has been argued that sellers sometimes disclose information which consumers do not have the experience to analyse about the quality of the goods.[50] This may make it difficult for consumers to interpret the declared information prior to making a decision which will be based objectively on an informed analysis. Consequently, the consumer ends up making a decision possibly without adequate analysis and proper judgement of the declared information regarding the quality status of the goods. This may invariably deny the buyer the benefit of the disclosure.

As noted above, the essence of excluding the seller from liability for disclosed defects is premised on the presumption that the defects when disclosed places the

---

[45] Twigg-Flesner (2004); Ramsay (2012); Miller et al. (1998); Ziegel (1973), p. 190.

[46] Busch (2015), p. 223.

[47] Howells (2005), p. 358; See also, Marotta-Wurgler (2014), pp. 63–74; Twigg-Flesner (2004), p. 12.

[48] Ben-Shahar and Schneider (2011), pp. 647–749; Twigg-Flesner (2004); Hadfield et al. (1998), pp. 131–169.

[49] Howells (2005), p. 358; Wendlandt (2005), p. 67; Hadfield et al. (1998), pp. 131–169.

[50] Bar-Gill and Ben-Shahar (2012), The authors particularly noted at pp. 15–16 that sellers give information: 'without regard for people's cognitive abilities and literacy levels, they disregard people's reluctance to read texts that are unfamiliar and imposing. They misconstrue people's objective, thinking of consumers as guzzlers of technical information, not as users of products. They tell people stuff about matters that most people have no experience with, which require a theoretical framework to analyse' p. 11.

buyer on an equal level of knowledge similar to the seller about the particular state of the goods. It can therefore be concluded that though it is important for the seller to disclose information on known defects, it might not remedy the information asymmetry especially where the consumer is unable to make sense of the impact of the information about the quality of the goods. As clearly shown in the discussion, the inability of the consumer to appreciate the overall impact of the disclosed defects may result in the consumer taking an unfavourable purchasing decision. This therefore raises an important question as to what extent the seller's liability exclusion will be granted without jeopardising the interest of the consumer. In other words, the extent to which information failures might be resolved before allowing the seller to escape liability remains unsettled. This is especially crucial particularly taking into consideration the chances of a consumer purchasing goods that are of substandard quality or defective without appreciating the import of the faults that the seller has previously declared in the goods.

It is however important to state that the uncertainty seems more pronounced especially in matters relating to sales contracts. In the given case of hire purchase in particular, the regime insists that the seller's liability exclusion should be subjected to not only the seller declaring the defects but also the seller explaining to the buyer the impact or effect of the defect.[51] Though this requirement stipulated under the hire purchase has not be commented on by the courts, it would be helpful if strictly applied by the courts to ensure that a seller only escapes liability if it is clear that the buyer understood the effect or impact of the seller's declared defect at the time of the contract.

In the case of sales contract such a requirement does not exist. It therefore remains unclear as to how the possible failure of the consumer to appropriately process the declared defects could be addressed especially in sales contracts as indicated earlier. This leaves the disclosure regime in contract of sales with uncertainties that need resolving in order to ensure that consumers in Ghana are better protected. Addressing the uncertainty will be particularly useful in ensuring that consumers are protected when they buy substandard or defective goods without properly appreciating the defective information the seller declares at the time of the contract formation.

[51] Section 14 (4) to (5) (a), the Hire Purchase Act, 1974, NRCD 292 – it is particularly provided that the implied merchantable quality will not be applied where the goods are supplied subject to a particular defect which the seller had brought 'to the notice of the hirer or buyer and made its effect clear to him'.

2.3.2 *Where the Seller Will Not Be Liable for Defects Owing to the Buyer's Examination of the Goods*

From the discussion set out earlier, a supplier of goods has an obligation to deliver goods that are free from defect in a sales contract and of a merchantable quality in a hire purchase or conditional sales agreement. In effect, the seller will be liable where the goods supplied are defective as earlier noted. However, the seller's liability will be excluded where prior to the contract the buyer examines the goods. This is specifically provided under.

Section 13 (1) (a) (i) and (ii) of the SGA as follows:

> (i) Where the buyer has examined the goods, in respect of defects which should have been revealed by the examination; (ii) in the case of sale by sample, in respect of defects which could have been discovered by a reasonable examination of the sample.[52]

In addition, section 14 (3) of the HP law states that:

> where the hirer or buyer has examined the goods or a sample of the goods before delivery, the term referred to in subsection 1 (merchantable quality under the HP law) shall not be implied in respect of defects which the examination ought to have revealed.[53]

The legal position regarding when the buyer examined the goods before the contract or at the time of the contract was summed up in the non-consumer case of *Continental Plastics Engineering Co. Ltd. v. IMC Industries – Technik GMBH.*[54] Especially, the Supreme Court firmly submitted that: '[w]hen the buyer has examined the goods the seller cannot be held liable for defects which ought to have been discovered on examination, as for example, patent defects.'[55] Similarly, in *G. A. Sarpong& Co. v. Silver Star Auto Ltd*,[56] the highest Court of the land reproduced its earlier position as contained above that once '…the buyer has examined the goods, the seller is not liable for defects, which should have been revealed by the examination.'[57]

The Court's observations above seem to mean that the seller's liability exclusion is only to the effect of where the buyer has examined the goods. However, the above position seems to have been overruled by the latest determination of the Supreme Court as regards the buyer's examination of the goods. In the matter of the non-consumer case of *Pyne & Associates v African Motors*[58] recited earlier in particular,

[52] Sale of Goods Act, 1962, Act 137, Sect. 13 (1) (a) (I &ii).

[53] Hire Purchase Decree, 1974, NRCD 292.

[54] (2009) SCGLR 298.

[55] Continental Plastics Engineering Co. Ltd. v. IMC Industries – Technik GMBH (2009) SCGLR 298, p. 304.

[56] (2014) SCGLR.

[57] (2014) SCGLR p 9 of judgment; See also, New Lucky Electrical Limited v. Startrack Int. Ghana Limited and Isaac Acquah (2010), Suit No. 49/08, p4; See also, Ansa-Asare (1980), p. 73; See also, Mills (1978–1981), p. 172.

[58] (2017) unreported judgment of the Supreme Court, CA. No. J4/38/2013, p. 14.

it was submitted by the Supreme Court that the plaintiffs had the responsibility to have inspected or examined the vehicle especially if they were conscious of the fact that their purchase of the vehicle was for travel on rugged terrain and long distances as part of their construction work. It was further stressed that 'the defects from which the vehicle suffered ... could have been easily detected if the plaintiffs had taken advantage of their rights to inspection and examination as is granted under the law.' Consequently, the plaintiffs' action against the backdrop of defects the vehicle was allegedly riddled with, was unsuccessful; for their failure to have exercised their rights of inspection of the vehicle before accepting it as found by the court. The recent observation of the Supreme Court seems to revive and corroborate an earlier submission of the High Court in the non-consumer case of *New Lucky Electrical Ltd. v. Startrack Int. Ghana Ltd and Isaac Acquah.*[59] The Court had particularly stated that 'the warranty of freedom from defects is lost where examination would make them evident.' The court went further to indicate that 'a buyer who is aware of defects in a product and chooses to buy same doe that ... *at* his own will and the seller should not be deemed to have a duty to protect that buyer.'[60]

The authorities seem to be pointing out that the buyer at all time has a duty to examine the goods so as to enable him to discover possible defects and to decide whether to buy the goods or not. It can also be seen that if the defects are the type that the buyer's examination should have revealed, the seller's liability would be excluded whether or not the buyer actually examined the goods. It is worth noting that the decisions requiring the buyer to exercise as a right in carrying out an examination of the goods were made in respect of non-consumer case law. It is however important to state that whilst commercial buyers may likely have relevant technical knowledge to be able to exercise much higher degree of diligence in carrying out any examination, a consumer may either have little or lack the relevant technical knowledge to be able to carry out such examinations with precision. In effect, adopting the approach as contained in the non-consumer case law above in consumer matters will likely be detrimental to the interest of consumers in Ghana.

It would be detrimental in that the moment defects in the goods are classed as capable of being revealed on examination, the burden shifts to the buyer whether he actually examined the goods or not. Clearly, applying a similar approach where a consumer who did not examine the goods which his examination could have discovered would not be helpful to consumers in Ghana. This would broadly limit the degree of protection for consumers against faulty goods in Ghana.

Another issue of concern in the exclusion of the seller's liability in respect of the buyer's examination of the goods relate to where the goods are 'experience' goods[61]

[59] (2010), unreported judgment of the High Court, Suit No. OCC 49/08, p. 4.

[60] Emphasis, mine.

[61] Examples of 'experience' goods include; television set, radio set, and home appliances like fridges, microwaves, and blenders among others. For further details, See, Leahy and Howard (2005), p. 45; See also, Men-Andri Benz (2007), pp. 1–5.

rather than 'search' goods.[62] In particular, it has been observed that recognising the quality level of particular goods largely rests on whether the goods are 'search' goods or 'experience' goods.[63] Whilst the quality attributes of 'search' goods may be discovered during the pre-purchase examination, the attributes of 'experience' goods can only be discovered when the goods are in use.[64]

It has also been submitted that 'experience goods are technically complex and consumers are usually not able to discover any defects by simply inspecting the goods. This makes it difficult, if not impossible, to discover quality defects in such goods.'[65] The ensuing difficulty in establishing the quality attributes of experience such as a fridge, a washing machine, a microwave, or a television set imply that a consumer's examination of the goods would definitely not be able to reveal defects in such class of goods. This leaves room for defects in such goods to manifest after the purchase. The instant case of a consumer buying 'experience' goods therefore leaves alive the question as to how the non-liability of the seller as regards defects in the goods which the buyer is said to have examined prior to the contract will be enforced without undermining the interest of consumers in Ghana.

In sum, the present determination of the concept of examination to the effect that a buyer who does not examine the goods where an examination could have revealed the defects will be detrimental to consumers if similarly applied in the case of consumer disputes in Ghana. This implies that the question as to how the trader's liability might be excluded without jeopardising the interest of consumers has not been addressed. The need to address this critical question is further heightened in instances where the goods the buyer purchased are experience goods in which his examination of the goods might as well not aid the discovery of defects in the goods. The question as to how the trader's liability exclusion will not affect the rights of the consumer needs to be addressed so as to instil certainty into the regime. This is important to clearly guarantee consumers of the extent to which they may be protected under the law in Ghana.

2.4 Fitness of Goods for the Particular Purpose of the Buyer

In addition to the quality obligation, the seller also has an implied duty to supply goods which are fit for the particular purpose of the buyer where the buyer has expressly or impliedly communicated his particular reason for buying the goods before or at the time of the contract. This section of the chapter further explores the

---

[62] Example of 'search' goods include; household furniture and furnishings, clothing, footwear, building materials among others. For further details, See, Leahy and Howard (2005), p. 45; See also, Men-Andri Benz (2007), pp. 1–5.

[63] Twigg-Flesner (2004); See also, Hadfield et al. (1998), pp. 131–169; See also, Akerlof (1970), p. 488.

[64] Ibid.

[65] Twigg-Flesner (2004), p. 2.

adequacy of this requirement for the protection of consumers in Ghana. Before engaging with the analysis, it is appropriate to set out the provision as captured under the statutes to keep in sharp focus the point of law being discussed. Specifically, section 13(1)(b) of the Sale of Goods Act stipulates that:

> where the goods are of a description which are supplied by the seller in the course of his business, and the buyer expressly or by implication makes known the purpose for which the goods are required, there is an implied condition that the goods are reasonably fit for that purpose[66]

Also, section 13 (2) of the HP law provides that:

> where the hirer or buyer, whether expressly or by necessary implication, (a) makes known to the owner or seller, or to a servant or agent of the owner or seller, the particular purpose for which the goods are required, or (b) in the course of the antecedent negotiations has made that purpose known to a person by whom those negotiations were conducted, or to a servant or agent of that person, it is an implied term, subject to section 14 (implied term as to merchantability), that the goods are reasonably fit for that purpose.[67]

The various issues arising from the above provision will be relayed for further discussion directed at highlighting the issues that need to be addressed to make the regime more responsive to the concerns of consumers in Ghana. The discussion will particularly consider the aspects of the regime that need to be enhanced to provide a better and well-improved system of protection for consumers against the incidence of faulty goods in Ghana. The various issues are discussed below with respect to the seller's obligation to supply goods which are fit for the purpose of the buyer.

2.4.1 *The Duty of the Buyer to Communicate the Purpose of Buying the Goods*

As observed above, the seller has an implied obligation to deliver goods which are fit for the particular purpose of the buyer. However, the implied undertaking of the seller hinges on the buyer expressly or by implication making known to the seller the intended purpose for which he/she is buying the goods. The accompanying responsibility of the buyer to expressly or impliedly disclose the intended purpose for the goods is especially provided as follows:

> where … the buyer expressly or by implication makes known the purpose for which the goods are required there is an implied condition that the goods are reasonably fit for that purpose[68]

[66] Sale of Goods Act 1962, Act 137.

[67] Hire Purchase Decree 1974, NRCD 292 – the emphasis (implied term as to merchantability) is mine.

[68] Section 13 (1) (b), Sale of Goods Act 1962, Act 137.

While the above recital is provided under the 1962 SGA, the Hire Purchase Act 1974 has similarly stipulated that:

> where the hirer or buyer, whether expressly or by necessary implication, (a) makes known to the owner or seller, or to a servant or agent of the owner or seller, the particular purpose for which the goods are required, … it is an implied term, … that the goods are reasonably fit for that purpose.[69]

In the non-consumer case of *Andreas Bschor GMBH v. Birim Timbers Ltd,*[70] it was stated by the Supreme Court that to give rise to the application of the implied condition regarding the fitness of the goods for the particular purpose of the buyer, 'the buyer should have made the seller aware of the purpose for which he requires the goods.'[71] In the instant case, the plaintiff had supplied a reconditioned saw-mill in return for the defendant to supply him with timber products. The saw-mill plant main carriage drive however broke down 2 months into operation in the presence of the plaintiff Managing Director. This was after the plant had broken down and been repaired eleven (11) days following its installation. The court accepted the view of the defendants that since they had made known the purpose of buying the saw-mill plant, the seller was under the obligation of supplying them with a plant that is fit for its intended purpose. Similarly, in *New Lucky Electrical Ltd. v Startrack Int. Ghana Ltd and another,*[72] also, a non-consumer case, it was held by the Court that the seller's liability for goods which are not fit for the use for which they were acquired applies only where the buyer had made it known to the seller before the contract. The Court therefore went further to hold liable, the seller who had admitted that he had been informed by the buyer that his purchase of the excavator was for the purpose of mining when the excavator was unfit for mining. Also, it was stated in the *Bschor GMBH*[73] case cited above that the buyer who made known the purpose of buying the goods was a demonstration that the buyer was fully relying on the seller's skills and knowledge to deliver to him goods which are fit for his purpose the law aims to protect.[74]

Essentially, the emphasises have been that the buyer's entitlement to demand that the goods should be fit for his purpose is subject to him/her communicating the particular purpose to the seller at the time of the purchase. The requirement for the buyer to communicate his expected use of the goods to the seller to hold him liable in the event of a breach has so far not been determined with respect to the buyer's communication of the purpose by implication. However, it is likely expected that where evidence clearly points to implied communication of the purpose of purchased goods, the courts may have no difficulty in holding the seller liable. Similarly, where the goods have a single use and the buyer fails to state his reason for buying

[69] Hire Purchase Decree 1974, NRCD 292.

[70] *Andreas Bschor GMBH v Birim Timbers Ltd* [2016] unreported CA. No. J4/9/2015, [9].

[71] Ibid. [9]; See also, *Yirenkyi v Tormekpey* [1987–1988] 1 GLR 533 CA, [537].

[72] [2010] unreported HC, Suit No. OCC 49/08 [5].

[73] [2016] unreported CA. No. J4/9/2015 [8].

[74] *Bschor GMBH v Birim Timbers Ltd* [2016] unreported CA. No. J4/9/2015 [10].

the goods, it is equally likely that the court may hold the seller to the effect that the goods should be fit for their known single purpose.

Nevertheless, one key element of uncertainty has to do with the instance of idiosyncratic needs of the buyer. In particular, it remains unclear as to what the law would be regarding where the buyer of the goods has a peculiar need for the goods which slightly departs from their normal use. The question as to whether the buyer will be protected where due to the abnormality of the buyer's situation the goods are unfit for the intended purpose which he had declared remains unresolved under the present regime.

Another unsettled area is where the goods the buyer is acquiring are meant for multiple uses. The question is, will the buyer have to itemise each use of the goods for which he is buying the goods, or will it suffice for him to mention that he/she is acquiring the goods for their known purposes? This question equally remains unresolved.

In short, the extent to which the requirement for the fitness of goods would be applied in matters where the consumer has peculiar needs which he has disclosed, and the question surrounding where the goods have multiple uses are both unresolved. Addressing the uncertainties is crucial in ensuring that the regime is explicitly clear to assist the course of consumers in Ghana. This is particularly important in ensuring that consumers in Ghana are better protected when they are supplied with faulty goods which are not fit for their intended purpose.

2.4.2 The Seller's Statements About the Particular Purpose of the Goods

As discussed above, the seller has the duty to supply goods which are fit to meet the particular purpose of the buyer. Before the seller's implied statutory duty will have application, however, the buyer should have disclosed to the seller the particular purpose for which s/he requires the goods, before or at the time of the contract as already mentioned above. Whilst the seller's liability for the unfitness of the goods is indexed to the buyer's disclosed reason for buying the goods, the question regarding the seller's claims about the goods fitness is unresolved. Essentially, the regime is silent on claims about the particular purpose of the goods made by the seller prior to the contract. This is especially where the buyer's purchasing decision is guided by the seller's express statements in relation to the given use of the goods. The question to ask is, will the seller be made liable for the unfitness of the goods for the purposes which he had expressly advanced before the contract? As indicated above, this has not been addressed under the regime.

Whilst it may be argued that the buyer can bring an action on grounds of misrepresentation, he may nevertheless confront other challenges in getting a remedy. In particular, a statement of misrepresentation within the framework of common law is not a promise and does not give effect to a breach of contract.[75] It is within this remit that *Benjamin's Sale of Goods* clearly posited that a right to discharge the contract or to the claim of damages does not arise in respect of a seller's misrepresentation which is not incorporated into the contract as a term.[76] In effect, a consumer may not be able to bring a claim under contract law in respect of a seller misrepresented claims. It is nevertheless, important to state that the right of a claimant may lie in tort on account of deceit or breach of duty as regards fraudulent and negligent misrepresentation respectively. It is also worth noting that within the principle of equity, a representee may be able to rescind the whole contract on account of fraudulent, negligent or innocent misrepresentation.[77] However, these rights may be cut short if the consumer is deemed to have affirmed the contract, and where restoring the trader to his original position is impossible on account of the destruction of the goods. Moreover, the primary focus of the present analysis is concerned with the rights available for consumers in contract law in respect of false claims of the seller that induce the consumer into the contract. Unlike English law, as will be seen later in Chap. 5, which provides further statutory cover for consumers under contract law,[78] such added protections do not exit under the law in Ghana.

Nevertheless, as observed above, a buyer can lay claim to the seller's misrepresented statements if the claims are found to be incorporated as terms of the contract under common law. However, a buyer who seeks to rely on such claims will need to establish a breach in relation to a fundamental aspect of the contract. In the non-consumer case of *New Lucky Electrical Ltd. v Startrack Int. Ghana Ltd and another,*[79] it was particularly noted that before a buyer can succeed in a claim of fraudulent misrepresentation, his burden is not only to '…prove the fraud, but *he* must *also* prove that the misrepresentation went to a fundamental term, being a condition of the contract.'

Clearly the conditions attached to the common law concept of misrepresentation do not seem suitable for dealing with consumer matters as regards attributes of the goods the seller claims which does not reflect the true fitness of the goods. Moreover, as mentioned earlier, a consumer claim may only lie under tort law for negligent or fraudulent misrepresentation but not in contract law, which is the primary concern of the present analysis of the Ghanaian law.

It can be seen that consumers may have difficulty in successfully navigating through to hold sellers liable for misrepresentation where the goods they purchase on the basis of claims made by the seller are unfit for the purpose for which they bought the goods. This may likely leave many consumers without redress. It is therefore submitted that the lack of express stipulation in respect of sellers' liability

---

[75] Goode and Mckendrick (2016), para. 3.95.

[76] Bridge (2017), para. 12.002.

[77] Goode and Mckendrick (2016), para. 3.95.

[78] The Misrepresentation Act 1967 of the English law provided under section 2(1) the right for claimants to maintain actions for the breach of a collateral contract in respect of a seller's misrepresentation.

[79] [2010] HC Suit No. OCC 49/08, [15] emphasis added.

for claims they make about the fitness of the goods they sell is not helpful to consumers in Ghana. This will need to be resolved to ensure that consumers are protected when they rely on traders' claims with respect to the particular purpose(s) of the goods in buying the goods, which eventually are unfit for the declared purpose(s).

2.5 Instances Where Sellers' Obligations for the Quality and Fitness of Goods Do Not Apply

This section mainly examines instances under which the implied obligations of traders regarding the requirements for the quality and fitness of goods, as examined above, may not be applicable. There are mainly two main circumstances where the implied duties of both quality and fitness of the goods will have limited application. The first situation under which both provisions will have restricted application is where the sale was not carried out in the ordinary course of the seller's business. The second instance is where the seller introduces an exemption clause that seeks to exclude him/her from liability for the non-conformity of the goods. These two instances are broadly examined below.

2.5.1 Sales which Are Not in the Ordinary Course of the Seller's Business

As examined earlier, the seller has an implied duty to supply goods that are free from defects, which he has not disclosed to the buyer before or at the time of the contract. The seller is, however, excluded from the implied obligation to supply goods that are free from defects where the goods are not sold in the ordinary course of his business. It is especially provided to the effect that the implied duty of the seller to supply goods that are free from defects will not apply 'where the goods are not sold by the seller in the ordinary course of his business, in respect of defects of which the seller was not, and could not reasonably have been aware of'.[80] The legal effect of the provision was stated in the non-consumer case of *G. A. Sarpong & Co. v. Silver Star Auto Ltd*[81] that: '...where the seller is not a dealer in the kind of goods sold and it is established that he did not know or could not reasonably have been aware of the defects complained of, he escapes liability.' Also, the Court of Appeal in the non-consumer case of *Andreas Bschor & Co. KG v. Birim Wood Complex Ltd*

[80] Section 13 (1) (a) (iii) Sale of Goods Act 1962, Act 137.

[81] *G. A. Sarpong & Co. v Silver Star Auto Ltd* (2014) SCGLR [9]; See also, Dowuona-Hammond (1995).

and Another had stated that: 'the evidence does not disclose that the appellants' normal course of business included the sale of 'Sawmilling machinery'. They could, therefore, not have been in breach of … any fundamental obligation as to quality and fitness of the machines.'[82] Whilst this observation was overruled on the basis of the fact that the appellants had sold similar machinery to other buyers following an appeal to the Supreme Court, it nevertheless contributes to enriching the discussion as regards the extent to which the principle could be applied to exonerate sellers of liability for defects in the goods sold outside the scope of their mainstream business.

The main question, however, is, what constitutes a sale in the ordinary course of a trader's business? For instance, will a seller who sells his/her used business assets or goods such as a car, or laptop mainly to acquire new ones for the continuation of his principal business be considered to be selling in the ordinary course of his business? In other words, the question of whether a seller who is making a one-off sale of an article or only disposing off his unwanted goods will be regarded as engaging in a sale in the course of the business is uncertain. Addressing the questions is crucial to help in affording consumers with a more clarified regime to better deal with issues of defective goods when sold to them through such sales outlet by the supplier. Resolving the uncertainty will further help in promoting the interest and confidence of consumers especially when they know approximately what is closely required under the law.

As also pointed out above, the trader's obligation to supply goods which are fit for the particular purpose of the buyer applies where the seller sells the goods which are of a description in the ordinary course of his business[83] similar to the seller's implied undertaking to supply goods which are free from defects as noted earlier. In the non-consumer case of *Bschor GMBH v. Birim Timbers Ltd*,[84] the Supreme Court particularly took the view that: 'the grounds for the condition as to fitness for purpose to be applicable are that the seller should sell the goods in the normal course of his business ….' The Court further accepted the view that the implied duty applies where the seller sells the goods in the ordinary course of his business description irrespective of whether the goods are sold as new or second hand.[85] In a recent non-consumer case of *Pyne & Associates v. African Motors,*[86] the question came up as to whether the sellers were dealers in the class of goods in contention. The Court, upon a perusal of the issues, explicitly observed that: '[t]he facts and circumstances of this case show clearly that the Defendants have been well known in the business of selling four-wheel drive vehicles of the type in contention.'[87] The issue is that the

[82] [2008] 4 GMJ [214].

[83] Section 13(1) (b), Sale of Goods Act 1962, Act 137.

[84] *Andreas Bschor GMBH v Birim Timbers Ltd* [2016] CA. No. J4/9/2015 [9]; See also, *Pyne & Associates v African Motors* (2017) CA. No. J4/38/2013, [15]; See also *Yirenkyi v Tormekpey* [1987–88] 1 GLR 533 CA [537].

[85] *Bschor GMBH v Birim Timbers Ltd* [2016] unreported CA. No. J4/9/2015 [8].

[86] [2017] unreported Supreme Court judgment, CA. No. J4/38/2013 [16].

[87] *Pyne & Associates v African Motors,* [2017] unreported Supreme Court judgment, CA. No. J4/38/2013, [16].

seller should be a dealer in the class of goods sold to give effect to the implied obligation with respect to the fitness of the goods.

It is important to highlight that there seems to be a sharp distinction between the instance for the exclusion of the seller's liability in the implied undertaking to supply goods that are free from defects observed above and the implied fitness obligation with respect to the doctrine of sale in the ordinary course of the trader's business. Thus, whereas the trader's statutory duty to supply goods that are free from defects is where the goods are supplied in the ordinary course of the seller's trade as examined above, it appears that the implied fitness obligation of the seller is confined to where the goods are of a description which the seller supplies in the ordinary course of his business. In other words, whilst the goods do not need to be in the trader's course of business in the case of the requirement for the goods to be free from defects, the goods need to be within the description of the trader's business in order to give effect to the operation of the goods' implied fitness for the particular purpose of the buyer. Moreover, under the implied duty of fitness, the buyer should have made known the purpose for which he requires the goods so as to give effect to the seller's obligation as will be seen shortly, but this is not required in the case of the duty to supply goods which are free from defects as examined earlier.

More importantly, the question of what constitutes sales in the ordinary course of the seller's business description has been a subject of judicial discussion, particularly in recent times.[88] For instance, in the non-consumer case of *New Lucky Electrical Ltd. v Startrack Int. Ghana Ltd and Another,*[89] the question that fell to be determined was 'where the goods are of a description which are supplied by the seller in the course of his business' in respect of the requirement for the seller to supply goods which are fit for the particular purpose of the buyer. The court, in this case, took the view that the provision in Ghana is an equivalent stipulation as found in the English 1979 SGA, which reads as 'where the seller sells the goods in the course of his business,' with respect to the seller's obligation to supply goods that are fit for the particular purpose of the buyer. Whilst the argument of whether the court's reading accurately reflects the Ghanaian text is beyond the scope of the present book, there seems to be, with respect, some linguistic differences in the recitals of the provision in the two regimes.

Significantly however, the court, after heavily relying on the English Courts[90] and the sixth edition of *Benjamin's Sale of Goods*, held that the provision covered sales which are an integral part of the trader's business and sales which incidentally are carried out by the trader with a degree of regularity even if the sale was one that

---

[88] *Andreas Bschor GMBH v Birim Timbers Ltd* [2016] unreported CA. No. J4/9/2015; See also, *Pyne & Associates v African Motors* [2017] unreported Supreme Court judgment, CA. No. J4/38/2013; *New Lucky Electrical Ltd. v. Startrack Int. Ghana Ltd and Isaac Acquah* [2010], unreported judgment of the High Court, Suit No. OCC 49/08; See also *Yirenkyi v Tormekpey* [1987–88] 1 GLR 533 CA.

[89] [2010], unreported judgment of the High Court, Suit No. OCC 49/08 [4].

[90] The English case law which the Court relied on are: *Ashington Piggeries v Christopher Hill Ltd* [1972] AC 44; *Stevenson v Rogers* [1999] QB 1028.

was happening for the first time in the nature of the seller's business. The court also contended that the provision included a one-off sale with a view to profit in the context of the seller's business. Within this context, the court concluded that the seller, who was in the habit of renting out heavy-duty equipment, including tipper trucks and excavators, sold the excavator to the buyer in the ordinary course of his business. The court, therefore, held that the seller was liable for defects in the excavator that rendered it unfit for its purchased purpose, which the buyer had declared before the contract.[91]

Similarly, the fundamental question that was placed to be addressed before the Supreme Court in the non-consumer case *of Bschor GMBH v. Birim Timbers Ltd* was what is meant by 'where the goods are of a description which are supplied by the seller in the course of his business.' The Supreme Court noting the absence of authority on the subject resorted to a number of English judicial authorities for persuasive guidance. The Court, after an exhaustive review of the English authorities,[92] made the following submission in respect of how the phrase should be read in the context of Ghana as follows:

> we will therefore broadly construe Section 13 (1) (b) of the Act 137 and give effect to the purpose of the provision by including any sale where there is an element of regularity showing the seller has been selling goods of that description as part of his business, whether it is his main business or not; or where the seller accepted an order from the buyer to supply goods of that description.[93]

This essentially sets out an expanded scope of what constitutes sales in the ordinary course of a seller's business description. In effect, sales in the principal business of the seller, sales in response to orders s/he has taken, and sales s/he carries out in regularity in his/her business adventures which may not be part of his/her core business, are all constituents of sales in the ordinary course of the seller's business description in respect of the doctrine of fitness. It is, however, important to note that the court went further to state that the provision is not applicable 'where the goods were sold on a 'where is' basis or as a private sale'[94] The court also discounted a one-off sale from the confines of the provision.[95] This in effect, excluded the seller's

[91] [2010] unreported judgment of the High Court, Suit No. OCC 49/08 [5].

[92] The various English cases that were cited for persuasion purposes included *Ashington Piggeries Ltd v Christopher Hill Ltd* [1972] A.C. 441; *Davies v Summer* [1984] 3 All ER 831 and *R & B Customs Brokers Co Ltd v United Dominions Trust Ltd (Saunders Abbott) (1980) Ltd, third party* [1988] WLR 321; *Jones v Bright* [1829] 130 ER 1167 [1171].

[93] *Bschor GMBH v Birim Timbers Ltd* [2016] unreported CA. No. J4/9/2015 [10–11]; see also, *Pyne & Associates v African Motors* [2017] unreported Supreme Court judgment, CA. No. J4/38/2013 [16].

[94] *Bschor GMBH v Birim Timbers Ltd* [2016] unreported CA. No. J4/9/2015 [10–11]; see also, *Pyne & Associates v African Motors* (2017) unreported Supreme Court judgment, CA. No. J4/38/2013 [16].

[95] This was done in *Bschor GMBH v Birim Timbers Ltd* [2016] unreported CA. No. J4/9/2015 [10] while relying on the English judicial pronouncements in *Davies v Summer* [1984] 3 All ER, 831; *R & B Customs Brokers Co Ltd v United Dominions Trust Ltd (Saunders Abbott (1980) Ltd, third party)* [1988] WLR 321.

liability for one-off sales that are carried out by the seller in the course of his business. This observation by the Supreme Court seems to discontinue the earlier observation by the High Court in the *New Lucky Electrical Ltd* case noted above that a one-off sale was to be viewed as a part of the description of goods in the seller's business that will give effect to the application of the implied fitness of goods for the buyer's purpose.

It can be seen that whilst the courts have widened the scope of sales in the ordinary course of the seller's business description to include sales the seller habitually undertakes with regularity and sale of goods in response to an accepted order, the regime nevertheless excludes one-off sales and private sales from its ambit. This implies that a consumer who obtains his/her goods from a seller who sells the goods to him/her in a one-off instance or private sale has no protection under the regime.[96] In the case of a private sale, it may be argued that parties in a private sale will have equal bargaining power and the goods may be of a lower value, and for that matter, the courts should not be overburdened with such disputes.

However, the exclusion of a trader's one-off sale from the confines of sale in the cause of a trader's business seems problematic to the generality of consumer protection in Ghana. In particular, the position of the law leaves doubts under the regime as to whether a seller disposing of his/her used assets to enable him to replace new ones falls within the ambit of sale in the ordinary course of the seller's business. Similarly, there remains uncertainty pertaining to where the seller decides to resell goods s/he bought as fixed assets for the running of his/her business in a one-off instance. Finding a solution to the uncertainty regarding a seller's sale of his old business assets or goods bought for the business in a one-off manner is important to ensure that consumers are afforded a very clear regime which will instil in them the confidence to operate in the market. This will boost the confidence of consumers, particularly in dealing with problems of defective goods, which raises questions about being sold in a one-off instance.

2.5.2 The Seller's Exemption from the Implied Liability for the Quality and Fitness of Goods

As discussed above, sellers of goods are under implied obligations to supply goods which are free from defects and fit for the purpose of the buyer in both sales contract and hire-purchase transactions in Ghana. However, there are instances, as recognised under the law, in which sellers may be able to exempt themselves from liability for the non-conformity of the goods they supply. In particular, sellers may be able to exclude themselves from liability where they expressly make the specific exemption aspect of the goods and its expected effects known to the buyer before or

[96] Yidana (2021).

at the time of the contract. The legal basis upon which sellers may be able to exclude themselves from the quality or fitness liability is explicitly stated as follows:

> The condition implied by paragraph (a) of subsection (1) is not affected by any provision to the contrary in the agreement where the goods are of a description which are supplied by the seller in the ordinary course of his business and the condition implied by paragraph (b) of subsection (1) is not affected by any provision to the contrary in the agreement unless the seller proves that before the contract was made the provision was brought to the notice of the buyer and its effect made clear to him.[97]

In *Bartholomiew & Co. Ltd. v. Adu-Gyamfi,*[98] the Supreme Court made an important statement in reference to the possibility of a seller to introduce an express liability exemption provision in a contract that excludes the implied quality or fitness requirements as discussed above whilst making the buyer aware of the exclusionary provision and its effect. This was particularly stated by the Court as follows:

> It is … settled law that there are certain terms implied in hire-purchase agreements such as … (c)implied condition or warranty of fitness for the purpose for which the goods are expressly hired or for which from their character the owner must be aware they were intended to be used. All the implied terms however are subject to the express terms of the agreement and within limits they may be excluded or modified if apt words are used; provided the party relying on such exempting clause carries out his contract in its essential respect, in other words, he does not commit a breach fundamental to the terms of the contract[99]

It is important to state that the statutory provision cited earlier is with respect to contracts of sale, whilst the judicial authority is to the effect of hire purchase agreements. Nevertheless, the judicial citation provides illuminating guidance with respect to how the statutory provision might be determined in relieving a seller from liability where the exclusion is clearly brought to the attention of the buyer and the effects explained or made known to him/her.

Whilst the above observation of the Court is a clear highlight of the possibility of a seller to exempt himself/herself from the quality and fitness failures of the goods supplied in a contract, it remains unclear the extent to which this might be carried out without jeopardising the position of the consumer. It has been suggested that what might be required of the seller is to specifically inform the consumer of the exact defect or unfitness of the goods for which the seller wishes to relieve himself/herself of any liability flowing from that and further explain to the buyer how that might affect his/her rights before the contract.[100] This observation seems to reflect the express submission of the Court in *Ashitey v. Ghana Industrial Holding Corporation,*[101] although this did not relate to a sales contract but to a bailment in

---

[97] Section 13 (2), Sale of Goods Act 1962, Act 137.

[98] [1962] 2 GLR 62; See Also, *KPeglo v Scoa Motors* [1962] 2 GLR 82, P87.

[99] *Bartholomiew & Co. Ltd. v Adu-Gyamfi* [1962] 2 GLR 62 [66]; See also, *KPeglo v Scoa Motors* [1962] 2 GLR 82 [87].

[100] Oninku (2022); Dowuona-Hammond (1995), p. 115; See also, Dei-Anang (1967); Nsubuga et al. (2024).

[101] [1989–1990] 1 GLR 474 [477].

which the plaintiff had brought his boat to the workshop for repairs but had his propeller misplaced by workshop owners. In this particular case, the court rejected the reliance on an exemption clause displayed in the defendant's workshop. It was particularly stated by the Court that it was the duty of the defendants to bring such liability exemption clause to the full knowledge and understanding of the plaintiff. The Court further added that the defendants needed to have explained to the plaintiff, who was not literate in English in the local language, to ensure that he fully understood the nature and consequences of the notice, without which the defendants could not escape the liability.

The requirement for the seller to show the exclusion and explain its implication to the buyer to be able to benefit from the liability exemption is important in helping to ensure that the buyer who is not aware of such exclusions is not deprived of the protection. However, the question as to whether such exemption clauses may always be fair to consumers remains unanswered. Ensuring that this is addressed is important to avoid the interests of the consumers being unfairly jeopardised under the pretext of liability exemption terms. This is particularly important as a substantial amount of available evidence suggests the predominant use of exclusion clauses that are greatly unfavourable to the general interest of consumers in Ghana. For instance, it is widely noted as a common practice for sellers to emboss clauses in their business premises, such as the company accepts no liability for defects in goods, goods purchased are not returnable, and money paid is not refundable, among others.[102] These clauses leave consumers in an unclear position as to whether they have any right of protection when the goods they buy are faulty.[103] The plight of consumers is further heightened by the absence of any form of control over the fairness of those terms presently under the Ghanaian regime.

The extent to which the fairness of such exemptions could be controlled is therefore critical for ensuring that sellers do not easily sidestep their fundamental obligations of supplying goods which are free from known defects and fit for the buyer's purpose. Addressing this will further ensure that consumers in Ghana are better protected.

2.6 Conclusion

This Chapter mainly examined the adequacy of the existing requirements for the quality of goods as regards the obligations of traders for the protection of consumers in Ghana. The analysis was essentially to answer the first research question regarding whether the regime requirements for the quality obligations of traders of goods are adequate to afford sufficient degree of protection to consumers when they are supplied with faulty goods. The discussion revealed that a number of limitations and

[102] Nkansah (2015).; Dowuona-Hammond (1995); Aborchie-Nyahe (2014).

[103] Dowuona-Hammond and Atuguba (2006).

uncertainties leave the regime in a deficient state of affording adequate protection to consumers in matters of disputes over faulty goods in Ghana. The definition of the standard for the quality of goods was found to be inadequate to appropriately help in dealing with the concern of consumers. In addition, the operation of the different standard terms of quality (free from defects or non-defective and merchantable quality) depending on whether the goods are purchased in a sales contract or hire-purchase transactions was revealed to have the tendency of creating confusion in the minds of the average consumer in Ghana as to what to expect. Similarly, the scope of assessing the quality of goods was found to be confined to latent defects which leave the regime handicapped to be able to respond to the quality concerns of consumers.

Regarding the implied requirement of fitness of goods for the particular purpose of the buyer, it was revealed that the extent to which the law will be applied in respect of a buyer's idiosyncratic needs is not clear. The issue of how the law may be applied in matters of multi-purpose of goods and claims made by the seller are also left unaddressed. In addition, the confinement of seller's liability to goods sold in the ordinary course of his business excluding one-off sales was found to limit the available protection for consumers in Ghana. This concern was particularly observed to premise on the fact that it is only sales that are carried out in the course of the trader's business that will give effect to the application of the implied requirement of quality and fitness of the goods. On this basis, as noted in the analysis, the exclusion of one-off sales from the ambit of sale in the ordinary course of the seller's business is not helpful to consumers who might obtain their goods in such instances. Similarly, the possibility of sellers introducing exemption clauses in respect of defects or unfitness of the goods by making buyers aware of the effects of such clauses was found to have the tendency of undermining the interest of consumers. The absence of measures to control unfair terms under such exemptions was seen as not helpful to the cause of consumers in Ghana.

The extent to which the various limitations and uncertainties could be addressed will further be explored in Chap. 3 below. This will be carried out in comparison with English law and its European experience while taking into account the domestic circumstances in Ghana.

References

Aborchie-Nyahe I (2014) The State of Consumer Protection in Ghana, presented at the Sixth Annual African Dialogue on Consumer Protection Conference, availabe online at https://view.officeapps.live.com/op/view.aspx?src=https%3A%2F%2Fwww.ftc.gov%2Fsystem%2Ffiles%2Fdocuments%2Fpublic_events%2F316871%2Fghanaireneaborchie.pptx%3Futm_source%3Dchatgpt.com&wdOrigin=BROWSELINK access 20/10/2025

Ackah I, Bukari D, Banye EZ, Bobio C (2021) Transitioning towards cleaner cooking fuels: an analysis of consumer preferences in Ghana's cookstoves market. Environ Sci Pollut Res 28(39):54936–54949

Akerlof GA (1970) The market for 'lemons': quality uncertainty and the market mechanism. Q J Econ 84:488–500

Ansa-Asare K (1980) Case for a comprehensive framework of consumer protection in Ghana. Rev Ghana Law XII & XIV:73

Bar-Gill O, Ben-Shahar O (2012) Regulatory techniques in consumer protection: a critique of European consumer contract law. Coase-Sandor Institute for Law & Economics Working Paper No. 598

Ben-Shahar O, Schneider CE (2011) The failure of mandated disclosure. Univ Pa Law Rev 159:647–749

Benz M-A (2007) Experience and credence goods—an introduction. In: Strategies in markets for experience and credence goods. DUV, Wiesbaden, pp 1–5

Bridge MG (2017) Benjamin's sale of goods, 10th edn. Sweet & Maxwell

Busch C (2015) The future of pre-contractual information duties: from behavioural insights to big data. In: Twigg-Flesner C (ed) Research handbook on EU consumer and contract law. Edward Elgar, Cheltenham, pp 221–240

Cartwright P (2004) Consumer protection and the criminal law: law, theory, and policy in the UK. Cambridge University Press, Cambridge

Dei-Anang KK (1967) Caveat Venditor Ghaniensis. Univ Ghana Law J 4:90

Dowuona-Hammond C (1995) Protecting the purchaser of goods under Ghanaian law. Rev Ghana Law 19:105

Dowuona-hammond C, Atuguba R (2006) The policy and legal framework for consumer protection in Ghana. Friedrich Ebert Foundation (FES)

Energy Efficiency Standards and Labelling (Household Refrigerating Appliances) Regulations (2009) LI 1958

Energy Efficiency Standards and Labelling (Non-Ducted Air Conditioners And Self-Ballasted Fluorescent Lamps) Regulation (2005) LI 1815

Goode R, Mckendrick E (2016) Goode on commercial law, 5th edn. Penguin

Hadfield GK, Howse R, Trebilcock MJ (1998) Information-based principles for rethinking consumer protection policy. J Consum Policy 21:131–169

Howells G (2005) The potential and limits of consumer empowerment by information. J Law Soc 32(3):349–370

Leahy AS, Howard W (2005) Search and experience goods: evidence from the 1960s and 70s. J Appl Bus Res 21(1):45–54

Marotta-Wurgler F (2014) Even more than you wanted to know about the failures of disclosure. Jerusalem Rev Leg Stud 11(1):63–74

Miller CJ, Harvey B, Parry D (1998) Consumer and trading law. Oxford University Press, Oxford

Mills JEA (1978) Rockson Armah: a case of caveat emptor, caveat Venditor or neither. Univ Ghana Law J 15:168

Nkansah LA (2015) Consumer protection in Ghana: an appraisal of the law. Joseph Ayo Babalola Univ Law J 2(1):185–200

Nsubuga LF, Naatu F, Kaaka DZ (2024) Consumer protection in hire purchase transactions: a case study of Ghana's legal framework. J Law Sustain Dev 12(10):e3972–e3972

Oninku EA (2022) A comparative study of the control of exclusion clauses in consumer contracts: lessons for Ghana. UCC Law J 2(1):37–60

Pascaud L, Thivillon T (2014) Ghana Consumer Segmentation Study: Global Alliance for Clean Cookstoves. <http://cleancookstoves.org/resources_files/ghana-consumer-segmentation-exec-summary.pdf>, [7–8] Accessed 30 June 2025

Ramsay I (2012) Consumer law and policy: text and materials on regulating consumer markets. Hart Publishing, Oxford

Twigg-Flesner C (2004) Information disclosure about the quality of goods—duty or encouragement? In: Howells G, Janssen A, Schulze R (eds) Information rights and obligations: a challenge for party autonomy and transactional fairness. Ashgate, Aldershot, pp 67–84

Wendlandt B (2005) EC Directives for self-employed commercial agents and on time-sharing: apples, oranges and the core of the information overload problem. In: Howells G, Janssen A, Schulze R (eds) Information rights and obligations: a challenge for party autonomy and transactional fairness. Ashgate, Aldershot, p 67

Yidana N (2020) The consumer in the midst of two distinct terms for the quality of goods in Ghana: can the law be simplified. J Law Policy Global 94:168

Yidana N (2021) Sale in the ordinary course of business under Ghana law: recent developments and lessons from the UK. Bus Law Rev 42(3)

Yidana N, Nkansah LA (2024) Consumer law in Ghana. In: Ghio E, Perlingeiro R (eds) Are legal systems converging or diverging?: lessons from contemporary crises. Springer Nature Switzerland, pp 101–125

Ziegel J (1973) The future of Canadian consumerism. Can Bar Rev 51:190

Chapter 3
Quality Requirements of Goods Under English Law: Resolving the Shortfalls of the Law in Ghana

3.1 Introduction

The previous Chapter examined the requirements for the quality of goods in consumer contracts in Ghana, mainly focusing on the extent to which the law protects consumers against faulty goods. The analysis identified a number of shortfalls that appeared to limit the degree of protection available for consumers in Ghana. This current Chapter seeks to address the uncertainties and limitations of the quality requirements for the supply of goods to consumers in Ghana. In particular, the terms (s) for the quality of goods in sales contracts and hire purchases are different and could confuse consumers as to what exactly to expect from the goods they buy. In addition, the standard terms for the quality of goods are not defined under the law and have been applied restrictively to the exclusion of critical quality features such as durability and appearance and finish, cherished by consumers in the goods they buy in Ghana. The extent to which the law may be applied to absolve the seller of liability for the supply of faulty goods in instances where the buyer examines the goods and where the seller discloses the defects in the goods was also uncertain. The question of how the law may be applied in matters of multipurpose goods claims by the seller and peculiar circumstances of the consumer with respect to the fitness of the goods for the particular purpose of the consumer was also found to be unsettled in Ghana. The court's definition of sale in the course of the trader's business was similarly found to be limited, especially where the seller is excluded from liability for one-off sales. It was also of concern that the possibility for parties to contract out of the statutory obligations under the law in Ghana could potentially undermine the degree of protection available to consumers.

The concerns with the quality requirements for the supply of goods, as was indicated, are unhelpful in providing consumers adequate protection in Ghana. This was found to be of great concern in view of the likelihood of consumers buying faulty goods in Ghana. The limitations and uncertainties, therefore, need to be addressed

N. Yidana, *Consumer Law and Policy on Faulty Goods*, Ius Gentium: Comparative Perspectives on Law and Justice 134,
https://doi.org/10.1007/978-3-032-08700-3_3

to clearly define a more enhanced regime for better protection of consumers in Ghana, as noted earlier in Chap. 2. The present Chapter seeks to address these concerns, taking guidance from English law but with due regard to the domestic perspectives in Ghana. This is particularly in response to the question regarding the extent to which English law requirements for the supply of quality goods to consumers can contextually help resolve deficiencies in the requirements for the supply of quality goods to consumers in Ghana. The basis for using English law for this comparative discussion has already been set out in Chap. 1 of this book.[1]

Before examining the highlighted concerns in Ghana through the lens of English law, it is important first to define the boundaries which will constitute the focus of the analysis concerning the use of English law for the present purpose. As already noted in Chap. 1 of this book, the quality requirements for the supply of goods to consumers under English law are presently found in the UK Consumer Rights Act 2015.[2] As noted in Chap. 1, the relevant provisions are mainly transposed from the pre-2015 regime but with some modifications, as the discussion below will show. Despite the identical nature of the rules to the pre-2015 regime, there exists a sharp distinction in terms of the range of contracts to which the rules apply in both regimes. In particular, whilst the pre-2015 regime applied to business-to-business (B2B) buyers, business-to-consumer (B2C) buyers[3] and consumer-to-consumer (C2C) buyers' matters, the CRA applies only to B2C contracts with the pre-2015 regime remaining the applicable law to B2B and C2C transactions.[4] The split of the regime to have more focused rules specifically dealing with B2C matters appeared to be centred on the settled view that consumers are always in a weak bargaining position, suffer information asymmetry about the quality of the goods, and have limited resources for asserting their rights when dealing with business traders and therefore need protection, which is not complex to understand.[5] It has be argued that the CRA dealing specifically with B2C is premised on the fact that: '[t]he buyer by

[1] For justification of the use of the English law for the present comparative discourse, see, Chapter One of this book on: 'The rationale for the use of the English law for the comparative analysis', para. 1.4.

[2] Herein refer to us, CRA.

[3] This has now been repealed in the case of business to consumer contracts by the inception of the CRA, 2015.

[4] This is clearly specified under the Explanatory Notes to the CRA 2015, para 24 under the title, 'Impact on Existing Legislation', p7; See also, Barry et al. (2016), para. 3.07.

[5] It worth stating that the essence of devoting this study to dealing with the extent to which consumers in Ghana could be better protected resonates with the settled position that consumers generally have a weak bargaining power, information asymmetry about the quality of goods they buy, inadequate wherewithal to assert their rights and therefore need protection. For detailed discussion; See, Brown (2016); See also, Ramsay (2012), p. 41; See also, Howells (2005); See also, Twigg-Flesner and Schulze (2010), p. 130; See also, Twigg-flesner (2004); See also, Twigg-flesner (2008); See also, Department for Business, Innovation and Skills (2014) Consumer Rights Bill: Statement on Policy Reform and Responses to Pre-Legislative Scrutiny, p. 10.; Department for Business, Innovation and Skills (2013) 'Draft Consumer Rights Bill: Government Response to Consultations on Consumer Rights' [5] & [40].

virtue of haste, ignorance, gullibility, inferior bargaining position or simple imprudence enter into transaction in which the goods supplied or the terms of the contract, or both, are unsatisfactory to him: and in many circumstances, it may be felt that he is deserving of protection whatever he may appear to have agreed. … These sorts of concerns have led to the construction of an elaborate body of law for the protection of consumers….'[6]

More significantly, given that the CRA provisions are restatements of the pre-2015 regime, as noted above, case law decided prior to the enactment of the CRA may be drawn upon to assist in appreciating the likely effect of the provisions under discussion. This is necessary as there are relatively few cases presently on the CRA 2015. It is also essential to state that decisions of both the English Courts and the Scottish Courts may be drawn to support the analysis. This is borne out of the fact that most of the relevant provisions on the quality requirements have a UK-wide application of equal magnitude. However, where Scottish case law is used in this book, it would be identified as such in the case citation. It is also worth clarifying that in resorting to the pre-2015 case law in the analysis, a degree of care will be applied where the Court's decision was made in the context of business-to-business matters. This caution is necessary because decisions of the courts on business-to-business matters have no binding effect on purely business-to-consumer issues, which is the primary focus of the CRA and, of course, the main concern of the present discussion. It is also vital to indicate that decisions of the Court of Justice of the European Union (CJEU) may also be helpful in supporting the analysis, especially in relation to aspects that implemented Article 2(2) of the EU Consumer Sales Directive.[7]

This chapter is organised into five principal sections including this introduction. The part following this introduction addresses the issues regarding the standard term for the quality of goods. This part starts with a layout of the provision on the standard of quality under the English law. This is followed-up with addressing the concern of the different standard terms being applied to sales contracts and hire-purchase transactions in Ghana. The section also seeks to resolve the problem of the definition of the standard term for the quality of goods in Ghana through the lens of English law, focusing mainly on the primary definition of satisfactory quality. This part also discusses the extent to which the limited scope of quality problems in Ghana may be resolved through the lens of the aspects of quality under the English law. The third part goes further to address the uncertainties regarding the requirements for the goods to be fit for the particular purpose of the consumer. In particular, the issue of multipurpose use of the goods, the issue of the consumer idiosyncratic purpose, and the issue of seller's claims are all been addressed in this section. The fourth part further resolves the issues relating to the exclusion of one-off sales from the trader's liability for the quality of the goods in Ghana and the issue of parties contracting out of the statutory obligations. The fifth part provides a conclusion.

---

[6] Bridge (2017), para.14.001.

[7] Section 9 of the CRA 2015; See also, Twigg-Flesner et al. (2016), p. 502.

This section provides a highlight of the findings of this chapter. Below is the requirement for the quality of goods to consumers under the English law mainly to resolving the shortfalls of the law in Ghana.

3.2 Quality Standard of Goods Under English Law: Resolving the Identified Issues in Ghana

This section seeks to analyse the issues pertaining to the standard of quality of goods to consumers in Ghana through the lens of the English law. Before the analysis, however, it is necessary to provide a highlight of the quality requirements regarding the standard of quality of goods under the English law. The quality framework for the supply of goods under the English law is contained under section 9 of the UK Consumer Rights Act, 2015. The Act provides that goods that are supplied in the course of a contract should be considered to include a term that the goods are of satisfactory quality.[8] The Act goes further to lay out a basic principle for the test of satisfactory quality of goods and complements the principle with a set of non-exhaustive lists of aspects of quality which may only have application in relevant circumstances. In particular, the Act states the basic requirement for the quality of goods as follows:

> [t]he quality of goods is satisfactory if they meet the standard that a reasonable person would consider satisfactory, taking account of – (a) any description of the goods, (b) the price or other consideration for the goods (if relevant), and (c) all the other relevant circumstances.[9]

Regarding the non-exhaustive requirements for the quality of goods, the Act states that:

> [t]he quality of goods includes their state and condition; and the following aspects (among others) are in appropriate cases aspects of the quality of goods – (a) fitness for all the purposes for which goods of that kind are usually supplied; (b) appearance and finish; (c) freedom from minor defects; (d) safety; and (e) durability.[10]

In addition to the various non-exclusive criterions, the Act also provides that public statements in respect of the quality characteristics of the goods may as well be taken into account under relevant circumstances in the determination of the satisfactory quality of goods.[11] The Act further clarifies that public statements made by the trader, his agent or the manufacturer of the goods as regards the quality characteris-

[8] Section 9 (1) of the United Kingdom Consumer Rights Act 2015.

[9] Section 9 (2), Consumer Rights Act 2015, United Kingdom.

[10] Section 9 (3), CRA 2015, UK.

[11] Section 9 (5), CRA 2015, UK.

tics of the goods may all come into play under relevant circumstances in the test for the satisfactory quality of goods.[12]

The above provision for the test of the satisfactory quality of goods is mainly a restatement of the pre-2015 regime as already noted in Chap. 1 and restated above.[13] The extent to which the above provision might be useful in resolving the problems of the regime in Ghana is explored below.

3.2.1 *Resolving the Use of Different Implied Standard Terms for the Quality of Goods in Ghana: Insights from English Law*

In Chap. 2 of this book, it was observed that the requirement for the quality of goods in a contract of sale and in a hire-purchase or conditional sales agreements uses different implied standard terms under the regime in Ghana. In particular, whilst the expressed implied standard term for the quality of goods in a contract of sale was that the goods should be free from defects, the implied standard term for the quality of goods in a hire-purchase or conditional sales agreement related to where the goods are of merchantable quality. The operation of the two distinct standard terms for the quality of goods was however argued as having the tendency of posing difficulties to consumers, especially regarding the standard term they should expect in the goods they buy. In other words, the standard term to expect in the goods may create confusion in the mind of the average consumer regarding which standard term to expect at any point in time. It was, therefore, suggested that a uniform standard term that reflects the quality of goods in consumer transactions in both sales and hire-purchase contracts might generally be more helpful to consumers than the present varied implied standard terms. It was further contended that resolving the issue of the different standard terms that are relevant to both channels of transactions was critical to ensure that consumers are afforded a more consistent and certain regime.

In comparing with the experience of the English law, the standard expected of goods delivered to consumers is that the goods should be of a satisfactory quality. This standard for the quality of goods is provided for in section 9 (1) of the CRA

[12] Section 9 (5), CRA 2015, UK.

[13] Specifically, section 9 of the CRA 2015 transposes section 14 (2A) and (2B) of the Sale of Goods Act, 1979 as previously noted in Chapter One. This was inserted into the 1979 Act by the Sale and Supply of Goods Act 1994 which itself originated from the 1893 Sale of Goods Act amended first in 1973 and consolidated in the 1979 Act before the 1994 revision. Moreover, public statement as a relevant circumstance for the determination of the quality of goods similarly originates from the 1979 Act. Public statement was first introduced into the 1979 Act (section 14(2D) and (2E), Sale of Goods Act,) through the Sale and Supply of Goods to Consumers Regulation 2002 which implemented the EU Directive 1999/44/EC.

2015 which itself is a restatement of section 14 (2) of the SGA 1979 as noted above. The proviso states that: '[e]very contract to supply goods is to be treated as including a term that the quality of the goods is satisfactory.'[14] The range of contracts covered for which satisfactory quality is to be treated as a term for the supply of goods to consumers include; sales contracts, contracts for the hire of goods, hire-purchase agreements and contracts for the transfer of goods.[15] It is important to indicate that conditional sales have been recognised as a sales contract under the CRA.[16] In *Atiyah and Adams' Sale of Goods*, it is submitted that: 'wherever a contract between a consumer and a trader involves the supply of goods (whether that is a sale, hire-purchase or hire) the same provisions will apply, although there are minor modifications for certain contracts.[17] In the CRA 2015 Explanatory Notes, it has similarly been clarified that sales contracts as an element of contracts to supply goods include conditional sales 'where goods are paid for in instalments and the trader retains ownership of the goods until the conditions in the contract have been met, whether the consumer has possession of the goods in the meantime or not.'[18] In any of these types of contracts to supply goods, the required standard term is that the goods should be of satisfactory quality as mentioned above. The application of uniform rules (including the standard of quality for the present purpose) to various transactions in consumer contracts has been extolled as a welcome development.[19]

The critical issue that triggers the above presentation of the English law is the guidance that may be drawn to address the confusion that might arise in the face of having two distinct standard terms in the different types of transactions in Ghana. This is particularly important to help ensure that any ambiguity the different standards might have is resolved for the benefit of consumers in Ghana. As observed above, the standard of satisfactory quality under the English law uniformly applies to the wide range of transactions involving consumers. The English law usage of one single term for the quality of goods in respect of the many transactions is very helpful in that when consumers become familiar with the term, they would not confuse it with other competing requirements, as is possibly the case with the different standard terms of quality in Ghana. The important question, however, is which standard term should the regime in Ghana use that would be sufficiently relevant and cover both transactions appropriately? Should the regime adopt one of the already existing standard terms of quality or it should consider the English standard term for the quality of goods in Ghana?

---

[14] Chapter 15.

[15] Section 3 (2), the UK CRA 2015.

[16] Section 5(3), the UK CRA 2015.

[17] Twigg-Flesner et al. (2016), p. 499.

[18] Explanatory Notes to the Consumer Rights Act 2015, para 58; See also, Department for Business, Innovation and Skills, 'Consumer Rights Act: Goods, Guidance for Business' (September 2015) <https://www.businesscompanion.info/sites/default/files/CRA-Goods-Guidance-for-Business-Sep-2015.pdf>. accessed on the 15/07/2025 [5].

[19] Twigg-Flesner et al. (2021), p. 473.

Drawing further guidance from the English law, it is worth noting that prior to the term of satisfactory quality as the standard term for the quality of goods, the standard term for the quality of goods was merchantable quality under the English law as provided in respect of the hire-purchase transactions in Ghana. This was, however, replaced with the current satisfactory quality standard term through the 1994 amendment to the1979 SGA which has now been restated under the CRA 2015 as noted previously. The merchantable quality was broadly found to be more appropriate to transactions involving retailers and wholesalers instead of consumer transactions.[20] It was also argued that the term was more attuned to natural products than complicated machinery which is the characteristic of the present-day products in the market.[21] Other criticisms were to the effect that the term has fallen out of general use and not suitable to consumer transactions. These criticisms consequently resulted in the Law Commission recommending its displacement.[22] Although the Law Commission's recommendation was to the effect of replacing 'merchantable quality' with 'acceptable quality',[23] the legislature nevertheless gave preference to 'satisfactory quality'.[24] The satisfactory quality as was introduced into the SGA 1979 by the SSGA, 1994 amendment is what has been transposed into section 9 of the CRA 2015 as noted earlier. The legislative favour for satisfactory quality had been argued to succeed in avoiding the potential confusion of the then proposed acceptable quality with its element of circularity which had manifested in the pre-1994 amendments of the 1979 SGA.[25]

The criticisms meted out to the 'merchantable quality' concept which led to its replacement under the English law raises the important question as to whether its adoption as the standard term of quality of goods in both sales contracts and hire-purchases transactions in Ghana would be appropriate to provide consumers with a clear regime? The highlighted criticisms of the merchantable standard term for the quality of goods under the then English law seem to begin to manifest in the case of Ghana in respect of consumer matters. In her more recent article in particular, Dowuona-Hammond posited that: 'the standard of merchantable quality ... is quite archaic, and not useful, in view of the uncertainties associated with its definition and scope.'[26] In an earlier commentary, the commentator had observed that the Sale of Goods Act 1962, 'Act 137 scrupulously avoids the use of the term "merchantable quality" with its definitional problems and inherent uncertainty of scope and instead

[20] See, The Law Commission, *Sale and Supply of Goods* (The Law Com. 160 and Scot. Law Com. No. 104, 1987) para. 3.10; See also, Willett (1993) [220]; Bridge (2003); Bridge (1995); Scott et al. (2000), p. 159.

[21] Bridge (1995).

[22] The Law Commission (1987) para. 3.19 – 3.22.

[23] ibid. para. 3.19–3.22.

[24] Section 14(2), the Sale of Goods Act, 1979 as amended by the Sale and Supply of Goods Act, 1994.

[25] Bridge (1995); Peter (1995).

[26] Dowuona-Hammond (2018).

refers specifically to "defects" in the goods ….'[27] Moreover, Mills had also argued that with the term of merchantable quality, goods may be bad or of inferior quality but yet fulfil the statutory requirement of being of merchantable quality. He therefore argued that the term was specifically alien to sale of goods transactions and that its application to the sale of goods in determining the quality of goods tends to lower the available protection under the Sale of Goods statute in Ghana.[28]

It is clear from the above submissions that using merchantable quality as the express standard term for the quality of goods in both sales and hire-purchase transactions will not be suitable in consumer transactions in Ghana. The question then is, should Ghana consider adopting the English law standard term of satisfactory quality or employ the requirement that the goods should be free from defects which is already the required standard under the sales contracts in Ghana as noted earlier? Taking first the standard term of satisfactory quality under the English law, the term has further been enlightened with a primary definition requiring the appraisal of the quality of goods to be carried out through the lens of a reasonable person, the description, and price of the goods including various aspects of quality criterion in relevant circumstances as will be examined shortly. This broad array of elements through which to test the conformity or otherwise of goods to the standard term of satisfactory quality seems to highlight the practical educational utility of the English regime. In particular, it was observed in the pre-CRA 2015 that while consumers might have difficulty in appreciating the degree of protection predating the inception of the satisfactory quality term, they may be 'more confident that their view of what constitutes 'satisfactory quality'is just as valid as that of the seller.'[29] While referring to the clarification of the relevant circumstances of the satisfactory quality term before the 2015 Act, it was similarly contended that the regime will better enable consumers to effectively bargain with traders.[30]

While the above observations properly positioned the doctrine of satisfactory quality capable of being well applied for the benefit of consumers in the UK, it is worth stressing that its educative content is clearly revealed in the broad spectrum of the definition that follows the standard term which will be explored further below. The express statement of the standard term itself does not seem to offer sufficient educative function to which consumer needs may be properly served. The editors of *Atiyah and Adams' Sale of Goods* have particularly observed that the term of satisfactory quality itself like its predecessor is a vague statement and that all vague terms tend to be meaningless or vacuous in practice.[31] The editors further contend that such a vague standard term gives 'little guidance as to what kind of defects or damages will render goods unsatisfactory … and are unhelpful in the practical

[27] Dowuona-Hammond (1995).

[28] Mills (1978).

[29] Howells and Weatherill (2005), p. 170.

[30] Willett and Morgan-taylor (2004); Ramsay (2012), p. 523.

[31] Twigg-Flesner et al. (2021), p. 141; Howells and Weatherill (2005), pp. 170–171.

application of the law'.[32] The term, therefore, turns to survive by employing the test of reasonableness to introduce the element of flexibility in its application. It has, however, been stressed that: '[t]ests which depend so heavily upon standards of reasonableness tend to be somewhat circular in practice.'[33] It has similarly been contended that the term of satisfactory quality is '... a phrase which as elaborated is little more than circular for any dispute."[34] However, the application of the test of reasonableness requires the court to fully evaluate each case with the primary sense of preserving justice.[35] This, therefore, underlined the standard term of satisfactory quality being juxtaposed with what a reasonable person would regard as satisfactory quality. The various elements of satisfactory quality, which will be discussed shortly, further adds up to make the standard term a viable statutory measure with the potential of affording the right fit criterion for the determination of the quality of goods.

As indicated above, the standard term of satisfactory quality has a recognised prominence that could afford very clear guidance to stakeholders in the determination of the satisfactory quality of goods. The question however is, will the standard requirement that the goods should be free from defects under the sales contracts in Ghana not aid the cause of consumers for both sales contracts and hire-purchase transactions in Ghana to warrant its displacement as a standard term for the quality of goods? Essentially, the prima facie disposition of the standard term that the goods should be free from defects goes to the point that the goods should be supplied without faults in them unless the faults are declared as previously examined in Chap. 2 of this book. On account of this, it has been argued that the standard term of quality that the goods should be free from defects preserves a very high standard degree for the quality of goods in Ghana with respect to sales contracts.[36] This has recently been affirmed by the Supreme Court that the sales law in Ghana 'imposes a heavier responsibility on sellers of goods'[37] regarding the required standard of quality expected of goods to purchasers. The standard term of quality that the goods should be free from defects clearly seems to self-evidently carry some educational value that might generally be useful to consumers. In particular, it has been advised that a statutory standard term of quality must move beyond 'a dispositive purpose' to a 'didactic purpose of educating the consumer or consumer rights organization reading the statute' in order to be properly a meaningful quality standard in consumer matters.[38]

From the discourse so far, it seems clear that the existing quality standard term requiring goods which a trader supplies to be free from defects remains practically relevant to securing a good degree of protection to consumers in respect of sales

---

[32] Twigg-Flesner et al. (2021), p. 141.

[33] Twigg-Flesner et al. (2021), p. 141; Ervine (2004).

[34] Ervine (2004).

[35] Twigg-Flesner et al. (2021), p. 141.

[36] Dowuona-Hammond (1995); MILLS (1981).

[37] *G. A. Sarpong v Silver Star Auto. Ltd* [2014], Suit No. J4/43/2013, [9].

[38] Bridge (2003).

contracts in Ghana. In effect, the need does not appear to arise to argue for the displacement of the current standard of quality under a contract of sale in Ghana. It may, therefore, be argued that the standard of quality requirements that demand traders to supply goods which are free from defects may accommodate not only sales contracts but also, hire-purchase transactions and conditional sales agreements in a suitable manner, if adopted. The adoption of the same quality standard term will ensure that consumers are offered a uniform express standard term of quality they should expect in the goods they buy. This will further address the chances of confusion that may result on account of the present different standard terms. This is significant to help provide a regime with more certainty to consumers in Ghana. This will be useful in safeguarding consumers when they are supplied with faulty goods in Ghana.

3.2.2 Resolving the Definition Shortfall of the Quality Standard in Ghana in the Light of the English Law

One other major issue of the standard of quality as noted earlier in Chap. 2 and restated above is the issue of the definition of the standard term for the assessment of the quality of goods in Ghana. As highlighted above, the recorded discussion in Chap. 2 bemoaned the absence of a clear definition for the assessment of the quality of goods in Ghana. This was noted as not being practically helpful for the safeguarding of consumer rights in Ghana. It was consequently highlighted that the limitation of the law needed to be addressed to ensure that consumers are better protected. This subsection will, therefore, examine the extent to which the English law might be helpful in providing the needed guidance to resolve the deficiency of the standard of quality definition within the context in Ghana. This is particularly useful to help in ensuring that consumers are afforded with an enhanced system of protection in Ghana.

As highlighted earlier, section 9 of the UK CRA does not only lay down a standard for the quality of goods to meet but also sets out a definition as a guideline for the determination of the quality of goods. The English law particularly requires that the basic requirement for the quality of goods is that the goods should be assessed within the context of a reasonable person having regard to the description of the goods, the price or consideration of the goods (if relevant) and other relevant circumstances.

The test is essentially an objective test, which is expected to be based on a hypothetical reasonable person with the relevant knowledge pertaining to the background facts of the goods.[39] It is within the construct of the reasonable person that a '…

[39] This observation had been made prior to the CRA 2015 in *Bramhill v Edwards* [2004] EWCA Civ 403 at [39] per Auld L.J.; The holding of Auld L.J. was followed in *Cembrit Ltd, Dansk Eternit Holding A/S v Apex Roofing Services LLP, Roy Alexander Leader* [2007] EWHC 111 (Ch); see

judge is required to evaluate the quality of the goods.'[40] From this background, the quality of the goods is expected to be examined having regard to the description attached to the goods at the time of the sale including the goods price (if relevant) and other circumstances that are deemed relevant in appropriate instances.

Guidance on the implementation of the provision can be seen from the judicial circles prior to the CRA 2015. Taking new goods first for example, Hale L.J. in *Clegg v Olle Andersson T/A Nordic Marine*[41] predating the 2015 Act had noted that a buyer of a brand new boat of a highly priced quality product costing nearly 'quarter of a million pounds,' is reasonably 'entitled to expect that it is free from even minor defects, in other words, perfect or nearly so.'[42] Similarly, in *Lamarra v Capital Bank plc,*[43] which also predates the 2015 Act, the buyer had agreed to a hire purchase price of £51,550.00 for a new Range Rover but the vehicle was subsequently detected with a series of defects a few days after delivery. With particular reference to the vehicle being very expensive and sold as a top of the range car, the Inner House of the Court of Session was satisfied to uphold the dictum of the Sheriff Principal that a reasonable person would be expected to receive such a car without any defects.[44] In a non-consumer case also predating not only the 2015 Act but also the 1994 amendment, the House of Lords had observed that what a buyer who paid a higher price is entitled to is reasonably something in line with the payment made 'if not to the value of his money, at least to a grade not entirely and hopelessly out of line with what he has paid'.[45]

It seems clear from the above illustrations that in considering the requirement of the provision set out earlier, a higher standard of quality is to be expected of new goods sold at a relatively higher price. It is important to further note that prior to the 2015 Act the courts were of the view that the overall ambit of the provision reflected a 'general standard which goods are required to reach' in a contract for the supply

also, the earlier case of *Clegg v. Anderson* [2003] EWCA, Civ 320; [2003] 1 All ER (Comn) 721, [2003] 2 Lloyd's Rep 32.

[40] Before the 2015 CRA, this had been expressed in *Kelly v Jewson Ltd* [2003] EWCA Civ 1030; [2004]1 Lloyd's Rep. 505 at [78].

[41] [2003] EWCA Civ 320; [2003] 2 Lloyd's Rep 32 at [72–73].

[42] [2003] EWCA Civ 320; [2003] 2 Lloyd's Rep 32 at [72]; See also, the pre-1994 case of *Rogers v Parish (Scarborough)* [1987] QB 933, where Mustill L.J. had similarly pointed out that the buyer of the new Range Rover which price was well above the level of an ordinary saloon car was entitled to have value for money.

[43] [2006] CSIH 49; 2007 S.C. 95; 2006 S.L.T. 1053; 2007; S.C.L.R. 719; 2006 G.W.D. 33-686; The Inner House of Court of Session heavily relied on the dictum of Mustill L.J. in *Rogers v Parish* while acknowledging the variation of the regime. The principle was merchantable quality in the pre-1994 regime in which *Rogers v. Parish (Scarborough) Ltd* [1987] QB 933 was decided, but the principle during the *Lamarra v. Capital Bank Plc* is the term of satisfactory quality as retained under the CRA, 2015.

[44] See also, *Kynaston-Mainwaring v GVE London Ltd*, 2022 WL 10712475 (2022).

[45] *BS Brown Ltd v Craiks Ltd* [1970] 1 W.L.R. 750 at [760] HL, per Viscount Dilhorne.

of goods.[46] In line with this, the courts essentially contended that the principal goal is to provide protection to consumers in 'the sale of substandard goods' thereby requiring the test to always take into account the intrinsic quality of the goods.[47] This, therefore, seems to set out the philosophical basis for the defined general standard the goods must reach in order to satisfy the requirement of being of satisfactory quality objectively taking into account the description, price and other relevant circumstances pertaining to the goods.

The requirement of the English law that the quality of goods assessment should be viewed from the perspective of a reasonable person, taking into account the description and price of the goods, may aid the cause of safeguarding consumers against the substandard quality of goods in Ghana if the test is replicated. This is because the underlining philosophical essence of the English law directly reflects the problems of consumers in Ghana. In Chap. 1 of this book, in particular, substandard goods were noted to inundate the market in Ghana, which largely exposes consumers to the possibility of buying poor quality goods. It will, therefore, be relevant that in resolving the definitional limits of the standard of quality in Ghana, a measure that is directed towards protecting consumers in the event that they encounter substandard goods is practically useful. This makes the initiative of the English defined criterion directly relevant to appropriately respond to the situation of consumers in Ghana. Especially, requiring that the test for the goods should be examined through the lens of a reasonable person within the remit of the description and price of the goods if adopted in Ghana will likely ensure that goods which are really shown to be substandard are rendered as defective goods.

The critical question, however, is should the same standard be applied in the case of second-hand goods in applying a similar test in Ghana? Addressing this question is important because consumers are not faced with only new goods but also confront on a daily basis second-hand goods in Ghana. It is, therefore, necessary to clarify in advance whether a similar demand should be expected or a less stringent standard test of quality should be anticipated for goods described as second-hand goods and sold at a fairly lower price within the reasonable person's standard in adopting a similar criterion in Ghana.

Some guidance from how the law has been applied by the English courts may be crucial here. In terms of the application of the test to second-hand goods before the courts in the UK, the case of *Thain v Anniesland Trade Centre*,[48] predating the CRA

---

[46] This had been expressed prior to the CRA 2015 in *Jewson Ltd v Kelly* [2003] EWCA Civ 1030; [2004] 1 Lloyd's Rep. 505; [2004] 1 C.L.C. 87; [2004] B.L.R. 31, para 46 and para. 77; see also, the non-consumer case of *Balmoral Group Ltd v Borealis (UK) Ltd* [2006] EWHC 1900 (Comm), [2006] 2 Lloyd's Rep. 629, at 140.

[47] This had been expressed prior to the 2015 CRA in *Jewson Ltd v Kelly* [2003] EWCA Civ 1030; [2004] 1 Lloyd's Rep. 505; [2004] 1 C.L.C. 87; [2004] B.L.R. 31, para 46 and para. 77; see also, the non-consumer case of *Balmoral Group Ltd v Borealis (UK) Ltd* [2006] EWHC 1900 (Comm), [2006] 2 Lloyd's Rep. 629, at 140.

[48] [1997] SLT [Sh Ct] 102, 106; see also *Richford v Parks of Hamilton (Townhead Garage) Ltd* [2012] GWD 24 – 505, Hamilton Sheriff Court) – where it had been maintained that a buyer of second hand goods should expect the goods to be of a lower standard than where they are new

2015, provides an illustration to this effect. In the particular case, *Thain* had purchased a second-hand car for £2995. The car had covered 80,000 miles as was shown on the odometer. Two weeks after the purchase, the car gearbox developed a fault. In determining the matter, the Sheriff Principal in Scotland gave much of his weight to the covered mileage of the second-hand car prior to the time of which the plaintiff bought the vehicle and its lower price. The court arrived at the point that the quality of the vehicle had been lowered and the defect expected and assumed by the buyer. The court particularly stated that: '[p]eople who buy second-hand cars get them at less than their original price in a large part because second-hand cars have attached to them an increased risk of expensive repairs. The price of the Renault, £2,995, was considered reasonable because there was the risk of expensive repair attached to the Renault.'[49] While second-hand goods can hardly be expected to be in perfect condition as new goods as observed, they are, however, expected to be 'reliable and capable of giving good service and fair performance.'[50]

From the pre-2015 application of the provision as exemplified above, second-hand goods which are often sold at a relatively lower price may reasonably have an acceptable low degree of quality and manifestation of defects after purchase may be tolerated. It is also clear that a high standard of quality is expected of new goods that are sold at a relatively higher price as against a less strict standard test of satisfactory quality in the case of second-hand goods sold at a fairly lower price under the English law.

Adopting a similar standard as contained under the English law stands the chance of better serving the interest of consumers in Ghana. First, a similar objective standard premised on the description and price of the goods as the basis for the assessment of the quality of goods in Ghana will create a fair and balanced system for both traders and consumers. This would largely ensure that the determination of the quality of goods is objectively assessed on the basis of a reasonable person having in mind the description and price of the goods without merely serving the interest of individual parties. The associated benefit this could generate is the guarantee that only truly substandard or faulty goods would be declared unsatisfactory. This would potentially discourage traders in selling substandard or faulty goods to consumers especially when they come to know that such goods (depending on their description and price) may be declared unsatisfactory from an objective standard of a reasonable person. This will consequently spare consumers of having to put up with being

goods; See also an earlier case of *Bartlett v Sidney Marcus*, [1965] 1 WLR 1013 where Lord Denning in his judgement then observed that '… a buyer, when he buys a second hand car, should realise that defects may appear sooner or later.' This observation was made in reference to a minor defect that had appeared after coverage of about 300 miles which cost of repair was about £45 more than the expected cost before the transaction. The Court therefore maintained then that the repair cost being higher than expected did not imply a breach of the implied conditions of quality.

[49] [1997] SLT [Sh Ct] 102, 106; see also *Richford v Parks of Hamilton (Townhead Garage) Ltd* [2012] GWD 24 – 505, Hamilton Sheriff Court); See also *Adam v Moneybarn* No.1 Ltd.[2025] SC DUM 6, [2025] 2 WLUK 206, [2025] G.W.D. 8-69.

[50] Carswell J. in *Lutton v Saville Tractors (Belfast) Ltd.* [1986] 12 NIJB 1: This observation predates the 2015 Act including the 1994 amendments.

faced with unsatisfactory goods without a guaranteed assurance of reliable protection to fall on as was noted in Chap. 1 of this book.[51]

Secondly, applying a similar test in Ghana will afford the needed guidance to serving the needs of consumers in the determination of the quality of goods. This is particularly relevant to resolving the charge that the regime in Ghana lacks such guidance on account of the absence of a clear criterion of the quality standard shown in the discussion in Chap. 2 earlier. In particular, the quality regime clearly spelling out that the expected standard for the quality of the goods indexes the objective reasonable person's standard to the relevant description and price of the goods is vital to offer guidance regarding the main criterion for the determination of the quality of the goods in Ghana. This will ensure that goods that failed to conform to the quality specification from the premise of such a set-out criterion will be held to be in breach of the stipulated standard of quality.

For instance, in taking what a reasonable person would regard as satisfactory, a brand-new car sold at the full market price would certainly be required to be of a high standard of quality compared to a second-hand car sold in the Ghanaian market at one-third of its market price. This implies that a consumer who buys second-hand goods will not reasonably expect the same level of stringent standard of quality in like manner as a purchaser of new goods. Deficiencies such as dents and scratches for example, which may be unacceptable in goods of a new description, might otherwise be acceptable in the case of second-hand goods. The effect will be that purchasers of new goods will always be entitled to expect that the goods they buy are of the stated quality. This will not only offer clear guidance but will as well inspire consumer confidence in the market. Largely, dissatisfied consumers can clearly rely on the plain provision of the regime if adopted to seek redress, especially where they are supplied with substandard goods that fail to conform to the stated quality of the goods.

Moreover, one important part of the definition requiring the quality of goods assessment to be viewed through the lens of a reasonable person that may as well be useful to resolve the issue of lack of a definition of the standard of quality in Ghana is the recognition of other relevant circumstances in appropriate instances. The question of what other relevant circumstances may entail has been stated to include public statements in the form of advertising or labelling, among others, regarding the quality characteristics of the goods by the seller, the manufacturer, or their representatives.[52] A public statement as a part of other relevant circumstances originates from the 1979 SGA which itself was the implementation of the EU CSD through the 2002 Regulation.[53] It was observed in the pre-2015 regime that public

[51] See Chapter One, para. 1. 2 'The Problem Statement and brief review of the law' where a survey carried out by the Consumer Watch revealed that about 90% of respondents reporting to have had problems with the goods the purchased but did not put up any challenge on the basis of uncertainty of the regime.

[52] Section 9 (5) and (6), the UK CRA 2015.

[53] The phrase 'other relevant circumstances' was previously left to be determined by the Courts but the amendment to the Sale of Goods Act 1979 effected by Regulation 3 of the Sale and Supply of

statements as a part of relevant circumstances may possibly heighten the bargaining potential of consumers where the statement has actually been made. It was further contended that holding traders accountable for statements made by manufacturers which they did not repeat is an expansion of the degree of liability for the benefit of consumers.[54]

The only circumstance under which the seller may be able to escape liability for statements regarding the quality of the goods is where the seller is able to show that he was unaware and could not reasonably be aware of the statement in question, or the statement had been withdrawn and corrected especially if its earlier version was misleading or incorrect, or the buyer's purchasing decision could not have been influenced by the said statement.[55] The seller may nevertheless face forensic difficulties in being able to prove that the consumer decision to buy the goods was not influenced by the statements about the quality of the goods.[56] In effect, statements which are made regarding the quality of the goods when relevant might be used as the basis for the determination of whether the goods conform to the test of satisfactory quality or not.

The clarification of other relevant circumstances to include statements that are publicly made through advertising or labelling among others as being required to be considered in the assessment of the quality of goods when relevant will similarly be critical in providing a very clear response to the limitation of a definition of the standard of quality in Ghana. Undoubtedly, consumers mostly get to know about the quality characteristics of the goods from the suppliers of the goods. The very claims or statements by either the sellers or manufacturers or their agents is what often influences the consumer in making his purchasing decision. The introduction of a similar requirement in defining the standard term of quality will, therefore, ensure that where these statements are actually made, consumers are protected in Ghana. Especially, while introducing new goods into the market, suppliers of goods make claims about the particular consumer needs the goods are meant to satisfy highlighting the quality characteristics of the goods as their selling point. Similar rhetoric is continuously made about existing goods so as to maintain a constant increase and retention of a reasonable market share of consumers. The particular purposes of both new and existing goods are mostly communicated to consumers through diverse channels so as to attractively persuade customers to buy the goods.[57] It is for

---

Goods to Consumers Regulation 2002 which implemented the EC Directive 1999/44, however, defined other relevant circumstances as currently contained in the Consumer Rights Act 2015.

[54] Willett and Morgan-taylor (2004), p. 94.

[55] Section 9 [7] (a), (b) and (c).

[56] Bridge (2014), para 7.79.

[57] Traders reach out to consumers about the functions of their products through multidimensional communication channels such as: personal selling in the markets, door-to-door selling, outreach sales promotion, brochures or flyers, billboards, radio and television advertising among others. Through these channels the particular purpose of the goods is often well expressed and mainly informs the consumer buying decision making. For details see, Duncan (2016); Iddris and Ibrahim (2015); Mwaawaaru (2009).

instance not uncommon for traders to rehearse the specific purpose of the goods to consumers to induce them into making purchasing decisions in their face to face personal selling which is rated as one of the most efficient and trusted sales routes presently in Ghana.[58]

A consumer who relies on such statements about the quality and purposes of the goods in buying the goods will be better protected if the regime in Ghana introduces a similar requirement. This should have the effect of requiring the test of quality to be based on the perspective of a reasonable person on account of not only the description of the goods and price but also other relevant circumstances that equally reflect statements that are made about the quality characteristics of the goods. In short, the test for the quality of goods as being free from defects should be framed on the principle of reasonableness through the lens of the goods description, their price, and other relevant circumstances (embracing among others public statements about the quality characteristics of the goods). This is particularly important to ensure that consumers are well protected in instances where they place full reliance on the statements that are publicly made about the goods by the seller, or the manufacturer or their agents and the goods eventually fail to meet the degree of quality espoused. This is necessary to ensure that sellers who seek to outsmart consumers are not allowed to escape liability regarding claims they made about the quality of the goods. It is also vital to safeguard consumers against the substandard quality of goods in the Ghanaian market as was highlighted in Chap. 1. This will largely build the confidence of consumers in the law to afford them sufficient protection.

3.2.2.1 Resolving the Problem of the Limited Scope for the Assessment of the Quality of Goods in Ghana through the Lens of the English Law

In Chap. 2, it was observed that the criterion for the assessment of the quality of goods is confined to latent defects. Other crucial quality requirements such as durability, safety, aesthetic qualities among others which consumers expressly cherished in goods they buy were however found to be precluded from the regime in Ghana. This was argued to leave the regime in an unsatisfactory state in providing the needed breadth of protection to consumers in Ghana. The present section, therefore, seeks to explore the extent to which the English regime might be helpful in resolving the express limitation of the law in Ghana. This is especially critical to ensure that the issue is resolved to make the regime directly useful in meeting the expectations of consumers in Ghana.

As discussed above, the English law defined the standard term of satisfactory quality to mean what a reasonable person would regard as satisfactory taking into account the description of the goods, the price (if relevant) and all other

---

[58] Export. Gov. (2017) 'Ghana – Selling Factors and Techniques' <https://www.export.gov/article?id=Ghana-Selling-Factors-and-Techniques> accessed 02/05/2018; see also, Sarah (2016).

circumstances in appropriate instances. As also highlighted earlier, upon the primary definition of the standard term of satisfactory quality, the English regime proceeded further to state that the quality of goods among others includes the state and condition of the goods and other aspects such as the fitness of the goods for all the purposes for which goods of that kind are usually supplied, appearance and finish, freedom from minor defects, safety and durability in appropriate instances.[59] While the previous section demonstrates the extent to which the primary definition of satisfactory quality could be useful in addressing the lack of a definition of the standard term of quality in Ghana, the present discussion explores how the various aspects of quality criterion might be able to assist in resolving the limited scope of the criterion for the quality of goods under the regime in Ghana as stated above.

The practical application of the English law aspects of quality as set out above can be drawn from the pre-2015 judicial construction of the quality aspects for guidance. For instance, in *Bramhill v Edwards*[60] prior to the 2015 Act, the question that arose before the Court was whether a vehicle the width of which was in excess of the width requirement of the Road Vehicle Regulations which the authorities had ignored amounted to a breach of the satisfactory quality. Whilst the excess width of the vehicle appeared to have raised safety concerns, it was nevertheless held by the Court as having no effect on the quality of the vehicle due to the absence of the risk of prosecution. The observation obviously appeared to have dispelled safety as a relevant circumstance. In the subsequent case of *Lowe v W Machell Joinery Ltd.,*[61] Lloyd L.J., while referring to the *Bramhill* case, the Court observed that but for the fact that there was no real risk of prosecution for the exceeded width, the vehicle would have been held in that case not to be of satisfactory quality.[62] However, the Court's verdict in the *Bramhill*'s case was criticised as a missed opportunity to treat it as a policy issue and to require that if goods cannot lawfully be used for a particular reason, they should not be of satisfactory quality irrespective of the absence of prosecution.[63] The point worth emphasising is that the application of any of the aspects of quality to the determination of the quality of goods under the English law is based on the relevance of each criterion to the particular case.

A further illustration can be seen in the matter of *Lamarra v Capital Bank plc,*[64] where the Inner House of the Court of Session had emphasised that all the other relevant circumstances prescribed by the law potentially had a very wide scope. The Court went further to stress that the relevant circumstances must only reflect circumstances that actually have a direct bearing upon the quality of the goods in question. Moreover, in the non-consumer case of *Balmoral Group Ltd. v Borealis*

[59] Section 9 (3) (a) to (e) of the UK Consumer Rights Act 2015.

[60] [2004] EWCA Civ 403; [2004] 2 Lloyd's Rep. 653.

[61] [2011] EWCA Civ 794; [2012] 1 All E.R. (Comm) 153; [2011] B.L.R. 591; 138 Con. L.R. 48; [2011] N.P.C. 72 Per Lloyd LJ., para. 44.

[62] Lloyd LJ. In *Lowe v W Machell Joinery Ltd* [2011] EWCA Civ 794; [2012] 1 All E.R. (Comm) 153; [2011] B.L.R. 591; 138 Con. L.R. 48; [2011] N.P.C. 72.

[63] Twigg-Flesner (2005).

[64] *Lamarra v Capital Bank plc* [2006] CSIH 49; [2007] SC 95 at 73–76.

(UK) Ltd[65] reflecting the dicta of the pre-2015 Act, it was observed that while fitness for all possible purposes is required, the requirement would be too wide where the goods have a broad range of possible uses and therefore only requires flexible application taking account of the relevant facts of the case. Similarly, whilst durability of goods requires that the goods should continue to endure for a reasonable time after supply, in the case of the *Thain v Anniesland Trade Centre*[66] as noted earlier, the vehicle was held to be of satisfactory quality although it had broken-down 2 weeks after delivery. The vehicle apparently was not durable. However, the description of the vehicle as a second-hand car of about 6 years old, and the lower purchase price of £2995 as highlighted previously had displaced durability from being a relevant circumstance in the instant case.

From the practical application of the law, it seems clear that goods will not inevitably be unsatisfactory just because they don't "tick" one of the relevant circumstances. It is perfectly possible for an item with short durability to be of satisfactory quality if sold at a lower price, whereas a similar item at a higher price might be expected to be more durable—especially if the former were described as "used" and the latter as "new". So, the point is that depending on the relevance of a given criterion to the particular case, the goods may be rendered unsatisfactory on the basis of their lack of durability, safety, fitness, and appearance and finish under UK law. The application of any of the complementary aspects of quality to the declaration of goods as satisfactory or unsatisfactory is only subject to when the said factor or a non-listed related factor is deemed relevant or otherwise in the particular case.[67] More importantly, the aspects of quality criterion are mainly observed to essentially constitute a further clarification of the requirement of 'other relevant circumstances' that may be essential in appropriate instances to the determination of the satisfactory quality of goods.[68] The various aspects of quality which may be adopted as guidelines in evaluating the quality of goods have also been argued to constitute primarily the most important expectations of consumers.[69]

Whilst the basic substance of the aspects of quality under the English law seems practically useful to consumers in Ghana, the approach to the various aspects of quality would need to be tailored towards the domestic circumstances of consumers in Ghana to ensure that they are well protected. In particular, the itemised non-exclusive guidelines for the determination of the quality of goods under English law are similarly relevant at two levels in resolving the problems of consumers in Ghana. First, consumers in Ghana are broadly identified to be more concerned about the durability, aesthetic, safety, functional reliability of the goods among others in making their purchasing decisions of various products in the market as was observed

[65] [2006] EWHC 1900 (Comm); [2006] 2Lloyd's Rep. 629 at [40]–[41].

[66] [1997] SLT [Sh Ct] 102, 106.

[67] Howells and Weatherill (2005), p. 180.

[68] *Lamarra v Capital Bank Plc* [2006] CSIH 49 at 69; [2007] S.C. 95; 2006 S.L.T. 1053; 2007 S.C.L.R. 719; 2006 G.W.D. 33-686.

[69] Bradgate and Twigg-Flesner (2003), p. 49.

earlier in Chap. 2 of this book.[70] In effect, the aspects of quality under the English law set-out above will similarly be useful meeting the highly desirable consumer expected requirements in goods they buy in the Ghanaian market if the aspects of quality are adopted in Ghana. Secondly, the inclusion of the various aspects of quality as guidelines is desirable in terms of giving a wider spectrum of clear quality specifications that could enhance the protection of consumers in Ghana. This will boost the confidence of consumers in Ghana while purchasing goods in the markets as they can rely on any quality criterion relevant to the goods they buy to hold the seller liable where the goods are not in conformity with the contract if adopted. The overall usefulness of a similar quality criterion in Ghana is that it will help to ensure that consumers are afforded enhanced protection. This is significant to safeguard consumers against defective goods in Ghana.

As indicated above, however, the approach to the aspects of quality will need to be modified to directly suit the circumstances of consumers in Ghana. It is important to note that whilst the problem of consumers regarding faulty goods might be similar in both Ghana and the UK as noted in Chap. 1, the literacy levels of consumers in both regimes are markedly different. In particular, majority of consumers in Ghana are within the illiteracy brackets. Moreover, the literate consumer population are equally less informed about the laws governing their rights and often see the law as a complex regime, broadly compared to their counterparts under the English law. It is therefore, important that the adoption of similar aspects of quality in Ghana is framed with the aim of avoiding potential ambiguities to render them more practically suitable to the needs of consumers. In particular, the application of any of the aspects of quality under the English law is mainly dependent on the relevance of the given quality criterion to the particular case in question as noted previously. The adoption of this approach of the English law *sensu stricto* in Ghana requiring the aspects of quality to apply only when a given criterion is relevant, might introduce elements of uncertainty to many consumers taking into account the class of most consumers in Ghana as noted above. In particular, consumers may have doubts as to whether the particular aspect of quality in issue will be taken as a relevant factor to secure a favourable determination in an action. Such an uncertainty may consequently discourage consumers from contemplating initiating actions when they are supplied with defective goods especially if the English law approach is adopted, as it is, in Ghana.

What might be more helpful to consumers in Ghana is to require that goods which are sold as new goods should always satisfy the various aspects of quality including the already settled view of the absence of latent defects to render the goods as being free from defects. The adoption of the aspects of quality in Ghana to include latent defects may nevertheless indicate clearly that where the goods are bought as second-hand goods, the application of any of the aspects of quality should be subject to the test of the particular quality criterion being a relevant factor similar to the approach of the English law. In short, the aspects of quality should be met in

[70] For details, see Chap. 2, para 2.2.1.1.

the case of new goods but vary on the basis of any of them being relevant in a given instance of second-hand goods. In effect, a consumer who is buying new goods should be entitled to require that the goods the seller supplies him are fit for all their known purposes, reflect their expected appearance and finish, are free from minor defects, are safe, durable and are without latent defects. This will largely ensure that consumers obtain a high degree of quality goods when they buy new goods in the market in Ghana. When buying second-hand goods on the other hand, the application of any of the various aspects of quality should be subject to the particular aspect of quality being relevant taking into consideration as earlier examined, the description and price of the goods in the light of a reasonable person's standard. This will allow a flexible application of the various elements in the case of second-hand goods. The adoption of this approach in Ghana will possibly provide a more simplified regime for the collective benefit of both consumers and traders. Disputes over an aspect of quality being a relevant factor may also be reduced.

Admittedly, however, it is not discounted that the provision as it is in the English law may produce a similar outcome in respect of new goods as envisaged in the proposed modification in the context of Ghana. For example, in *Ward v MGM Marine Ltd,*[71] which predates the CRA 2015, the issue of fitness for all purposes for which the goods were supplied, including safety and durability were the crucial factors for the assessment of the quality of the goods. In the instant case, a luxury motor yacht caught fire and exploded 15 min after delivery. While the cause of the fire could not be identified with precision, it was held that the fire source, without doubt, resulted from a deficiency associated with the yacht implying that it was not of satisfactory quality. In the said case, fitness for all purposes, durability and safety were all relevant factors which the new goods failed to satisfy. In a recent case of *Peebles v Rembrand Builders Merchants Ltd*[72] decided on the previous text of the law, the plaintiffs purchased tiles and carried out work in their residential home which was expected to retain their appearance between 15 to 20 years. The colour of the tiles, however, deteriorated 5 years after usage. From the evidence, the court observed that the defects existed before the date of delivery as latent defects and only took 5 years to manifest. The tiles were therefore held to have failed the test of appearance, of finish, of durability and, ultimately, of being of satisfactory quality.

As shown above, the English text on the aspects of quality could produce outcomes similar to what the proposed modification could generate for the benefit of consumers in Ghana. Nevertheless, it will still be more practically beneficial to the tailored needs of consumers in Ghana if the provision is replicated to expressly require the standard of goods to be goods which are free from defects to confirm that the goods have actually met the various aspects of quality in respect of new goods, while entertaining variation as regards second-hand goods similar to the English law requirement. This will simplify the regime to assist the course of consumers in Ghana. Moreover, the advantage of expressly stipulating for a consistent application

[71] [2012] EWHC 4093 QB.

[72] [2017] SC DUN 28; [2017] WL 01831372, para. 56.

of the various aspects of quality in the determination of the quality of new goods will dispel possible uncertainties that may greet the question of when each quality aspect would be a relevant conception in the Ghanaian context as noted earlier. This will further forestall the potential disputes that may characterise the relevant based regime. This will also ensure that the regime reflect the tailored circumstances of consumers in Ghana.

While considering modifying the aspects of quality to better serve the needs of consumers in Ghana, it is crucial to state that the listed aspects of quality may still fall short of affording consumers in Ghana with a sufficient degree of protection in view of the situation in Ghana. As clearly observed in Chap. 1, there are alleged incidences of substandard goods in the markets in Ghana. It will therefore be more helpful to extend the coverage of the scope of the proposed aspects of quality criteria in Ghana to expressly include technical regulatory standards expected of the various goods in the market in Ghana. Although it cannot be ruled out that there are no substandard goods in the UK, the degree to which the problem has reached in Ghana seems to be relatively different. In particular, the problem of substandard goods in Ghana has recently been argued to be a national crisis as noted in Chap. 1 of this book.[73] The situation in Ghana, therefore, demonstrates the need for the inclusion of technical standards as aspects for the determination of the quality of goods that are supplied to consumers. Essentially, the inclusion of technical standards requirements for goods to meet will broaden the liability of sellers of goods regarding the quality expectation of goods they sell. This will ultimately discourage sellers from dealing with substandard goods in Ghana to avoid incurring liability to consumers. This will similarly support the existing efforts of regulatory institutions in the control of the spread of substandard goods in the market in Ghana.

It is, however, important to state that whilst regulatory standards are not expressly listed as an aspect of quality under the English law, they may not be discounted as an aspect of quality when considered as relevant factors on a case by case basis in the English legal regime. Predating the 2015 CRA for example, the question of whether a staircase, which was ostensibly of satisfactory quality but could breach building regulations if installed, was placed before the Court in *Lowe v W Machell Joinery Ltd.*[74] It was held by the Court of Appeal that a reasonable buyer would not find the staircase to be of satisfactory quality. Twigg-Flesner had also argued that the failure of goods to comply with technical regulatory requirements should give rise to the goods being rendered to be of unsatisfactory quality as was observed

[73] See Chap. 1 of this book, para. 1.0.

[74] [2011] EWCA Civ 794; [2012] 1 All E.R. (Comm) 153; [2011] B.L.R. 591; 138 Con. L.R. 48; [2011] N.P.C. 72; See also, the non-consumer case of *Britvic Soft Drinks v Messer UK Ltd* [2002] EWCA Civ 548; (2002) 2 All ER Comm 321 (CA); See also, the non-consumer case of *Medivance Instruments Ltd. v Gaslane Pipework Services Ltd (2) Vulcana Gas Appliances Ltd* [2002] (unreported)- Here, it had been observed that goods will generally not pass the test of satisfactory quality where they do not correspond with the appropriate technical standards. This observation is very much in tune with the Lowe case and it is likely that a similar stance may continue under the CRA 2015.

earlier. It is clear, therefore, that under the English law, technical standards could play important role in the quality assessment of goods particularly when deemed as a relevant factor.

However, the underlying rationale for the argument to expressly include technical regulatory standards as aspects of quality in Ghana rest on the ground that the proposal for the introduction of the aspects of quality criteria in the regime in Ghana is to the effect of the provision having a constant application in matters of new goods. The inclusion will therefore avoid the possibility of it being conceived that the expected quality of goods excludes that of regulatory standards. As already noted, the inclusion of regulatory standards to elements of quality criteria will directly help consumers to be able to seek redress when supplied with substandard goods which are considered to be at a crisis level in the market in Ghana. This will ensure that consumers are afforded with a more tailored protection in Ghana.

In short, the requirements for goods to be free from defects as regards their state and condition in Ghana will mean that the goods are fit for all their known common purposes, safe, durable, free from minor defects, good in appearance and finish, free from latent defects and comply with the required technical standards. In the matter of second-hand goods, their application will vary depending on the relevance of any of the criteria.

3.3 English Law on Disclosed Defects and Examined Goods: Lessons for Resolving the Concerns in Ghana

As mentioned earlier, the implied standard of quality expected of goods under the Ghanaian law do not apply where the seller had disclosed the particular defects to the buyer and where the buyer had examined the goods in respect of defects which the examination ought to reveal. In both circumstances, the seller will be precluded from liability in respect of defective goods which a buyer may eventually seek to complain about. However, two important general observations as was discussed called to question the extent to which the exceptions could be applied so as not to prejudice the interest of consumers in any given case. For clarity: In particular, even where the seller disclosed, at the pre-contractual stage, defects in the goods, it is much uncertain that the buyer would be in a position to properly appreciate the import of the disclosure of the defects so as to take informed decisions respecting the goods. Also, in terms of examination, a consumer may not be able to easily discover defects during the pre-purchase examination where the goods are ‘experience’ goods in which defects in such goods will only manifest when the goods are in use for) a while, as discussed in Chap. 2. These observations raised the important question regarding the extent to which the exceptions may be applied without jeopardising the interest of consumers in Ghana. As was argued, resolving this fundamental question is critical to ensure that consumers are better protected in Ghana.

The present discussion will therefore explore the extent to which the English law might contribute to resolving the uncertainty on this subject in Ghana.

In seeking to analyse the limitation of the law in Ghana in the light of the English law however, it is imperative to first set out the requirements of the English law regarding where the seller's quality obligations may be excluded. This will provide the impetus to further lay down in brief the background of the exclusions before the discussion of the relevant parts in connection with the issues raised in the Ghanaian case. Section of 9 (4) of the CRA, 2015 particularly states that the requirement for goods to be of satisfactory quality does not apply to any matter which makes the quality of the goods unsatisfactory:

a. which is specifically drawn to the consumer's attention before the contract is made.
b. where the consumer examines the goods before the contract is made, which that examination ought to reveal, or.
c. in the case of a contract to supply goods by sample, which would have been apparent on a reasonable examination of the sample.[75]

Before analysing the implementation of this provision which is similarly provided under the law in Ghana as noted above, it is essential to note that the related provision of CRA above mainly re-enacts section 14(2C) of the SGA 1979 as was amended by the Sale and Supply of Goods Act 1994. While the disclosure exemption was the results of the 1973 Act re-formulation with minor modifications under the 1994 Act, the examination exclusion originated from the 1893 Act with a slight rewording under the 1994 Act. As already indicated, the 1994 formulation of the satisfactory quality exceptions is what has been re-transposed under the CRA, 2015. Following this background, the issues arising from the context of the regime in Ghana are further explored below in light of the English law. The analysis will especially highlight the extent to which the English law might be helpful in resolving the concerns that were identified in the regime in Ghana.

3.3.1 Goods Examined by the Consumer Under English Law: Guidance for the Resolution of the Concerns in Ghana

In Chap. 2 as re-stated above, it was made clear that the seller's duty to supply quality goods that are without defects do not apply where the buyer had examined the goods for defects which the examination ought to reveal. This was interpreted by the courts to mean that the buyer has a right or responsibility to always inspect the goods he buys and where he fails to do so, the seller cannot be liable for defects in the goods which could have been revealed if the goods were examined in respect of the defects. While the courts' determination was in respect of non-consumer case law, it was nevertheless argued that a similar pattern in consumer matters would be detrimental to the rights of consumers in Ghana. The critical question as to what

[75] Section 9 (4) (b) & (c), Consumer Rights Act, 2015.

pattern would be followed in purely consumer matters was left unresolved. The anxiety of the uncertainty was specifically linked to where the consumer is dealing with ‘experience’ goods rather than ‘search’ goods. As was noted in Chap. 2, while defects in ‘search’ goods are easy to discover in a pre-purchase examination, defects in ‘experience’ goods may only be discoverable when the goods are in use. The increasing complexity of the uncertainty as was similarly indicated in the Chap. 2 is intensely found worrying when indexed to the mushrooming of the substandard quality of goods or defective goods in the Ghanaian market adumbrated in Chap. 1 of this thesis. It was therefore contended that the uncertainty is not helpful in safeguarding the rights of consumers in Ghana to acquiring goods that are of high standard of quality. The uncertainty was therefore highlighted to require redress in order to clarify the law to guarantee that consumers will be better protected where the issue of examination of goods arises respecting defects concerns. This was noted to be necessary, a fortiori, to ensure that the application of the exclusion in purely consumer matters is carried out without putting the consumer in a disadvantaged position. The extent to which the English law might be helpful in providing guidance to resolving the uncertainty for a more clarified (and enhanced) regime for the protection of consumers in Ghana is therefore explored below.

As clearly established above, the English law has equally provided for the exclusion of the seller from liability where the buyer examined the goods before the sale, similar as the case in Ghana. In the instant case of Ghana as highlighted above, the provision has not benefited from being applied in consumer matters except in non-consumer case law, leaving doubts as to how the regime will be applied in purely consumer matters as shown in the restatement of the discussion in Chap. 2. In the context of the English law however, the provision has had the benefit of being applied particularly before the 2015 CRA. In *Bramhill v. Edwards,*[76] the buyer had examined the interior part of the vehicle before purchase. The width of the vehicle was subsequently discovered to exceed the approved limits of the Road Vehicle Regulations. The trial Court in its obiter statements in reference to a buyer’s examination as a defence observed that the buyers’ have had the privilege of living in the motor home for some few days before the purchase, and ought to have revealed the width excessiveness. On appeal, the seller sought to amend his pleadings to take the benefit of the buyer’s examination of the vehicle as a defence. The Court of Appeal however noted that the seller amendment of his pleadings was not necessary under the circumstance but went further to state that if there was basis for the seller to rely on examination, the court would not have departed from the trial court verdict.

[76] [2004] EWCA Civ 403; [2004] 2 Lloyd’s Rep. 653; See also, Thornett and Febr v. Bears and Son (1919) 1KB 486 – where a representative of the buyer conducted a surface examination hastily on the outer part of the goods with the excuse of turning in late for the inspection appointment. The seller was held not liable despite the non-conformity of the goods which a proper examination would have revealed. This however, has been criticised as resurrecting the buried common law rule (in Jones v. Just [1868] LR 3, QB 197) where a buyer who has had the opportunity of inspecting the goods before purchase but failed to utilised same loses the right of the implied quality regime.

The above *obiter* of the Court of Appeal seems to imply that the moment the buyer had the opportunity it does not matter whether he in fact examined the goods, it was enough for him to have discovered the excessive width. This view of the English courts seems to similarly resonate with the determination of the Ghanaian courts as discussed in Chap. 2 and briefly restated above. However, as argued in Chap. 2 and reiterated above, a similar application to deal with consumer matters in Ghana would be detrimental to the interest of consumers. This will expose consumers to more adverse consequence where they are buying unfamiliar goods for the first time. In the case of Ghana, the situation may further be exacerbated in view of the range of substandard goods in the markets as was revealed in Chap. 1.

It is however important to state that the above obiter of the English Court of Appeal had been criticised as an oversight reading which should not be followed in subsequent matters.[77] It had therefore been argued that: 'there is no obligation on a consumer to make an inspection. If the consumer chooses to inspect the goods, liability will only be excused for defects which that examination ought to have revealed.'[78] Consequently, in *Macdonald v. Pollock*[79] predating the 2015 Act, the buyer bought a fishing vessel for £75,000 after a 30 min sea trial following his engineer superficial inspection which did not extend below the engine's floor plates where the defect resided. On a sea trial, the defect manifested and repairs cost was valued at £50,000. The Court of the Inner House of Session set aside the Sheriff Principal verdict and restored the Sheriff decision particularly stating that the provision on examination exempting the seller of liability is mainly 'concerned with the examination which was in fact conducted and what that examination ought to have revealed'.[80]

Drawing inspiration from the Court of Session and the academic commentary above, it seems that the expected application of the provision is to the effect that the buyer's examination must be one that has actually been carried out and the defect should as well be one which that examination could and should reveal. Moreover, it can also be inferred that where the buyer's examination was not fully the type that could discover the defect, the seller may not be able to come under the defence of the provision to escape liability. This further supports the argument that the buyer's examination of the goods does not provide the seller a complete or comprehensive defence from liability for the seller's failure to supply goods of satisfactory quality.[81]

---

[77] Twigg-Flesner (2005), pp. 205–206; See also, Bridge (2017), para. 11-037, p. 559, fn.218 – where it has been described as probably been 'overlooked'; See also, Mckendrick (2010), para. 11.66, p. 330, note 139.

[78] Howells and Weatherill (2005), p. 182.

[79] [2012] CSIH 12; [2012] 1 Lloyd's Rep. 425; 2013 S.C. 22; 2012 S.L.T. 462; 2012 G.W.D. 8-162; See also, Twigg-Flesner (2005), pp. 205–206; See also, Bridge (2017), para. 11-037, p. 559, fn.218 – where it has been described as probably been 'overlooked'; See also, Mckendrick (2010), para. 11.66, p. 330.

[80] Macdonald v. Pollock [2012] CSIH 12; [2012] 1 Lloyd's Rep. 425; 2013 S.C. 22; 2012 S.L.T. 462; 2012 G.W.D. 8-162, para 34.

[81] Bradgate and Twigg-Flesner (2003), para. 3.3.4.3, p. 50.

The determination of the provision to the effect that the buyer's actual examination of the goods should be the basis for excluding the seller from liability will as well be practically helpful in dealing with consumer matters in Ghana. In particular, requiring that sellers would only be relieve of liability where the buyer has actually examined the goods will ensure that consumers are protected against faulty goods where they have not examined the goods or where the examination was not the type that could reveal the defects in disputes. However, where the examination was the appropriate type to detect the defect but was not revealed by the buyer's examination that might nevertheless be the basis for denying the buyer the protection under the law. In effect, where the buyer chooses to carry out the examination, he is admonished to do so with sufficient degree of care and painstaking scrutiny.[82]

More importantly, it had also been argued that the provision does not in any way impose on the buyer the obligation to examine the goods, and even where the buyer has the opportunity to examine the goods but declined to carry out the examination, it will not relieve the seller of the obligation to supply satisfactory quality of goods.[83] This observation will be relevant in implementing the provision in Ghana in consumer matters.

Basically, applying the law in this context will be very viable in ensuring that consumers who purchase 'experience' goods are not stripped off the right to demand that the goods conform to the quality stipulation. This is particularly essential as defects in 'experience' goods are only revealed when the goods are put to use as noted earlier. In effect, a consumer who is sold substandard or defective goods can still fall on the seller for a resolution of the problem. Applying the law within this framework has the positive tendency of significantly improving consumer confidence in the market. It may further discourage the sale of goods of substandard quality or defective goods in the markets especially when traders come to appreciate the fact that they cannot easily outsmart consumers and easily get away with it.

3.3.2 *Disclosure of Defects in Goods Under English Law*

As discussed in Chap. 2, the obligation of traders to supply goods which are free from defects to consumers ceases to apply where prior to the conclusion of the contract, the trader disclosed the defects in the goods to the consumer. It was further revealed that the courts' application of the doctrine of seller's disclosure of defects as a window to be excluded from liability so far was confined to non-consumer cases. It was therefore demonstrated that whilst non-consumer may have superior technical knowledge to be able to appreciate the nature and degree of the defects in the goods which the seller disclosed, same cannot be vouched for the consumer.

---

[82] Twigg-Flesner (2005), pp. 205–206.

[83] Macdonald v. Pollock [2012], para. 33; see also Bradgate and Twigg-Flesner (2003), para. 3.3.4.3, p50; See also, Twigg-Flesner (2005), pp. 205–206; See also, Mckendrick (2010), para. 11.66, p. 330.

Whilst the court's determination of the application of the theory of disclosure in non-consumers matters was found unsuitable in consumer's cases, the question of how the law will be applied in consumer disputes was left unresolved. Addressing this was therefore crucial to help in providing guidance on how the law should be determine so as not to undermine the interest of consumers. The English law will therefore be analysed for possible guidance in resolving the issue of how the provisions may be applied in purely consumer matters for the benefit of consumers in Ghana.

The English law, as in Ghana, stipulates for the non-application of the requirement of satisfactory quality where the buyer was aware of the defect in the goods or where the consumer attention was drawn to the defects before the contract was formed as recited earlier. In commenting on the English provision of where the buyer's attention was specifically drawn to the defect in *Bramhill v. Edwards*[84] the Court of Appeal accepted the argument of the defendant's counsel that the seller's representation of the interior width should have alerted the buyer to the effect that the external width of the vehicle was greater than the permitted limit.

Applying a similar view held by the English Court of Appeal in Ghana will largely disadvantage the buyer and undermine the protection given to consumers under the regime. The overall effect will not be helpful to safeguarding the rights of consumers with respect to substandard and defective goods in the markets in Ghana. This is mainly because, in such application of the provision, buyers of goods will always be burdened with the duty to draw inference, for example, from general statements from sellers in coming to terms as to whether a material fact about the goods has been brought to their attention or not. As Twigg-Flesner rightly argued, such application of the provision 'would be too generous to a seller at the expense of the buyer'[85] In discouraging reading un-particularised defects statements into the intent of the provision, Goode and Mckendrick have argued that general statements of the seller that the goods are sold subject to defects or that the goods are in a poor condition are largely not enough to qualify drawing the buyer's attention to a known defect.[86]

Whilst there has been less case law on the subject of disclosure of defects, it is however refreshing to note that leading commentators have however made significant observations regarding the possible legislative intent. For example, Twigg-flesner had contended that the provision largely 'require a fairly precise identification of the particular defect' to be drawn to the attention of the buyer.[87] A similar observation has been expressed by Goode and Mackendrick that the particular defect to which the buyer complains should have been pointed out to him by the seller.[88] In Benjamin's Sale of Goods commentary, Bridge added that the defects that are

[84] [2004] EWCA Civ 403; [2004] 2 Lloyd's Rep. 653.

[85] Twigg-Flesner (2005), p. 206.

[86] Mckendrick (2016), para. 11.64, p. 329.

[87] Twigg-Flesner (2005), p. 206.

[88] Goode and Mckendrick (2016), para. 11.64, p. 329.

pointed out are most likely to affect the description under which the goods are eventually sold and a seller seeking to bring himself within the exception must allege and show factual prove.[89] These observations are consistent with what Dei-Anang had long said about the possible requirement of the disclosure regime in Ghana as noted earlier in Chap. 2. He had particularly contended that the regime appeared to be requiring that sellers openly show known defect(s) to buyers' and interpret to them in order to escape liability.[90] It remains relevant that applying the law by clearly pointing out any known defect(s) to the buyer prior to reaching agreements is vital in ensuring that consumers are well informed to make better purchasing decisions.

While the seller pointing out a defect to the buyer will be useful to aid the buyer in making a well informed decision, the chances of the buyer making a decision without appropriately appreciating the implication or impact of the defect shown to him is not discounted as was noted in Chap. 2. The worry as noted earlier, however, is that the extent to which the law might be applied so as not to jeopardise the interest of consumers has not been settled.

While there is paucity of case law on the extent to which the principle could be applied without being detrimental to the rights of consumers, commentators of the English law have however put forward useful advice regarding how this could be achieved. In particular, it has been advised that: 'the courts should be vigilant to ensure that the consumers are aware of the nature of the defect and the consequence flowing from it, before they allow this avenue of escape for sellers.'[91] It has equally been suggested to the effect that a balanced application of the rule will require mainly establishing that the buyer was not misled as regards the nature of the declared defect as a possible guide.[92]

From the discourse, the expected application of the law in consumer matters under the English law seems to require the Courts to first ascertain that the buyer did understood the declared information about the relevant defects and its possible impact at the time of the contract before granting the liability exclusion of the seller. Similarly interpreting the provision in this manner in Ghana would be generally helpful to advancing the goals of consumers. It would particularly be useful in ensuring that the consumer's possible information processing failure about the defects which the seller had disclosed are fully taking into account before a seller could escape from the liability. In particular, this will mean that the application of the provision to exclude the seller from liability will only be permitted where the disclosure was such that it was capable of aiding the consumer to better appreciate the nature of the defects and the likely implications of the defects in the goods. This will provide the certainty that the information imbalance between the consumer and the trader is properly addressed before clearing the seller from liability of the defects

[89] Bridge (2010), para. 11.041, p. 559.

[90] Dei-Anang (1967), p. 103.

[91] Twigg-Flesner (2004); see also, Howells and Weatherill (2005), para. 3.5.6.1, p. 182.

[92] Goode and Mckendrick (2016), para. 11.64, p. 329.

in the goods. This will especially be useful in helping consumers to deal with defects in goods they are supplied with in Ghana.

3.4 Fitness for the Particular Purpose of the Consumer Under the English Law for Resolving the Problems in Ghana

In analysing the requirement for the goods to be fit for the particular purpose of the buyer in Chap. 2, a number of concerns were identified to be unhelpful to the regime's overall protection of consumers in Ghana. Specifically, whereas the buyer was required to make known the particular purpose for buying the goods to be entitled to hold the seller liable for the fitness of the goods, it was however unclear what the position of the law will be where the goods have multiple uses. The question as to whether the buyer will have to mention each application he intends to put the goods to before he can expect the goods to be fit for his purpose was unresolved. The question of claims which the seller makes about the goods resulting in the contract, which quality descriptions the goods failed to meet and therefore unfit for the purpose, was also not settled. Also shown in Chap. 2, the issue of what will be the position of a buyer whose goods are unfit for his particular purpose due to his peculiar circumstance which he had brought to the attention of the seller was found unresolved. As was observed in Chap. 2, resolving these legitimate questions are critical to bring certainty into the regime in Ghana as regards the fitness of goods for their intended purpose. This section therefore seeks to explore the English law for possible guidance in addressing the issues in Ghana while having in mind the unique circumstances in Ghana.

In the case of the English law, section 10 of the CRA 2015 lays down the obligation of the trader to supply goods that are reasonably fit for the particular purpose of the consumer. In particular, the aspect of section 10 which is relevant to the heart of the present discussion is stated as follows:

> (1) Subsection (3) applies to a contract to supply goods if before the contract is made the consumer makes known to the trader (expressly or by implication) any particular purpose for which the consumer is contracting for the goods.
>
> (2) Subsection (3) also applies to a contract to supply goods if – (a) the goods were previously sold by a credit-broker to the trader, (b) in the case of a sales contract or contract for transfer of goods, the consideration or part of it is a sum payable by instalments, and (c) before the contract is made, the consumer makes known to the credit-broker (expressly or by implication) any particular purpose for which the consumer is contracting for the goods.
>
> (3) The contract is to be treated as including a term that the goods are reasonably fit for that purpose, whether or not that is a purpose for which goods of that kind are usually supplied.
>
> (4) Subsection (3) does not apply if the circumstances show that the consumer does not rely, or it is unreasonable for the consumer to rely, on the skill or judgment of the trader or credit-broker.

The above provision is a restatement of section 14(3) of the Sale of Goods Act, 1979 specifically applicable to consumer contracts. [93] Section 10 mainly originates from the 1893 SGA which itself was a codification of the common law.[94] Few amendments were however made in 1973 and consolidated under the 1979 SGA.[95] The provision of the 1979 Act as stated above is what has now been restated under section 10 of the CRA to be applicable mainly to consumer transactions.

It is worth noting that there are chances of overlap in the application of the satisfactory quality requirements of goods as examined earlier and fitness of goods for the particular purpose of the consumer under English law. In particular, "fitness for all common purposes" of the goods is one of the factors for the satisfactory quality test, but the failure of an item to be fit for all its common purposes would not automatically result in the conclusion that the goods are not of satisfactory quality as examined previously. On the other hand, fitness for the particular purpose of the buyer is mainly concerned with unusual purposes or for very specific purpose where the fitness of the goods for that purpose is crucial. The dividing line between satisfactory quality and fitness for purpose was clearly set out in *Jewson Ltd v Kelly*[96] prior to the 2015 Act. In this case, Clarke LJ stated that the function of satisfactory in contract with fitness for particular purpose 'is to establish a general standard of quality which goods are required to reach. It is not designed to ensure that goods are fit for a particular purpose made known to the seller. That is the function of *reasonably fit for purpose*.'[97] The standard of fitness for particular purpose will not apply where the buyer does not rely on the seller's skill and judgment or where it would be unreasonable for the buyer to rely on the seller's skill and judgment[98] but such limitation does not exist under satisfactory quality. Conversely, satisfactory quality does not apply where the defect was drawn to the buyer's attention or where the buyer had examined the goods for defects which the examination ought to reveal. This restriction does not also apply to fitness for the particular purpose of the buyer. Having set out the background pertaining to the doctrine of fitness for purpose under the English law, the extent to which the English law might be useful to assist in addressing the issues in Ghana is further examined below.

---

[93] There is however some minimal variation in the wording as can be seen in a contrast between section 10, CRA 2015 and section 14 (3) and (4) of the SGA 1979.

[94] This has been made clear per Lord Morris of Borth-y-Gest in *Henry Kendall & Sons (a firm) v William Lillico & Sons Ltd and Others*[1969] 2 AC 31, 91H; per Lord Diplock in *Ashington Piggeries Ltd and Another v Christopher Hill Ltd*[1972] AC 441, 501; Lord Justice Rimer in *BSS Group Plc v Makers (UK) Limited (t/a Allied Services)* [2011] EWCA Civ 809; [2011] WL 2747641; See also, Bridge (2017), para. 11-046; Twigg-Flesner et al. (2016), pp. 6–7.

[95] Ibid.

[96] [2003] EWCA Civ 1030; [2004] 1 Lloyd's Rep. 505, para. 68.

[97] *Jewson Ltd v Kelly* [2003] EWCA Civ 1030; [2004] 1 Lloyd's Rep. 505, para. 68 (Emphasis added).

[98] Ibid.

3.4.1 Resolving the Uncertainty Regarding Communicating the Purpose of the Goods

In examining the requirement for the fitness of the goods for the particular purpose of the buyer in Chap. 2 of this book, it was discovered that the buyer is only entitled to expect the goods to be fit for his purpose where he had made the purpose known to the seller prior to the contract. The question of whether a purchaser of goods will have to declare each use where the goods have a broad range of normal uses so as to benefit from the regime in the event of the goods being unfit was identified as remaining unresolved under the regime in Ghana. Also, the question of whether the seller will be liable for specific claims about the particular purpose of the goods that induces the buyer into buying the goods was equally found to be unresolved under the regime in Ghana as shown earlier in Chap. 2. The limitations of the regime therefore need to be resolved so as to provide a more simplified regime for the protection of consumers in Ghana.

Taking guidance from the English law, the CRA has similarly placed on sellers the duty to supply goods that are reasonably fit for the purpose for which the buyer expressly or by implication made known to them before the contract. The application of the requirement for the fitness of goods for the particular purpose of the buyer can be seen from the pre-2015 regime. In particular, in *Jewson Ltd v Kelly*[99] it was observed that before the seller could be held liable for the failure of the goods to be fit for the buyer's intended purpose, the buyer should have sufficiently communicated the specific purpose for which he was buying the goods to the seller either before or at the time of the contract. The buyer's explicit communication of the particular purpose of buying the goods imposes on the seller a *prima facie* duty for the goods to be fit for the buyer's particular purpose,[100] and this is very strict.[101] For instance, in the non-consumer case of *BSS Group Ltd v Makers (UK) Ltd*[102] predating the 2015 CRA Act, the seller had supplied plumbing materials to the buyer to be used for renovation works in a public house in Cambridge. The buyer was supplied with incompatible valves in his subsequent request for additional

[99] [2003] EWCA Civ 1030; [2004] 1 Lloyd's Rep. 505, para. 61 to 65; See also, the earlier case of *Slater v Finning* [1997] Ac 473, 486 D to E.

[100] Twigg-Flesner et al. (2021), p. 174; See the old case law which the present regime mainly retained; See, Lord Steyn *Slater v Finning* [1997] AC 473, 486C to D; see also Lord Justice Rimer in *BSS Group Plc v Makers (UK) Limited (t/a Allied Services)* [2011] EWCA Civ 809; 2011 WL 2747641, para. 41; see also, Lord Reid in an earlier case of *Henry Kendall v William Lillico* [1969] 2 AC 31, 79F; see also, *Preist v Last* (1903) 2KB 148; see also, *Bristol Tramsway v Fiat Motors Ltd* [1910] 2 KB 831; see also, *Cammell Laird & Co. Ltd. v. Manganese Bronze and Brass Co Ltd* [1934], HL, AC 402.

[101] Howells and Weatherill (2005), p. 186; see also, Lord Reid in *Kendal v Lillico* [1969] 2 AC 31, 84 - Where he noted that the duty '... covers not only defects which the seller ought to have detected but also defects which are latent in the sense that even the utmost skill and judgement on the part of the seller would not have detected them.'

[102] *BSS Group Plc v Makers (UK) Ltd (t/a Allied Services)* [2011] EWCA Civ 809, para. 37.

materials for the same project which made the system insecure under pressure after being fitted. The decision of the trial Court was accepted by the Court of Appeal that the valves supplied in the subsequent request were not reasonably fit for purpose on the basis of their incompatibility as Makers had made known expressly or at least by implication the purpose of buying the goods. Although this was not a consumer case, in a consumer context, a court is likely to be just as willing, if not more so, to take the view which the court took in *BSS Group.*

So far, the observations of the English courts seem to be consistent with the requirements of the law in Ghana as was observed in Chap. 2. That is, the buyer is required to unequivocally state the particular purpose(s) for his purchase of the goods to establish the basis for the seller's liability. As noted above, one of the main concerns of the law was that, in matters of multipurpose goods, the regime in Ghana has not clarified whether the buyer will have to state each purpose before he can demand the fitness of the goods for their purposes.

Drawing guidance from the English law, the *Blackstone's Guide* to the CRA 2015 observes that the buyer will be required to explicitly notify the seller of the intended reason for buying the goods where the goods have multiple uses in order to successfully claim against the seller for the supply of goods unfit for the purposes of the buyer.[103] The buyer notifying the seller of the purpose of buying the goods shifts the burden of responsibility to the seller to ensure that the goods supplied are fit for the indicated purpose of the buyer. However, where the goods have varied applications, the buyer is not obliged to specify each application he intends putting the goods into in communicating the purpose of buying the goods. The non-consumer case of *Kendall v Lillico*[104] decided on the basis of the 1893 Act provides a good illustration here. In that case, the buyer had bought Brazilian groundnut extraction for the purpose of compounding the extracts into feed-stuff for cattle and poultry. The extraction which was not dangerous to cattle, was however fatal to pheasant and partridge chicks as a large number of them died upon being fed with the feed. The extraction was held to be unfit for the purpose of the buyer. Lord Pearce had made the following observation:

> [i]n deciding the question of fact, the rarity of the unsuitability would be weighed against the gravity of its consequences. Again, if food was merely unpalatable or useless on rare occasions, it might well be reasonably suitable for food. But I should certainly not expect it to be held reasonably suitable if even on very rare occasions it killed the consumer. The question for the tribunal of fact is simply 'were these goods reasonably fit for the specified purpose?[105]

[103] Barry (2016), para. 3.55; Goode and McKendrick (2016). para. 11.106—where the buyer does not inform the seller, he may nevertheless be able to rely on the satisfactory quality where the goods are required to meet all their known common purposes.

[104] [1969] 2 AC 31 [115].

[105] [1969] 2 AC 31, [115]; see also, *Ashington Piggeries Ltd. v Christopher Hill Ltd* [1972] AC 441—where a Norwegian herring meal was mixed with preservatives rendering them harmless to most animals but deadly to mink. The meal was to be used for animal feed known to the suppliers, who were, however, unaware that the feed was to be used for mink. The House of Lords held there that the sellers should have contemplated that the meal might be included in the feed of any animal

This may likely remain relevant in the determination of matters pertaining to the CRA. It can be seen that upon the buyer's disclosure of the purpose for buying the goods, a very wide obligation then falls on the seller making him virtually liable to the buyer for failure of the goods to satisfy at least one use for which the goods are intended.[106] The seller will still be liable whether he was aware of the particular use the buyer was putting the goods to or not. It may be observed however that a seller may limit the extent of his or her liability by clearly specifying to the buyer the functional limits of the goods, if known.

While the settled authority of the English law could be helpful in dealing with the issue regarding the normal use of multipurpose goods in Ghana, it does not, however, seem to address the issue of claims made by sellers as regards the particular purpose for which the consumer acquires the goods. This implies that the English regime may not be helpful in resolving the issue of claims made by sellers regarding the particular purpose of the goods which induces the buyer into buying the goods, and for which the goods are not fit for the purpose stated by the seller. Although the call for the need to introduce statutory liability in Ghana against the seller for the supply of defective goods contrary to his statements about the goods draws guidance from the English law earlier, the proposal does not envisage having an automatic application. It would be applicable only where the seller's statement is treated as a relevant factor from a reasonable person's perspective.

Moreover, it might as well be argued that the consumer should be able to maintain an action against the seller under the common law doctrine of misrepresentation. In particular, in addition to the right of a consumer to maintain an action under the common law tort of deceit and breach of duty for misrepresentation as highlighted in Chap. 2 earlier, a consumer may also be able to bring a claim against a trader for misrepresentation through the aegis of section 2(1) of the Misrepresentation Act 1967 under English law. As similarly noted in Chap. 2 however, the opportunity for a consumer to maintain a claim for the seller's misrepresentation may cease to exist where the consumer is said to have affirmed the purchase[107] or where the trader's position in respect of the goods cannot be restored due to damage of the goods.[108]

It therefore remains that addressing claims by sellers that form the basis for the consumer's purchase of the goods for a particular purpose which the goods are not fit for, is crucial in the context of Ghana to ensure that consumers are well protected. Essentially, while to some extent the problems of consumers in the UK might be similar to the challenges facing consumers in Ghana, there is nevertheless the need to consider solutions that reflect the socio-economic and cultural realities of consumers in Ghana. In particular, whilst it is a common practice for sellers to make

by the buyers who were unaware of the toxins in the herring meal. The herring meal was, therefore, unfit for the buyer's purpose. The majority held the view that it was sufficient for the buyer to indicate requiring the meal for animal food but that the buyer did not have to individually specify the different animals for which the feed might eventually be given.

[106] Twigg-Flesner et al. (2021), p. 177.

[107] Long v Lloyd [1958] 1 W.L.R. 753 [760].

[108] Armstrong v Jackson [1917] 2 K.B. 822 [828]; see also, Hibbert and Chambers (2014).

claims about the specific purpose(s) of the goods they sell as already noted previously, many of these claims may often be exaggerated by traders in the case of Ghana. It has been noted that through 'advertisements and promotions,' some traders make misleading and untruthful claims about the efficacy and effectiveness of products they sell.[109] It has further been observed that traders mostly succeed in taking 'undue advantage of less educated individuals' in the consumer market in Ghana through these machinations.[110]

Whilst the above observations are specifically in relation to cosmetics, herbal products, drugs, medical devices and household chemical substances, similar situations may be witnessed in the diverse product sectors in Ghana. In *Rockson v Armah*[111] as noted in Chap. 2 for example, the seller initially claimed that the damage to the car which the buyer found after purchase was a mere graze on account of a brush against a garage but subsequently admitted in an idle moment to the occurrence of an accident which the buyer had strongly maintained was the possible cause of the state of the vehicle. In the matter of *Frafra v Boakye*[112] in addition, a tractor for haulage of timber was claimed by the owner to be in a very good condition capable of hauling at least 30 logs in a day but ended up hauling a maximum of a paltry 7 logs a day. Although the case was purely a matter of contract of hire, it nevertheless depicts the length to which owners of goods desirous of making sales could go in making claims about the functional purpose(s) of goods that could turn out to be a fiasco. The overall effect is that consumers are more prone to buying the goods mainly for a particular purpose which the trader had vouched for in his hype but the goods may clearly be unfit for the intended purpose the seller had declared.

It might therefore be appropriate that where the seller makes a particular statement about the purpose of the goods which forms the basis for the consumer's purchase of the goods, the seller is made liable for the particular unfitness of the goods for the purposes of the consumer. It will therefore be more helpful if the legislature in Ghana gives statutory status to claims made by sellers not only in reference to the quality of the goods, as argued for earlier, but also in relation to the fitness of the goods for the particular purpose of the buyer. This will ensure that a consumer who is unable to rely on the requirement for the goods to be free from defects as examined earlier, may be able to bring actions for the unfitness of the goods for their particular purpose which the trader had declared. This will also be helpful for consumers where they seek to rely solely on the fitness of the goods for their particular purpose like in the non-consumer case of *Bschor v Birim Timbers Ltd*[113] where the action was brought by the buyers relying only on the fitness regime.

---

[109] Ghana, Food and Drugs Authority, Code of Practice for sales, (2018), Doc. No. FDA/2018/01, para. 4.3.

[110] Ghana, Food and Drugs Authority (2018), Doc. No. FDA/2018/01, para. 4.5 (iii).

[111] (1975) 2 GLR 116.

[112] [1976] 2 GLR 332.

[113] *Andreas Bschor GMBH & Co. KG v Birim Wood Complex Ltd and Birim Timbers Ltd* [2016] CA. No. J4/9/2015.

In summary, it can be seen that it is a settled position under English law that the buyer only needs to state the purpose of buying the goods but not the multiple applications he intends to use the goods for where the goods are having a range of applicable uses. This appears to be helpful and the courts in Ghana may be urged to apply this in dealing with matters that raise questions of multiple applicable uses of goods in respect of the fitness of the goods. Moreover, consumers may be better protected if sellers are specifically made liable for the unfitness of goods for the purpose(s) of the consumer which the seller had noted. This is useful in view of the penchant of traders to often advance exaggerated claims about the purpose(s) of goods they sell in Ghana. In a nutshell, including claims the seller makes which the consumer relied on to buy the goods to operate alongside instances where the consumer clearly specifies his intended purpose for the goods will increase the protection for consumers in Ghana.

3.4.2 Resolving the Uncertainty Regarding Idiosyncratic Use of Goods in Ghana

As mentioned earlier, the analysis in Chap. 2 revealed that there was uncertainty regarding how the doctrine of fitness of goods will be applied in respect of idiosyncratic needs of consumers in Ghana. In particular, the question of whether a consumer will be protected in buying goods for a purpose different from the usual purpose of the goods which he/she disclosed was uncertain. The present subsection therefore seeks to further examine the extent to which the uncertainty could be resolved with guidance from the English law. This is important to ensure that consumers in Ghana are effectively protected.

Unlike the case of Ghana, the English law seems to be very explicit as regards the issue of peculiar circumstances for which goods are procured. In particular, section 10(3) of the CRA overtly states that the trader's duty to supply goods that are reasonably fit for the buyer's purpose holds '...whether or not that is a purpose for which goods of that kind are usually supplied.'[114] The provision seems to lay out specific directions to the effect that where the goods are not reasonably fit for their particular purpose, the seller may be held liable although the goods were bought by the buyer for an unusual purpose. Before the seller could be held liable however, the buyer should have discharged his cardinal role of sufficient disclosure of the intended use for which he is buying the goods so as to hold the seller accountable where the goods are not fit for that purpose. The failure of the buyer to clearly communicate the special purpose for acquiring the goods will deprive him/her of the benefit of the protection under the provision. For example, in *Jewson v Kelly*,[115]

[114] Section 10(3), CRA 2015.

[115] *Jewson Ltd v Kelly* [2003] EWCA Civ 1030; [2004] 1 Lloyd's Rep. 505; [2004] 1 C.L.C. 87; [2004] B.L.R. 31.

preceding the CRA 2015, a buyer purchased boilers which were installed in his converted flats meant for sale. While the boilers were performing well, the flats had poor SAP ratings resulting in their being less attractive to prospective buyers of the flats.[116] The poor SAP ratings were as a result of the unique characteristics of the building which had the effect on the flats' SAP ratings, but this was not sufficiently communicated to the sellers at the time of the contract. The sellers were therefore held not liable.

The buyer's responsibility of making the purpose known to the seller is heightened especially where the purpose of the goods is slightly different from the normal circumstances or where the buyer is dealing with a peculiar case. To this effect, the peculiar circumstance that departs from the normal purpose must be brought to the attention of the seller so as to invoke his liability in the event that the goods do fit for the declared idiosyncratic purpose. Prior to the 2015 Act for example, it was explained by the House of Lords in *Slater v Finning Ltd*[117] that a seller would not be liable for fitness for a particular purpose of goods where their unfitness arose out of the presence of features or idiosyncrasies which the buyer did not disclose to the seller at the time of the contract formation, whether or not the said idiosyncrasies were known to the buyer. Similarly, in an earlier case of *Griffiths v Peter Conway Ltd*[118] decided under the SGA 1893, the purchaser wore a customised coat and contracted dermatitis which would not have occurred but for the abnormally sensitive nature of his skin. The court of Appeal then observed that the seller was not aware of the purchaser's sensitive skin and that the buyer merely saying that she required the cloth for personal wear was not enough to make the seller liable. Consequently, the seller was held not to have breached the duty of ensuring that the goods were reasonably fit for the particular purpose of the buyer.

The express requirement of the English law for the goods to be fit for the buyer's purpose irrespective of whether the buyer is buying the goods for their usual purpose or not offers a very useful and clear direction for the benefit of consumers. This will similarly be relevant in resolving the uncertainty of the fit for purpose requirement in Ghana. In particular, a similar complementary stipulation in Ghana will address the unsettled question of whether a consumer who purchased goods for a purpose that departs from the usual purpose of the goods will be given protection. Essentially, the viability of a similar measure will come with the effect that consumers who are well aware of their idiosyncratic needs and make this known in advance will possibly be able to hold the supplier liable where the goods do not fit the declared purpose before a tribunal. This will consequently guarantee consumers protection where the unfitness of the goods is primarily as a result of the consumer's abnormal situation which he had brought to the attention of the trader before the contract.

---

[116] SAP ratings refer mainly to the Standard Assessment Procedure for determination of the energy efficiency level. The SAP rating is dependent on the particular features of the house its energy system.

[117] [1997] A.C. 473.

[118] [1939] 1 AII ER 685.

3.5 Resolving Issues Surrounding Instances Where Both the Quality and Fitness of the Goods Requirements May Not Apply

This section seeks to address the issues that were raised in Chap. 2 of this book regarding instances where both requirements for the quality and fitness of goods will not apply. In particular, where the sale is not carried out in the course of the seller's business and where the parties expressly exempt themselves from the statutory liability of quality and fitness of the goods. The various concerns that were raised fell on the scope of sale in the course of the seller's business and the chances of the liability exclusions to undermine the degree of protection that is available under the regime for consumers. The various issues are further explored in the light of the English law below regarding the extent to which it might provide helpful guidelines in resolving the concerns.

3.5.1 Resolving the Issue Surrounding Sale in the Ordinary Course of the Seller's Business

It emerged in Chap. 2 of this book that the seller's liability for the quality of the goods was only applicable where the transaction was carried out in the course of the trader's business under the law in Ghana. This was observed to have been interpreted by the Courts to exclude one-off sale. The exclusion of a one-off sale transaction from the seller's business definition was however argued to be unsatisfactory as it might deprive the consumer of the protection of the regime against faulty goods which are acquired through this channel. Addressing the issue is critical to ensure that a more enhanced regime is made available for consumers in Ghana. The extent to which the English law might be helpful in affording guidelines to resolving this concern is explored below.

In a review of the English law, the CRA requires that transactions to which the seller will be liable for the unsatisfactory quality and fitness of the goods are where the transactions are between a trader and a consumer.[119] The Explanatory Notes to the Act further re-affirmed that Part I of the Act to which the present discussion relates governs the relationship between traders and consumers under the English law.[120] Beyond clarifying the parties to which the regime applies, the Act went further to define a trader to mean 'a person acting for purposes relating to that person's trade, business, craft or profession, whether acting personally or through another

[119] Section 1, the UK, CRA, 2015.

[120] Explanatory Notes to the Consumer Rights Act 2015, para 1(1); See also, Barry et al. (2016 4), para. 2.01; Bridge (2017), para. 14-023.

person acting in the trader's name or on the trader's behalf.'[121] While the definition of a trader in this context relates to the EU Directives,[122] it has been argued that the term "traders" is a reflection of the pre-2015 requirement that the parties should be 'acting in the course of business' to give rise to the application of liability for the non-conformity of the goods to statutory requirement.[123]

While observing that the CRA is silent on whether a one-off sale by a trader of his old items would be caught as relating to the trader's business or trade or craft or profession, Barry *et al,* however, noted that the fact that the goods belong to the trader and profit will plough back into the trade imply that this might still be read as a part of the trader's business or trade or profession or craft.[124] This observation appears to have been motivated by the courts pre-2015 determination of the question of whether a one-off sale by a seller was in the course of his business to which the term trader now relates as noted above. In particular, in the pre-2015 Act in *Stevenson v Rogers,*[125] the question of whether a fisherman's sale of his fishing boat was carried out in the course of his business was placed to be addressed before the Court of Appeal. While setting aside the trial court's ruling that the transaction was not in any form of regularity to be in the course of the fisher's trade, the Court of Appeal held that regularity of habit was not what is required but rather a one-off sale in the course of the fisherman's business was sufficient to hold him liable. Similarly, in *MacDonald v Pollock*[126] in which the pursuer bought the defendant's former fishing vessel after causing a marine engineer to carry out a general survey of the vessel, which sea trial was only very limited. One of the questions that arose on appeal before the Court of Session was whether the sale was conducted in the course of the defendants' business. While accepting the earlier verdict of the Court of Appeal in *Stevenson v Rogers,*[127] it was observed by the Court that the notion of the need for some prior degree of regularity to exist to give rise to the sale being qualified as in

[121] Section 2 (2), the UK CRA, 2015; A consumer has also been defined in Section 2 (3) of the CRA, 2015 to connote 'an individual acting for purposes that are wholly or mainly outside that individual's trade, business, craft or profession.'

[122] See, Art 2(2), Directive 2011/83/EU of the European Parliament and of the Council of 25 October 2011 on consumer rights, amending Council Directive 93/13/EEC and Directive 1999/44/EC of the European Parliament and of the Council and repealing Council Directive 85/577/EEC and Directive 97/7/EC of the European Parliament and of the Council Text with EEA relevance; See also, Art 2 (c), Directive 1999/44/EC of the European Parliament and of the Council of 25 May 1999 on certain aspects of the sale of consumer goods and associated guarantees; See also, Art 2(c), Council Directive 93/13/EEC of 5 April 1993 on unfair terms in consumer contracts 1993; See also, Regulations 2, (2012, No. 3110), UK Consumer Rights (payment Surcharges) Regulation 2012; See also, Bridge (2017), para. 14-033; See also, Explanatory Notes to the Consumer Rights Act 2015, para. 34.

[123] Bridge (2017), para. 14-023.

[124] Barry et al. (2016) para. 2.12.

[125] [1999] QB 1028.

[126] [2012] CSIH 12, 2013 SC 22.

[127] [1999] QB 1028.

the course of the seller's business is unsatisfactory.[128] Later, the Court submitted that sale as an integral part of the seller's business 'will undoubtedly extend to cases where the seller sells goods of a kind in which he has not previously dealt and (*semble*) also to cases where he sells goods of a kind in which he does not ordinarily deal, e.g. where a store sells off one of its delivery vans.'[129]

As seen above, the settled position of the English law in the pre-2015 regime is that a one-off transactional sale by the trader will give rise to the trader's liability arising from the quality defects of the goods. It therefore seems very likely that disputes regarding whether the trader's one-off sale of his old assets relate to his trade or business or craft or profession will lead to a similar determination as the authors rightly argued above.

The example of the English law in which a one-off sale is classed as relating to the trader's business or trade or craft or profession or its former requirement of sale in the course of a business will similarly be helpful in resolving the concern that excluding a one-off sale as being an integral part of the seller's business in Ghana limits the protection available for consumers. The clear inclusion of a one-off sale as a part of the seller's business will expand the scope of transactions for which the consumer may be protected in Ghana. This is particularly critical as the trader who has been using the goods prior to the sale should have a better appreciation of the degree of quality of the goods than the consumer who is only acquiring the goods for the first time. As previously examined in Chap. 2 and earlier in this Chapter, however, the seller should be able to exempt himself from liability if he declares those defects that he is aware of before the sale. Another important justification for the seller to be made liable for defects in the goods is that his sale of the goods will add up to his accrued transactional income which he may as well reinvest in his business as similarly argued under the English law indicated above. For this underlying reason, it is appropriate that a one-off sale is rendered as a part of the seller's business under the law in Ghana especially in consumer matters.

3.5.2 Resolving the Issues Relating to the Use of Exclusion Clauses in Consumer Contracts in Ghana Drawing Guidance from the English Law

In Chap. 2 of this book, it was found that sellers may be able to exclude themselves from liability through the use of liability exemption clauses especially by showing such clauses to consumers. This was argued to be unsatisfactory especially in light of the inequality of power of the consumer to influence what is being introduced by the seller and may end up being exploited. Addressing the issue of how such exclusion clauses might be controlled so as not to undermine the rights of consumers in

[128] *MacDonald v Pollock* [2012] CSIH 12, [2013] SC 22 Para. 21.

[129] Ibid. para. 23.

Ghana was noted to be imperative particularly to avoid the tendency of traders supplying substandard quality of goods to consumers while having their liability excluded. The extent to which the issue might be resolved drawing guidance from the English law is therefore analysed below.

Under the English law, the CRA seems to explicitly prohibit any term in a consumer contract seeking to exclude or restrict the trader's liability arising from his supply of goods to consumers. In particular, section 31 states among others that: '[a] term of a contract to supply goods is not binding on the consumer to the extent that it would exclude or restrict the trader's liability arising under … goods to be of satisfactory quality; (and) … goods to be fit for particular purpose.'[130] The Act further maintains that a term of contract cannot also deprive a consumer of the right or remedy in respect of liability resulting from his supply of faulty goods.[131] The Explanatory Notes of the CRA particularly explain that the provision is intended to prevent any attempt by traders to contract out of the statutory rights of consumers under the Act. In particular, it has been stated that the proviso 'has the effect that any term in a contract which seeks to prevent the consumer from having access to the statutory rights and remedies, or to make exercising these rights less attractive to the consumer by either making it more difficult and onerous to do so, or by placing the consumer at a disadvantage after doing so, will be void.'[132] In a similar vein, the BIS Guidance for Business contends that traders cannot state in a transaction contract that they will not provide redress under the Act if the goods they supply do not meet the Act's requirements. The BIS also observed in its guidelines that even terms which are not expressed but carry the effect of excluding the trader's liability under the Act and which the consumer has agreed to, will not have a binding force.[133] In *Atiyah and Adams' Sale of Goods* it has been stressed that: '[t]he upshot is that the rights of a consumer under the Consumer Rights Act are mandatory and therefore non-excludable, and that any attempt to do so will be ineffective.'[134]

From the outline of the English law, it is clear that a trader's resort to the use of liability exemption terms to circumvent their liability that may arise from the non-conformity of the goods they supply in consumer contracts is vehemently prohibited. A similar legislative measure in Ghana will be significant in clearly discouraging the present widespread use of terms such as 'goods purchased are not returnable', 'money paid is not refundable', 'we accept no liability for defects in the goods', among others, as was noted in Chap. 2 of this book. In particular, similarly providing such outright prohibitions of the use of liability exemptions regarding the statutory requirements for the quality of goods will broadly render such clauses ineffective *ab initio* when traders still continue to use them. The introduction of these prohibitions is particularly important to help preserve the statutory rights of

130 Subsection 1 (a) and (b), the UK CRA 2015, emphasis added.

131 Section 31 (2), the UK CRA, 2015.

132 Explanatory Notes to the Consumer Rights Act (n 18) para 161.

133 Department for Business (2015), pp. 57–58.

134 Twigg-Flesner et al. (2021), p. 497.

consumers who may lose them without knowing it under the present regime. In effect, it will eliminate any tendency of a trader using such clauses to undermine the legislative rights of consumers in Ghana.

3.6 Conclusion

This Chapter mainly analysed the deficiencies that were identified earlier in Chap. 2 of this book regarding the quality requirements of goods in Ghana through the lens of English law. This was to address the question about the extent to which English law might be contextually helpful in resolving deficiencies in the requirements for the quality obligations of traders of goods in Ghana. From the analysis, it is clear that whilst the general approach of the English law will largely offer viable guidance to resolving many of the shortfalls of the law in Ghana, some modifications would nevertheless be required to appropriately tailor the solutions to the domestic needs of consumers in Ghana. In particular, the review of the English law revealed that the term satisfactory quality is the standard requirement for the quality of goods in all transactions involving consumers. Drawing guidance from this, the analysis argued that it would be more useful for Ghana to similarly adopt one standard term of quality to generally apply to consumer transactions. This is found to be crucial to help resolve the possible confusion the present different standard terms might cause to consumers. The analysis went further to suggest that traders' requirement to supply goods that are 'free from defects' should be adopted to cover all consumer transactions in Ghana. As the analysis has shown, the term that the goods should be free from defects, which is presently set out under the Sale of Goods Act 1962, Act 137, appeared to reflect the aspirations of consumers and has also been rated to command a high degree of protection for consumers.

Regarding the absence of a definition of the standard term of quality, it was shown that the basic definition of the term of satisfactory quality under English law would similarly be useful in resolving the present undefined standard term of quality in Ghana. In particular, testing the quality of goods through the lens of a reasonable person, bearing in mind the description of the goods, their price (if relevant) and all other circumstances, including public statements about the quality characteristics of the goods. This was found to be comprehensive in addressing the limitation of the term that the goods should be free from defects, as the standard term in the case of Ghana. The analysis, therefore, suggested that the approach of the English law will be helpful in resolving the definition deficit of the quality of goods term in Ghana.

On the issue of the scope of quality being confined to latent defects, the discussion revealed that English law has aspects of quality criteria which are to be considered in appropriate circumstances in the assessment of the quality of goods. These aspects of quality were found to constitute the state and condition of goods, including, among others, the fitness of the goods for their common purposes, appearance and finish, freedom from minor defects, safety and durability. Whilst the discourse found similar quality criteria to be useful in Ghana, the discussion, however, suggested that these will need to be expanded to expressly include the requirement that the goods should be free from latent defects and comply with technical standards in Ghana. The analysis points out that this will help ensure that the regime is better harmonised with the already settled position of the law and support the prevailing effort towards the protection of consumers in Ghana. Moreover, whilst the application of the various aspects of quality of goods under English law in the assessment of the quality of goods is dependent on the relevance of each factor, this will need to be modified to require all new goods to 'tick' each of the aspects of quality while allowing their flexible application only in second-hand goods.

Regarding instances where the seller will not be liable for disclosure of known defects, the comparative analysis with the English law similarly revealed that the courts have not had the opportunity to clearly define the application of the provision. However, leading commentators are found to suggest that the courts will need to establish that the precise defect the trader disclosed is the subject of the dispute and that the consumer was not misled in respect of the nature of the defects disclosed at the time of the contract. It was noted that a similar process of applying the law in Ghana was important to guarantee that consumers are properly protected. In particular, the court's reading of the provision to the effect that the defects in disputes precisely reflected what was disclosed and that the consumer was not misled regarding the disclosed defects before absolving the seller of the liability will be crucial to ensure that consumers in Ghana are not shortchanged. Similarly, on the issue of the buyer's examination of the goods, actual examination in respect of defects, which the examination should reveal as proffered under the English law, will equally be vital in better serving the interest of consumers when given equivalent reading by the courts in Ghana.

On the issue of communication of purpose to give rise to the application of the doctrine of fitness for the buyer's particular purpose, the English courts' determination that where the buyer communicates his requirement for the goods for their normal purpose, it suffices to impose liability on the seller for any of the particular range of uses he puts the goods to, will similarly be valuable in aiding the cause of consumers in Ghana. However, the law in Ghana will need to further clarify that a trader who made claims about the particular fitness of the goods and the goods are not fit for the purpose(s) could form the basis for a consumer to seek redress for the unfitness of the goods. The English law's requirement that where the buyer makes known the purpose of buying the goods, liability falls on the seller irrespective of whether that purpose is the common purpose of the goods will equally be useful in addressing the uncertainty as to what the law would be under idiosyncratic circumstances of consumers in Ghana.

Furthermore, the scope of sales to which the seller's liability applies, including a one-off sale under English law, will also expand the range of sales outlets with which consumers may be protected if adopted in Ghana. The English law's outright prohibition of the use of liability exclusions of the requirements for the quality of goods will be practically viable in ensuring that the statutory rights of consumers are not undermined in Ghana if replicated.

In summary, while English law offers important guidelines for resolving the various issues of the regime in Ghana, some modifications remain vital to ensure that the regime is properly tailored to the needs of consumers in Ghana, as noted previously. The adoption of the various measures will help clarify the uncertainties and limitations that were highlighted as not helpful in safeguarding consumers in the Ghanaian market. The introduction of the reforms, as indicated in the discussion, also has the potential incentive of simplifying the quality requirements for the supply of goods to consumers in Ghana.

The next chapter will focus on the adequacy of the existing consumer remedies for faulty goods under the law in Ghana. The analysis will seek to identify potential shortfalls of the law for a further comparative discussion with English law.

References

Barry D, Jenkins E, Lloyd D, Douglas-Jones B, Sumnall C (2016) Blackstone's guide to the consumer rights act 2015. Oxford University Press
Bradgate R, Twigg-Flesner C (2003) Blackstone's guide to consumer guarantees : a guide to the new provisions of consumer sales law. Oxford University Press
Bridge MG (1995) The sale and supply of goods act 1994. JBL 398
Bridge MG (2003) What is to be done about Sale of goods? Law Q Rev 119:173
Bridge MG (2010) Benjamin's sale of goods, 8th edn. Sweet & Maxwell, London
Bridge MG (2014) The sale of goods, 3rd edn. Oxford University Press
Bridge MG (2017) Benjamin's sale of goods, 10th edn. Sweet & Maxwell
Council Directive 93/13/EEC of 5 April 1993 on unfair terms in Consumer Contracts 1993
Dei-Anang KK (1967) Caveat Venditor Ghaniensis. Univ Ghana Law J 4:90
Department for Business, Innovation and Skills (2013) Draft Consumer Rights Bill: Government Response to Consultations on Consumer Rights
Department for Business, Innovation and Skills (2014) Consumer Rights Bill: Statement on Policy Reform and Responses to Pre-Legislative Scrutiny
Department for Business, Innovation and Skills (2015) Consumer Rights Act: Goods, Guidance for Business. <https://www.businesscompanion.info/sites/default/files/CRA-Goods-Guidance-for-Business-Sep-2015.pdf>. Accessed 15 July 2025
Directive 1999/44/EC of the European Parliament and of the Council of 25 May 1999 on certain aspects of the sale of consumer goods and associated guarantees
Dowuona-Hammond C (1995) Protecting the purchaser of goods under Ghanaian law. Rev Ghana Law 19:105
Dowuona-Hammond C (2018) Consumer law and policy in Ghana. J Consum Policy 41(4):333–354
Duncan DD (2016) Communicating with informal sector clients: a study of strategies employed by Ghana commercial Bank and Unibank Ghana limited. Stud Media Commun 4(1):1
Ervine WCH (2004) Satisfactory quality: what does it mean? J Bus Law 684
EU Directive 2011/83/EU of the European Parliament and of the Council of 25 October 2011 on consumer rights, amending Council Directive 93/13/EEC and Directive 1999/44/EC of the European Parliament
Explanatory Notes to the Consumer Rights Act 2015
Export. Gov. (2017) Ghana – Selling Factors and Techniques, <https://www.export.gov/article?id=Ghana-Selling-Factors-and-Techniques> Accessed 2 May 2025
Ghana, Food and Drugs Authority (2018) Code of Practice for sales, Doc. No. FDA/2018/01, para. 4.5 (iii)

Goode R, McKendrick E (2016) Goode on Commercial Law, 5th edn. Penguin Books
Hibbert W, Chambers H (2014) Sale of goods: defective goods. Thomson Reuters
Howells G (2005) The potential and limits of consumer empowerment by information. J Law Soc 32:349
Howells G, Weatherill S (2005) Consumer protection law, 2nd edn. Ashgate, Aldershot
Iddris F, Ibrahim M (2015) Examining the relationships between E-marketing adoption and marketing performance of small and medium Enterprises in Ghana. J Mark Consum Res 160
McKendrick E (2010) Goode on commercial law, 4th edn. Penguin Books, London
McKendrick E (2016) Goode on commercial law, 5th edn. Penguin Books, London. p 329, para. 11.64
Mills JEA (1978) Rockson Armah: a case of caveat emptor, caveat Venditor or neither. Univ Ghana Law J 15:168
Mwaawaaru S (2009) Marketing strategy in terms of promotion and communication for energy drinks in Ghana, case company' Sinebrychoff Brewery <https://www.theseus.fi/bitstream/handle/10024/5985/Mwaawaaru_Sarah.pdf?sequence=1&isAllowed=y>. Accessed 2 May 2025
Peter G (1995) The sale and supply of goods act 1994. Bus Law Rev 16(3):55
Ramsay I (2012) Consumer law and policy: text and materials on regulating consumer markets, 3rd edn. Hart Publishing
Sarah B (2016) Consumer credit relationships—protection, self-interest/reliance and dilemmas in the fight against unfairness: the unfair credit relationship test and the underlying rationale of consumer credit law. Leg Stud 36(2):230
Scott C, Black J, Cranston R (2000) Cranston's consumers and the law. Butterworths
The Law Commission, Sale and Supply of Goods (The Law Com. 160 and Scot. Law Com. No. 104, 1987)
The Sale and Supply of Goods to Consumers Regulation 2002 which implemented the EU Directive 1999/44/EC
Twigg-flesner C (2004) Information disclosure about the quality of goods – duty or encouragement? In: Howells RG, Janssen A, Schulze R (eds) Information rights and obligations: a challenge for party autonomy and transactional fairness. Ashgate, Aldershot, Chapter 8
Twigg-Flesner C (2005) Examination prior to purchase: a cautionary note. Law Q Rev 121:205
Twigg-flesner C (2008) Pre-contractual duties - from the acquis to the common frame of reference. In: Schulze R (ed) Common frame of reference and existing EC contract law. Sellier ELP, Munich
Twigg-Flesner C, Schulze R (2010) Protecting rational choice: information and the right of withdrawal', Handbook of Research on International Consumer Law. Edward Elgar Publishing
Twigg-Flesner C et al (2016) Atiyah and Adams' sale of goods, 13th edn. Pearson
Twigg-Flesner C et al (2021) Atiyah and Adam's Sale of Goods, 14th edn, Pearson Education Ltd.
Willett C (1993) The quality of goods and the rights of consumers. N Ir Legal Q 44:218
Willett C, Morgan-taylor M (2004) The sale and supply of goods to consumers regulations. J Bus Law 1979:1

Chapter 4
Consumer Remedies for Faulty Goods Under Ghana Law

4.1 Introduction

The previous chapter addressed the various issues that were raised in Chap. 2 regarding the deficiencies of the quality requirements of goods in Ghana, drawing from English law and its EU influence. The present Chapter examines the remedies for consumers where the seller is in breach of his undertaking to supply the required quality of goods in consumer contracts. The analysis of the remedies seeks to address the question of whether the remedies under Ghana law are sufficient to effectively afford consumers adequate protection when they are supplied with faulty goods. This examination of the adequacy of the remedies for consumers in respect of faulty goods is important as a complement to the review of the requirements for the quality of goods in Chap. 2. This will further provide the impetus for this book to holistically contribute to enhancing the degree of protection available for consumers in Ghana. In particular, the analysis of the prevailing remedies will underline potential limitations of the law in Ghana for a subsequent comparative discussion with the English law and its EU experience, but within the Ghanaian context, later in Chap. 5 of this book.

Before the analysis, it is important to restate, as noted earlier in Chap. 1, that the remedies for consumers for the purpose of this analysis are provided under the SGA 1962[1] and the HPA 1974[2] and are for the benefit of both consumers and non-consumers. Moreover, the government of the Republic of Ghana adopted a Consumer Protection Policy in 2014 to provide a more tailored regime for consumers. As mentioned in Chap. 1, this policy is currently before the Office of the Attorney General and Ministry of Justice to be prepared into a draft bill for

[1] Act 137.

[2] NRCD 292.

N. Yidana, *Consumer Law and Policy on Faulty Goods*, Ius Gentium: Comparative Perspectives on Law and Justice 134,
https://doi.org/10.1007/978-3-032-08700-3_4

consideration by Parliament. The analysis in this Chapter will focus on the prevailing remedies under the SGA and the HPA as the policy document is still being drafted into a Bill. It is also worth reiterating, as noted in Chap. 2, that there is a paucity of case law that specifically deals with the application of the rules on consumer matters in Ghana. As a result, the analysis will utilise case law on both consumer and non-consumer matters with respect to the application of the rules on the remedies for faulty goods for guidance in appreciating the text of the law. It is critical, however, to state that some level of caution will be applied when drawing guidance from non-consumer case law, as the courts may deal with a consumer matter more leniently. In summary, the case law of both consumer and non-consumer origin, in which the courts have commented on the application of the remedies in respect of faulty goods, will be used for guidance in the analysis, but with caution in drawing conclusions in non-consumer case law where necessary.

The chapter is divided into five parts. Part one is this introduction which embraces the setting of this Chapter and this outline of the Chapter structure. Part two provides a brief highlight of the remedies available under the regime for consumers where sellers are in breach of their quality obligations as discussed in Chap. 2 of this book. This part further sets out the non-availability of certain remedies as legal rights, which are, however, on offer voluntarily in very limited instances by some sellers and manufacturers. Part three discusses the buyer's right to reject faulty goods and highlights the underlining concerns. This part also examines the instance where the buyer may lose the right to reject faulty goods on the basis of being deemed to have accepted the goods under the law in Ghana. Part four discusses the circumstances under which a buyer may be able to claim damages against the seller. This part also provides highlights of the concerns arising thereto. The last part of this Chapter provides a conclusion to the entire discussion of the chapter. Set out below is an outline of the remedies for consumers when they are supplied with faulty goods in Ghana.

4.2 Outline of the Remedies for Consumers in Respect of Faulty Goods Under the Law in Ghana

As noted in Chap. 1 and reaffirmed above, the SGA and the HPA provide for the remedies that are available under the regime for consumers when they are supplied with faulty goods by traders in Ghana. The remedies are stipulated under sections 49 and 55 of the SGA[3] and sections 13(3) and 14 (6) of the HPA.[4] It is worth noting that the provisions in both the SGA and the HPA are to the effect of affording consumers the right to reject goods which are faulty or to make a claim for damages. The extent to which these provisions may be able to afford consumers who are

[3] Sale of Goods Act 1962, Act 137, Ghana.

[4] Hire Purchase Decree 1974, NRCD 292.

supplied with faulty goods with satisfactory remedies, however, remains unclear. This, therefore, calls for a detailed assessment of the extent to which the provisions may afford consumers the required protection in Ghana.

Before the substantive analysis, however, it is appropriate to first take stock of a number of remedies of critical importance to consumers, which are, however, unavailable as legal rights for consumers under the law in Ghana. This is especially crucial as consumers sometimes obtain these remedies from sellers or manufacturers in the form of voluntary warranties as either a part of the trader's business practice or on goodwill grounds. It is, however, important to mention that few traders proffer these voluntary warranties and goodwill remedies to consumers in Ghana. In particular, under the law in Ghana, there is no obligation on the seller to take steps to provide a remedy, such as repair or replacement or reduction of the price of the goods where the goods he supplied are found to be defective or faulty. In other words, there are no remedies of repair, replacement, and price reduction as options which buyers may access when they are supplied with goods that turn out to be faulty.

In some limited instances in practice, retailers and manufacturers offer voluntary guarantees reflecting these remedial options. One commentator has observed that where these guarantees are offered by the manufacturers or the retailers, consumers are able to rely on them in seeking redress before the courts.[5] Whilst some retailers and manufacturers offer these voluntary cures of repair or replacement or price reduction where the goods they supply are defective, the majority of traders do not offer such remedies to consumers. These private overtures are usually offered to consumers in the sale of expensive goods such as vehicles[6] and other durable products like electronic and electrical goods.[7]

It is significant to state that these remedies offer the most practical means of resolving disputes regarding the quality and fitness problems of consumer goods. This reflects the observations that the fundamental desire of most consumers is to have the defective goods which they are supplied repaired or replaced at no cost to them.[8] The absence of these options under the law in Ghana therefore leaves the regime in a state that does not entirely reflect the expectations of consumers.[9]

It is nevertheless important to better appreciate the extent to which the legal remedies presently available under the regime might operate to the benefit of consumers when they are sold defective goods. This will provide the needed impetus to contribute towards addressing the shortfalls of the regime and the apparent exclusion of the most desired remedies of repair, replacement, and price reduction. Below is a detailed analysis of the rights of rejection and claim for damages in matters of faulty

---

[5] Dowuona-Hammond (2018).

[6] This was especially the case in *G. A. Sarpong & Co. v Silver Star Auto Ltd* [2014] 72 G.M.J; See also, *Pyne & Associates v African Motors* [2017] CA No.: J4/38/2013.

[7] Dowuona-Hammond (2018).

[8] Ansa-Asare (1981), Dowuona-Hammond (1995, 2018).

[9] Ansa-Asare (1981), Dowuona-Hammond (1995, 2018).

goods with a highlight of possible concerns that need to be addressed to ensure that consumers are better protected in Ghana.

4.2.1 The Right of Consumers to Reject Faulty Goods

The present section seeks to discuss in detail the right of consumers to reject faulty goods under the regime in Ghana. The discussion will particularly provide a highlight of potential constraints that are likely to limit the extent to which consumers may benefit from exercising the right to reject faulty goods in Ghana. As noted earlier, the arising concerns will be subjected to a subsequent comparative analysis with the English law and its EU experience but in the context of Ghana. The right of a buyer to reject faulty goods and the issue of its limitation in respect of defects which do not amount to a breach of a condition of the contract is first examined below.

4.2.1.1 The Right to Reject Defective Goods and the Issue of Defects Which Do Not Constitute a Breach of a Condition of the Contract

As mentioned above, one of the primary remedies available for consumers when they are supplied with faulty goods under the regime in Ghana is to reject the goods. Section 49 of the SGA specifically states that:

> … the buyer is entitled to reject the goods and to refuse to pay or as the case may be, to recover, the price where – (a) the seller is guilty of a breach of a fundamental obligation; or (b) the seller is guilty of a breach, not being of a trivial nature, of a condition of a contract, ….[10]

Similarly, the HPA also provides in respect of the requirements of the goods to be of merchantable quality under section 14 (6) as follows:

> [a] breach of any provision of this section by the owner or seller shall give the hirer or buyer a right to rescind the agreement.[11]

In commenting on the above SGA provision, the High Court in the non-consumer case of *A. G. Sarpong v Silver Star Auto Ltd*[12,13] stated that: '… section 49 does not confer an automatic right on the buyer to reject goods simply because they are defective.' The court proceeded further to stress that '… the defect which entitles the buyer to reject the goods must be of a serious, substantial or of a fundamental

[10] Sale of Goods Act 1962, Act 137.

[11] Sale of Goods Act 1962, Act 137.

[12] [2010], Suit No. OCC10/2009, pp. 15–16 of judgement.

[13] [2010] HCGLR.

nature.'[14] Also, in an earlier case of *Rockson v Armah*,[15] the Court of Appeal took inspiration from the English case of *Cehave NV v Bremer Handelsgesellsschaft MBH*[16] and stated that: 'while a buyer was entitled to receive from his seller that which the seller had agreed to sell and deliver, it was not an essential corollary that any departure by the seller from his promise to the buyer should of necessity lead to the buyer being entitled to rescind the whole contract. A court should not be over-ridden, unless so required by statute or authority to construe a term in a contract as a condition any breach of which gave rise to a right to reject.'

The ground upon which a buyer may exercise the right to reject faulty goods was further clarified by the Supreme Court in the non-consumer case of *G. A. Sarpong v Silver Star Auto. Ltd*[17] when the case subsequently went before it on appeal. The Court stated that: '[a] breach of an obligation that would of necessity call for an election on the part of an innocent party to exercise his right of determination in the contract must fit into one of the following: (i) that which goes to the whole root of the contract and not merely part of it; or (ii) that which makes further performance impossible; or (iii) that which affects the very substance of the contract.'[18] Following this observation, the Court went further to hold that the defects in the vehicle which the sellers had sold to the appellant went to the root and substance of the contract. The court particularly stated that the vehicle in contention 'was inferior and fundamentally different from what the appellants had bargained for … and the respondents could not be said to have fulfilled their obligations…'[19]

From the submissions of the courts, it is undoubtedly clear that the buyer's right to reject goods that do not conform to the contract specifications is only possible where the seller's breach constitutes an essential part of the contract. In other words, the buyer's right to reject faulty goods will only arise where the seller or owner of the goods is in breach of his obligation, which is an essential part or condition of the contract. In effect, a consumer who buys goods with defects that do not amount to a breach of a condition will not be able to benefit from the remedy of rejecting the goods. It has been argued that the possible rationale for the exclusion of the buyer from the right to reject goods where the defects do not amount to a breach of a condition broadly seeks to encourage the performance of contracts with the right to reject only on matters of genuine defects which are serious.[20] The critical question, however, is what constitutes defects that are not serious enough to amount to a condition of the contract that a buyer of goods with such defects will not be permitted to reject under the law in Ghana. The High Court, in the non-consumer case of *A. G. Sarpong v Silver Star Auto Ltd*, as recited earlier, stated that to entitle the

[14] [2010] HCGLR, [15–16].

[15] [1975] 2 GLR 116 [123].

[16] [1976] QB 44; 3 ALL ER 739.

[17] *G. A. Sarpong & Co. v Silver Star Auto Ltd* [2014] 72 G.M.J. [12].

[18] *Ibid.*

[19] Ibid.

[20] Dowuona-Hammond (1995).

buyer to reject the goods, '[t]he defects complained of must not be trivial.' A commentator has also suggested that the provision is meant to prevent buyers from the tendency to play 'fast and loose' with rejection at the slightest non-conformity of the goods.[21] However, the question of what amounts to trivial defects in goods to which a consumer may be deprived of exercising the right of rejection has not been defined under the regime.

While acknowledging the absence of a definition as to what amounts to defects as a whole, Dei-Anang pointed out that the task of making an objective assessment of defects as regards what is serious and what is trivial to different consumers is a difficult one.[22] This recognised difficulty consequently leaves consumers in frequent dilemma of deciding whether the defects in their purchased goods are trivial. The consumer predicament heightens when the defect is seemingly trivial but negatively compromises the consumer's use of the goods. Imagine, for example, a consumer buying a new jacket with a tipped zipper, which may result in struggles over time but not evident at the time of the purchase. Similarly, imagine a dining table with a slightly uneven leg, which is not easily noticeable but begins to wobble after a short while of use. One may also look at the case of a television remote control that works intermittently such that a change of batteries will not resolve the problem. The question is whether consumers with such defects can rely on the rejection remedy or the defects would be regarded as trivial, depriving them of the right to reject the goods. In considering the difficulty consumers may have, Dowuona-Hammond argued that the courts in Ghana may accept the buyer's version of the adverse effect of the defects on his overall purpose of acquiring the goods in the course of making a determination.[23] It is essential, however, to note that this critical question of what the courts may say regarding what constitutes trivial defects has, to date, not been determined by the courts in Ghana. In effect, the issue as to what will amount to trivial defects in goods for which a consumer may be precluded from the benefit of rejecting the goods has since remained unresolved. Under this situation, a consumer may be saddled with faulty goods but feel helpless and demotivated to seek redress. Apparently, the lack of clear guidance is broadly unhelpful to the agenda of consumer protection.

It is worth noting that the preceding discussion mainly concentrated on the buyer's right to reject faulty goods with a defect that is not trivial but a condition in sales contracts. Therefore, there is a need to look at the application of section 14 (6) of the HPA with respect to the right of the buyer to rescind a hire-purchase or conditional sales agreement. The examination of the application of section 14 (6) is especially required to be reviewed in the light of section 5 (1) of the HPA. The provision states that: '[a]t any time before the final payment under a hire purchase agreement or conditional sale agreements falls due, the hirer or buyer shall … be entitled to

[21] Dowuona-Hammond (1995).

[22] Dei-Anang (1967); Dowuona-Hammond (1995).

[23] Dei-Anang (1967); Dowuona-Hammond (1995).

terminate the agreement by giving written notice of termination to any person entitled to receive payments under the agreement.'[24]

The above provision finds application in the case of *Yayo v Nyinase.*[25] The Court of Appeal, in upholding the verdict of the trial court, specifically stated that: '[t]he object of ... (hire purchase) agreement is to ensure that the property in the goods remains in the owner during the whole period of bailment and to vest in the hirer the right to put an end to the bailment either by purchasing the goods or returning them.' Also, in *Badu v Fynn* cited in *Antwi and Another v Raman and Others*[26] with approval, the court observed that 'in a hire purchase agreement the property in a bus (goods) remained in the vendor until the payment of the whole purchase price....' In an earlier case of *Mensah v Osei*,[27] it was contended that '[e]very body is presumed to know the law, and I must presume that the plaintiff knew at all times of his right to terminate the hire purchase agreement if he wished.'

In the case of hire-purchase transactions, as observed above, the buyer can terminate the contract at any time during the life of the transaction prior to making a final payment. The caveat of the buyer being barred from rejecting the goods where the defects of the goods are not a condition of the contract does not apply until the final payment is made.[28]

It is nevertheless worth noting that per the law, a consumer may find himself in a similar situation as observed in the case of sales contracts if defects in the goods manifest shortly after the final instalment payment. That is to say, the defects the buyer complained about may be subjected to the test of whether the defects are a condition of the contract or trivial defects in consideration of the buyer's right to reject the goods. A consumer case may only fall into this bracket where the agreed instalment payment is to last for a short time period. Consequently, the limitation by the law of the buyer's right to reject the goods where the defects are not considered to affect a condition of the contract may also arise in the case of hire-purchase transactions.

It is therefore worth emphasising that the lack of a definition of trivial defects does not appear helpful in serving the interest of consumers, especially when they are supplied with defective goods. The apparent exclusion of the right of the

---

[24] Hire Purchase Decree 1974, NRCD 292.

[25] [1975] 1 GLR 422 [426] emphasis added.

[26] *Antwi and Another v Raman and Others* [1992] 1 GLR 253 [255] emphasis added in respect of goods.

[27] [1962] 1 GLR 261 [263].

[28] However, '[w]here the hirer or the buyer terminates the agreement ... without prejudice to any liability which has accrued before the termination, he shall be liable to pay the difference between the total of the sum paid and one half of the hire purchase or total purchase price, or if the agreement specifies a lesser amount, he shall be liable to pay the amount so specified' as per section 6(1), Hire Purchase Decree 1974. The rationale for this requirement was stated in *Kpeglo v SCOA Motors* [1962] 2 GLR 82 [82] that the hirer should not '... have free use of the car; he must pay for the use on a quantum *meriut* basis.' The Court further noted that '...the remedy of rescission ... should be accompanied by *restitutio in integrum*, the rents paid in the interim should be applied to the restoration of the car to its original condition.'

consumer to reject defective goods, which the court might determine as trivial, may further worsen the plight of the average consumer in Ghana. The exclusion of the consumer's right to reject goods with defects that are considered to be trivial creates a worrying situation in the light of the possible exposure of consumers to defective goods, as observed in Chap. 1. The current state of the regime on trivial defects is likely to jeopardise the interest of consumers where the particular defect is of significant importance to the consumer, as shown above. Addressing the issue of what constitutes trivial defects is, therefore, critical to ensure that consumers are better protected in Ghana. This is especially significant in the light of the substandard quality of goods in the market in Ghana which may expose consumers to defective goods within the realm of being trivial in nature.

4.2.2 The Right to Reject the Goods and Terminate the Contract But with no Alternative Options for the Consumer

As observed above, a consumer has a right to reject goods which a seller supplied to him in breach of the implied quality and fitness obligations which constitute a fundamental aspect of the contract. The critical question which immediately follows the buyer's rejection of the faulty goods is what remedy he may be able to pursue to have his purpose of buying the goods met. An answer to this very important question requires a further examination of the relevant provisions. As highlighted previously, section 49 of the SGA states that: '… the buyer is entitled to reject the goods and to refuse to pay or as the case may be, to recover, the price where – (a) the seller is guilty of a breach of a fundamental obligation; or (b) the seller is guilty of a breach, not being of a trivial nature, of a condition of a contract, …. '[29]

Essentially, the Courts have had the occasion to comment on the provision regarding the effect of what a buyer may opt to do upon rejection of faulty goods. In particular, in the recent non-consumer case of *Andreas Bschor GMBH v Birim Wood & another*[30] which facts have been recited previously, it was stated by the Supreme Court that: '[a] breach of either a fundamental obligation or a condition entitles the party not in default to repudiate the sales contract, and if it is the seller who is in breach, the buyer can reject the goods.'[31] Also, in the non-consumer case of *G. A. Sarpong* & Co. *v Silver Star Auto,*[32] the Supreme Court similarly observed

[29] Sale of Goods Act 1962, Act 137.

[30] [2016] CA, No. J4/9/2015 [5].

[31] [2016] CA, No. J4/9/2015 [5].

[32] *G. A. Sarpong & Co. v Silver Star Auto Ltd* (2014) 72 G.M.J; See also, the non-consumer matter in general contract law case of *Security Bank Ltd. v CBAM Services Inc.*, the Court came to the conclusion that a breach of an essential or fundamental term of a contract is one of the effectual basis for the agreement to be terminated.

that: '[u]pon a breach … of a condition, the innocent party is entitled to treat the contract as terminated and consider himself discharged from the obligation of further performance of the contract.'

Whilst the above authorities reflect non-consumer matters, similar observations have clearly been made about the buyer's entitlement to end the contractual agreement after having exercised the right to reject defective goods, for which defects are not trivial in nature in consumer matters. In particular, in the case of *Rockson v Armah,*[33] the Court of Appeal expressly pointed to the fact that where the breach is construed in the lens of a condition of the contract, the buyer would be entitled to reject the goods and as well rescind the contract.

Similarly, in the matter of *Yirenkyi v Tormekpey,*[34] the Court of Appeal in referring to the trial Court's verdict submitted that the 'judge seemed to be saying that the defendant breached the implied condition … that the vehicle was reasonably fit for the purpose the plaintiff required it and that the plaintiff was entitled to repudiate the contract, return the vehicle and claim a refund of the purchase price' as stipulated by the SGA. In the case of *Sackey v Fattal,* it was also stated that where a seller delivers inferior goods different from what was contracted for, the buyer could successfully assert 'a right to reject the whole of the deliveries and demand the return of the price … paid….'[35]

It seems clear from the above authorities, that the consumer's rejection of defective goods further entitles him to bring the contract to an end and to refuse to pay for the goods or demand a refund of any money which he had paid to the seller. It is important to note that the illustrations so far on the contemporaneous right of a buyer to reject faulty goods and to terminate the contract are confined to contracts of sale. The important question that comes into sharp focus is what will be the option of a buyer or hirer who similarly rejects faulty goods in the case of hire-purchase or conditional sales transactions? This question seems to have equally been addressed by the HPA regarding the requirements for the goods to be of merchantable quality. As already discussed earlier in particular, section 14 of the HPA, which prescribed the obligation of the seller to supply merchantable quality goods to consumers, further provides in subsection 6 of the same provision that: 'a breach … by the owner or seller gives the hirer or buyer a right to rescind the agreement'.[36]

So far, the existing judicial determination of the buyer's right of rescission in hire purchase transactions predates the HPA 1974. Especially, in the case of *Bartholomiew & Co. Ltd v Adu-Gyamfi,*[37] the Supreme Court had expressly stated that '[i]f the

[33] [1975] 2 GLR 116 [123].

[34] [1987 -88] 1 GLR 533 [537].

[35] [1959] GLR 176 [179]; See also, *Japan Motors Co. Ltd. v Randolph Motors Ltd* [1982-83] GLR 536 [543], where the Court has similarly maintained in a general contract of a non-consumer case that a purchaser is entitled to '… rescind the contract, return the property if already accepted, and recover the purchase price, if already paid, by action after demand and refusal.'

[36] Hire Purchase Decree 1974, NRCD 292.

[37] [1962] 2 GLR 62 [66].

breach goes to the root of the contract it may be rescinded by the party aggrieved.' In *Kpeglo v SCOA Motors*,[38] the Supreme Court similarly gave a categorical endorsement to the High Court's submission that it was open to the hirer or buyer '... to elect to repudiate the contract and return the car to the defendant's company' if he was supplied a different car from what was represented.[39] Whilst the case law predates the 1974 Act, it seems likely from the recital of the provision that a consumer might similarly be determined to be entitled to terminate the agreement and to return the goods to the seller under the present hire-purchase regime.

As seen above, the option available for the buyer after exercising the right to reject faulty goods under the Ghanaian regime is to terminate the contract. It might be argued that a consumer who rejects faulty goods and terminates the contract will be able to obtain similar goods from other suppliers or traders who sell the same goods to enable him to meet his requirement of buying the goods. The problem, however, is where there are limited suppliers of the kind of goods in question, or only one supplier has a monopoly over the particular description of goods. In such a situation, termination of the contract might not be helpful to the consumer.

The consumer might be better off if there is an alternative remedy on which he may rely to resolve the problem of the defective goods instead of ending the contract. In particular, remedies such as replacement or repair of the goods may be useful in helping the consumer to meet the primary purpose of buying the goods. Unfortunately, however, these remedies do not exist under the regime in Ghana as alternative remedies, as noted earlier. Presently, however, a consumer's only option is to keep the goods and seek damages, which itself might not be satisfactory, as will be discussed shortly in this Chapter.

In summary, whilst the right of the consumer to reject faulty goods and to terminate the contract is important, the absence of alternative remedies to termination of the contract as options after the rejection of defective goods does not seem satisfactory to affording consumers with a desirable mix of remedies in Ghana.[40] Addressing this limitation is critical to ensure that consumers are able to avail themselves of remedies that are more suitable to meet their needs upon rejecting faulty goods from a trader in Ghana. This is especially vital to help boost the degree of protection available under the regime for the benefit of consumers in Ghana.

---

[38] [1962] 2 GLR 82 [85].

[39] [1962] 2 GLR 82 [85].

[40] Nsubuga et al. (2024); Yidana (2020).

4.2.3 *The Buyer's Right to Rescind the Agreement in the Case of Hire-Purchase and Issues Arising*

As observed above, the buyer has a right to rescind the contract where the goods the seller supplied are defective. However, the buyer's right to rescind the agreement in a hire purchase contract only lies where the breach is in relation to the doctrine of merchantable quality.[41] In the case of the seller or owner's breach of the implied fitness of the goods under the Hire-purchase law, the displeased buyer can only avail himself of damages[42] as will be discussed later in this chapter. However, under the Sale of Goods Act, the seller's breach of both the implied obligations of quality and fitness of the goods could trigger the buyer's right to reject the goods and rescind the contract, as discussed above.

From the outset, a buyer has no right to reject goods which do not fit his particular purpose if he acquired the goods under hire-purchase, unlike in a sales contract where he can reject the goods. In effect, if a farmer, for example, buys a plough on hire purchase or conditional sale for the particular purpose of using it in rocky land, which turns out not to be fit for the rocky area, he will be unable to reject the plough under the current state of the law. This certainly does not seem helpful in safeguarding the interest of consumers in Ghana.

It might be more useful for consumers to reject goods which are unfit for their intended purpose, especially if this was made known to the trader at the time of the purchase. However, this is currently not the case as pointed out above. There is, therefore, the need for this to be addressed to ensure that consumers can avail themselves of the required remedies irrespective of whether the breach is with respect to the quality and fitness of the goods.

4.3 Limitation of the Consumer's Right to Reject Faulty Goods by Acceptance

As clearly pointed out above, the consumer has a right to reject faulty goods and terminate the contract where the seller is in breach of the implied terms of quality and fitness of the goods which goes to the root of the contract. However, the right of the consumer to reject faulty goods may be lost before he begins to contemplate availing himself of the remedy of rejection of the faulty goods and termination of the contract. In particular, the SGA provides that 'the buyer may not reject goods which the buyer has accepted.'[43] The Act went further to clearly state that the buyer will be deemed to accept the goods where the buyer: '(a) intimates to the seller that

[41] Section 14 (6), Hire-purchase Decree 1974, NRCD 292. For the import of the provision, see, *Bartholomew & Co. Ltd v Adu-Gyamfi* [1962] 2 GLR 62; *Kpeglo v SCOA Motors* [1962] 2 GLR 82.

[42] Section 13 (3), Hire-purchase Decree 1974, NRCD 292.

[43] Section 51 (1), Sale of Goods Act 1962, Act 137.

the buyer accepts the goods, or (b) does not, within a reasonable time after delivery of the goods, inform the seller that the buyer rejects the goods, or (c) wrongfully refuses or neglects to place at the disposal of the seller after notifying the seller that the buyer rejects the goods.'[44] Unlike the third exception, which appears not to pose serious concerns, the first two exemptions raise critical questions that need further consideration. Their consequences to the overall goal of protecting consumers in Ghana are examined below.

4.3.1 Issues of Uncertainty of the Time to Reject Faulty Goods in Ghana

As noted above, one of the instances under which a buyer will be considered to have accepted the goods to foreclose his right to reject faulty goods and to terminate the contract is where he failed to reject the goods after the lapse of a reasonable time after taking delivery of the goods. In particular, the buyer will be deemed to have accepted the goods where the buyer 'does not, within a reasonable time after delivery of the goods, inform the seller that the buyer rejects the goods'[45] as already set out above. The courts in Ghana have had the benefit of commenting on this very provision. For instance, in the recent non-consumer case of *Pyne & Associates v African Motors,*[46] the quest of the plaintiff to reject a vehicle due to alleged retention of complained defects after the defendants' repairs was refused by the Supreme Court. The Court particularly stated that: '… the retention of the vehicle by the plaintiff from November 2004 until October 2005 before attempting to reject same constitutes acceptance. The legal consequences are that, the property in the vehicle has passed to the plaintiff, and at the time he purported to reject same and requested the defendants to sell same and refund their monies to them, the defendants no longer owned the property.'

In a similar non-consumer case of *New Lucky Electrical Ltd v Startrack Int. Ghana Ltd & another,*[47] the plaintiff kept a second-hand excavator for a period of one year and one month before attempting to reject the vehicle. It was held that the plaintiff keeping the vehicle for that period was extremely unreasonable and it was not open to him to reject the vehicle. In the case of *G. A. Sarpong v Silver Star Auto,*[48] the High Court had stated that each case must be determined based on its own facts, and that the twelve (12) months duration was a reasonable time during which the buyer could justifiably reject the defective vehicle. The High Court's pronouncement which was set aside by the Court of Appeal was subsequently

[44] Section 52, Sale of Goods Act 1962, Act 137.

[45] Section 52 (b), Sale of Goods Act 1962, Act 137.

[46] *Pyne & Associates v African Motors* [2017] CA No.: J4/38/2013 [16].

[47] [2010] Suit No. Occ 49/08, [11–12].

[48] *G. A. Sarpong & Co. v Silver Star Auto Ltd* [2010] HCGLR.

restored by the Supreme Court on appeal.[49] While 12 months was a reasonable time to reject the goods in the latter illustration above, reasonable time had elapsed in the former two examples with about the same time duration from when the good was delivered, thus depriving the buyers of the right to reject the goods. However, as observed in the *Sarpong* case above, the facts of each case provide the criterion for the court to determine whether a right to reject is justifiable.

Further instances where the courts have made determinations regarding reasonable time during which a buyer may be able to reject faulty goods can be drawn from the non-consumer case of *Silver Star Auto Ltd. v Georgia Hotel Ltd.*[50] In this case, the buyer sought to reject the vehicle about two years after purchase due to concerns of defects in the car. The Court of Appeal submitted that: 'it does not appear reasonable for the respondents to claim or attempt to reject the car almost two years after purchase.' However, in *Andreas Bschor & Co. v B.W.C. Ltd*[51] the observation of the Court of Appeal per Abban, J.A., that the retention of the machine for 20 months 'must be equalled with acceptance of the transfer of the property in the goods and the assumption of all risk'[52] was subsequently set aside by the Supreme Court.[53] The Supreme Court particularly found it appropriate not to deprive the buyer of the right to reject the machine which initially broke down on the eleventh day, and later, two (2) months into the installation and were respectively repaired. These breakdowns and repairs, the court observed, were known to the seller prior to the buyer's attempt to reject the saw-mill 20 months into its installation.[54] In the immediate two authorities above, the reasonable time period during which a buyer may reject faulty goods again received varied interpretation by the courts.

It seems clear from the discourse so far, that the reasonable time for a buyer to reject faulty goods is a major source of uncertainty. However, it is worth noting that the above cited authorities are mainly drawn from non-consumer case law. Nevertheless, a similar trend is discernible in purely consumer transactions in which comparable disputes arose. For example, in *Rockson v Armah*,[55] the respondent purchased a Mercedes Benz Car from the appellant which was later discovered to have been damaged as a result of the car's involvement in an accident prior to the sales contract. The appellant accepted liability and carried out repairs employing the services of a 'wayside' fitter after finding the estimates of *Messrs RT Brisco Ltd* too high. Upon using the vehicle for two months, the defects persisted resulting in the

[49] G. A. Sarpong & Co. v Silver Star Auto Ltd [2014] 72 G.M.J.

[50] [2010-2012] 1 GLR 471.

[51] [2008] 4 GMJ.

[52] [2008] 4 GMJ [215].

[53] *Andreas Bschor GMBH & Co. KG v 1. Birim Wood Complex Ltd, 2. Birim Timbers Ltd* [2016] CA. No. J4/9/2015 [14–15].

[54] In particular, the whole plant had ceased operating 11 days after its installation and was repaired and its main carriage was also replaced barely two months after the installation due to its breakdown.; Ibid.

[55] [1975] 2 GLR 116.

respondent's rejection of the vehicle which was upheld by the High Court. In an appeal however, the Court of Appeal found that the respondent had lost his right of rejection after retaining the car for about two months. Specifically, the Court of Appeal stated that: 'any undue delay in rejection amounts to a positive assumption that the property in the goods has passed' as 'time is a material element for consideration where repudiation of a contract of sale is sought….' [56] The Court further stated that: '… retention of a second-hand car for almost two months was unreasonable and it was also not thereafter open to the respondent to avoid the transaction.'[57]

Also, in *Armah v Baffour,*[58] the buyer retained a Bedford engine for a five months upwards duration. His attempt to resist the seller's action for payment of the outstanding balance together with damages and interest was rejected by the Court. It was held that the buyer had clearly waived his right to reject the engine having kept it for an upward time-span of five months. Similarly, in *Christie Koranten v African Motors*,[59] the plaintiff sought to reject a vehicle after a period of one year. It was held by the Court that a long period of retention amounted to acceptance of the vehicle and the plaintiff could not be rejected thereafter. Also, in *Charles Frimpong v Godwin Akumah,*[60] the defendant took delivery of a vehicle and sought to reject it after a year, but this was objected to by the court.

The discourse so far points clearly to a degree of uncertainty associated with the exact time frame during which a consumer may be able to exercise the right to reject faulty goods. This is particularly evident from the judicial decisions explicated above. Thus, whereas the right to reject faulty goods may be exercised by the consumer within a prolonged period after the goods have been delivered in some instances, the right to reject defective goods could lapse so quickly in other circumstances. This is a real source of uncertainty which is not helpful in affording consumers with clear guidance as to when to reject non-conforming goods.

It is, however, worth noting that the above discussion so far has concentrated in pointing out the uncertainty of when to reject faulty goods in respect of sales contracts. It is therefore appropriate to examine the situation as regards the reasonable time within which to reject faulty goods that are acquired under the hire-purchase regime. Regarding the time frame to exercise the right of rejection of faulty goods in a given case of hire purchase or conditional sales, the buyer or hirer can at any point in time rescind the contract prior to making the final payment of the agreed instalment. The final payment is an indication of the buyer having bought the goods and the property in the goods having been transferred to the buyer. The buyer's right to withdraw from the contract is stipulated under section 5 (1) of the HPA as previously highlighted.[61] The provision states that: '[a]t any time before the final payment

---

[56] [1975] 2 GLR 116, [119].

[57] [1975] 2 GLR 116, [119].

[58] [1989–1990] 1GLR 207.

[59] [2008] 17th December.

[60] [2010] 20th July 2010 unreported.

[61] Section 5, Hire Purchase Decree 1974, NRCD 292.

under a hire purchase agreement or conditional sales agreement falls due, the hirer or buyer shall … be entitled to terminate the agreement by giving written notice of termination to any person entitled to receive payments under the agreement.'[62]

In *Bartholomiew & Co. Ltd v Adu-Gyamfi*[63] predating the 1974 HPA, the buyer had acquired three different vehicles from the plaintiffs' company under hire purchase in August, November, and December of the same year. The defendant used the vehicles for a period of over ten to twelve months covering a total mileage of 87,000, with an average of 3000 miles per vehicle per month in respect of the different transactions. The defendant then returned the vehicles to the plaintiffs' company alleging unsuitability of the vehicles. It was held by the Supreme Court that the hirer was not entitled to rescind the agreement after using the vehicles for over ten to twelve months. Korsah, the then Chief Justice of the Supreme Court in a resounding approval of the trial court's decision clearly stated that 'I must … refer to the learned trial judge's conclusion, with which I agree, thus: "[t]he vehicles having covered at least 87,000 miles, could not be said to be unfit for the purpose for which they were intended."[64]

Moreover, in *Kpeglo v SCOA Motors*[65] prior to the 1974 HPA regime, the plaintiff had entered into a hire purchase agreement in respect of a car with the defendant which was alleged to be brand-new. However, it was discovered to have some defects upon inspection by the plaintiff. The plaintiff nevertheless used the car for one year, and was involved in five accidents, fell into arrears, but refused the defendant's attempt to retake possession of the car. He later brought an action for the termination of the agreement and return of paid rents among other reliefs. His claim was however, turned down. The Supreme Court pointed out that the time duration the car had been put to use could not support the alleged unfitness of the car. The Court specifically stated that: '… when regard is had to the undisputed circumstances of the instant case, … that for the period of a whole year the plaintiff had the use of the car running it at an average of 2000 miles a month, it becomes obvious that the plaintiff's substantial complaint that the car was unfit for the purpose for which it was supplied can only be described as unfounded and frivolous.'[66] Although the judicial pronouncements on the question of the reasonable time (within which) to reject faulty goods predates the 1974 regime, it is nevertheless likely that the courts might follow the same pattern in making a decision in relation to the time frame for the buyer to reject faulty goods.

Under the hire-purchase regime as seen above, consumers may be able to reject goods they found defective during the life span of the agreement until the final

[62] Hire Purchase Decree, 1974.

[63] [1962] 2 GLR 62 [66].

[64] [1962] 2 GLR 62 [66].

[65] [1962] 2 GLR 82 [87]; See also, *Mensah v Osei* [1962] 1 GLR 261 [263] where buyer's concern about defects in the goods being the basis for his arears of payment of the hire-purchase instalment was rejected by the court. It was stressed by the court that the hirer could have terminated the agreement at any time if he wished.

[66] Ibid.

payment is made. However, a delay in rejecting the defective goods may result in the consumer being deprived of the right to reject the goods especially as the alleged defects will be contrasted with the period the goods have been in use after delivery as observed above. Moreover, as argued earlier, defects which manifest shortly after the buyer has made the final instalment payment may likely trigger uncertainties as to whether the buyer is still within the confines of a reasonable time frame to reject the goods. This may arise early where the instalment payment is to be completed within a short time period, for example, weekly instalment, for a period of four weeks. Consequently, the exact time frame during which a consumer may be able to return the goods to the seller and withdraw successfully from the contract remains an uncertainty under the hire-purchase regime in such circumstances. This similarly reflects the uncertainty of the effective period for consumers to be able to exercise the right to reject defective or faulty goods under the sale of goods contracts as noted earlier.

Broadly from the discourse, the time period during which a buyer may exercise the right to reject faulty goods and to rescind a contract has been shown to be a source of uncertainty. It is clear from the discussion, that the situation is not helpful to the plight of consumers when they are supplied with faulty goods. The Courts strongly maintained that '...the right to reject must be exercised within a reasonable time and that what is a reasonable time for a successful rejection of faulty goods to occur is a question of fact to be determined by the courts taking the substance of each case into account.[67] Under this settled position, however, consumers are continuously faced with uncertainties as to the appropriate time to reject non-conforming goods under the regime in Ghana as seen above. The acceptable period for a consumer to exercise the right to reject faulty goods has not only been a source of uncertainty to consumers but has also proved to exert undue anxiety on judges in Ghana. A confirmation of this anxiety evinced from the words of Justice Henry A. Kwofie's remarks in his judgment in the non-consumer case of *G. A. Sarpong v Silver Star Auto Ltd*[68] at the High Court. In referring to the question as to whether it was within a reasonable time for the buyer to reject the faulty vehicle, he stated as follows:

> I have considered whether having retained possession of the vehicle for 12 months, it was reasonable for the plaintiff to exercise its right to reject the vehicle. It is this fact which has exercised my mind and given me considerable anxiety.[69]

One of the practical consequences of the uncertainty of the exact reasonable time within which a buyer can reject faulty goods lies in the difficulty lawyers might have in being able to appropriately advise their clients as to when they stand to succeed in rejecting faulty goods their clients purchased. In addition, the fear of the

[67] *G. A. Sarpong & Co. v Silver Star Auto Ltd* [2010] HCGLR, [9] of judgment; *Rockson v Armah* [1975] 2 GLR 116 [119]; See also, *New Lucky Electrical Ltd v Startrack Int. Ghana Ltd & Isaac Acquah* [2010], Suit No. Occ 49/08, [13].

[68] *G. A. Sarpong & Co. v Silver Star Auto Ltd* [2010] HCGLR [16].

[69] *G. A. Sarpong & Co. v Silver Star Auto Ltd* [2010] HCGLR [16].

uncertainty of the outcome might discourage consumers who are supplied with faulty goods from maintaining legal action. The eventual effect is that many consumers, with the fear of uncertainty, may keep the defective goods without asserting their right to reject the goods.

It is undoubtedly clear from the analysis that the present uncertainty of the regime regarding when a consumer might be able to exercise the right to reject faulty goods is unhelpful to consumers in Ghana. The plight of consumers seems to be further worsened, especially in view of the prevalence of substandard goods in the market in Ghana, which increases the chances of consumers buying defective goods in Ghana. It will be more helpful that this uncertainty is resolved to ensure that consumers are provided with a more reliable and easily predictable time frame during which they can reject faulty goods they are supplied with.

4.3.2 *Loss of Right of Rejection by Intimation of Acceptance or by Conduct*

As observed earlier, whilst the buyer has a legal right to reject faulty goods under the law in Ghana, this right may be extinct where the buyer is deemed to have accepted the goods. As recited earlier in particular, section 51 of the SGA provides that 'the buyer may not reject goods which the buyer has accepted.'[70] On the issue of acceptance and preclusion of the right to reject faulty goods, the court had stated that: '... when the buyer accepts the goods then he may not exercise his right to reject the goods.'[71] The critical question is, when will a buyer be construed to have accepted the goods to give rise to his preclusion from exercising the right to reject non-conforming goods? This seems to have been addressed by section 52 of the SGA.[72] The provision has stated unequivocally that where the buyer 'intimates to the seller that the buyer accepts the goods',[73] it constitutes one of the instances in which he will be deemed to have accepted the goods to preclude him from rejecting the goods.

The Courts have had the opportunity to comment on where the buyer's intimation of acceptance of the goods to the seller may extinguish his right to reject the goods when he later, shortly after the intimation discovers them to be defective. For instance, in the matter of *Armah v Baffour*[74] the plaintiff who had sold a Bedford engine to the defendant brought an action to recover the weekly instalment on which the defendant had defaulted in payment. The defendant counterclaimed that the

[70] Section 51 (1), Sale of Goods Act 1962, Act 137.

[71] *A. G. Sarpong & Co. Ltd v Silver Star Ltd* [2010], Suit No OCC10/2009 [15–16]. This observation was especially made when the case was before the High Court.

[72] Sale of Goods Act 1962, Act 137.

[73] Section 52 (a), Sale of Goods Act 1962, Act 137.

[74] [1989–1990] 1GLR 207 [212].

engine was faulty, which he had to repair against the seller's assurance that it was new and faultless. It was observed by the court that the defendant had installed the Bedford engine on his vehicle and carried out the necessary repairs of the engine for his commercial purposes at the expense of exercising his right to reject the engine when he discovered the defects. The court therefore held that 'the defendant's conduct was more consistent with a willingness and readiness to accept the Bedford engine and *thus, would* be bound by the contract of sale rather than reject it.'[75]

Similarly, in an earlier non-consumer case of *Robin Hood Mill Ltd v Farah,*[76] the buyer entered into a contract to buy Robin Hood Flour from the defendants. When the flour was finally shipped to the plaintiff, a large consignment was found to be weevil infested. In view of this, the buyer surrendered the goods to the Port Health Authorities to dispose of the flour on the basis that the flour was unfit for human consumption. It was observed by the Supreme Court that the plaintiff's surrender of the flour to the authorities to have it destroyed were '... powers or rights exercisable only by an owner, the person in whom is vested title, possession, and control of the goods.' The Court therefore held that by the plaintiff's initiative to surrender the flour for destruction, '... he is deemed in law to have accepted the flour and is not entitled to refund of the purchase price.'[77]

It seems clear from the discourse that the determination of the buyer's intimation of acceptance of the goods is not confined to an express statement of the buyer that he accepts the goods, but that, his conduct could be taken as a manifestation of acceptance of the goods. The buyer's intimation of acceptance of the goods which possibly will be taken to have manifested in his conduct will consequently preclude him from exercising the right to reject the goods when they reveal defects thereafter.

It is important, however, to note that the preclusion of the buyer from exercising the right to reject faulty goods on the basis of his intimation of acceptance of the goods does not seem to operate where the revealed defects constitute a breach of a condition of the contract. In a lucid expression, the High Court had submitted that 'where the seller is in breach of a fundamental obligation then the acceptance of the goods will not deprive the buyer of his right to reject the goods.'[78] In an earlier seminal submission in the case of *Zakour v Pillsbury Mills Inc.*,[79] the Court had posited that irrespective of the buyer's acceptance and payment, '... he is not precluded from subsequently rejecting the goods ... for breach of the contract of sale if on examination the goods are found not to be in accordance with the contract.'

As clearly observed above, the extinction of the right of the buyer to reject faulty goods on account of his intimation of acceptance of the goods does not apply where the breach is of a fundamental condition of the contract. On the contrary, however, where the breach is not of a nature fundamental to the terms of the contract, the

---

[75] [1989–1990] 1GLR 207 [212] emphasis added.

[76] [1963] 2 GLR 149.

[77] *Robin Hood Mills Ltd and Another v Farah* [1963] 2 GLR 149 [154–155].

[78] *G. A. Sarpong v Silver Star Auto. Ltd.* [2010], HCGLR [9].

[79] [1961] GLR 401 [405].

buyer will be deprived of the opportunity of rejecting the goods upon intimation of acceptance of the goods. Whilst this standard of the law may be ideal in non-consumer matters, its strict application in consumer cases may be unhelpful to consumers. In particular, in the case of a non-consumer buyer, he may still use the goods for other purposes while maintaining an action for damages. In the case of purely consumer matters, the buyer's purchase of the goods is usually for the fulfilment of an identified need, which may make it practically difficult if the goods are unsuitable for the given purpose for which the consumer bought the goods.

The exclusion of the buyer from exercising the right to reject the goods upon intimation of acceptance, therefore, raises critical questions regarding whether the application of the law will be contingent on the buyer examining the goods. The opportunity for the buyer to examine the goods before his right to reject the goods is limited or excluded is fundamental to help him in determining the degree of conformity of the goods. This important question has clearly been left unresolved. Addressing the question regarding the possible opportunity for the buyer to examine the goods before being deprived of the right to reject the goods when he is said to have intimated acceptance is important to better define a clear and more enhanced system for the protection of consumers in Ghana.

4.4 The Claim of Damages for the Supply of Faulty Goods

Apart from the buyer's right to reject faulty goods as discussed above, the buyer may also be able to make a claim for damages where the seller is in breach of his obligation in respect of the quality and fitness of the goods. Section 55 of the SGA specifically states that: '[w]here the seller is guilty of his fundamental obligation or of a condition or warranty of the contract, the buyer may maintain an action against the seller for damages for the breach complained of or may set up a claim to such damages in diminution or extinction of the price.'[80] While referring to this provision in the recent non-consumer case of *Andreas Bschor GMBH v Birim Wood Complex Ltd and Birim Timbers Ltd*,[81] the Supreme Court observed that: 'the breach of a warranty cannot lead to repudiation or rejection of goods, but will entitle the party not in breach to only damages. But a party who is entitled under the Act to repudiation and rejection of goods may, nevertheless, waive that right and opt for damages instead.' The case where a buyer may accept faulty goods and bring an action for the claim of damages in a breach of a fundamental condition of the contract can further be seen in the non-consumer case of *Japan Motors Trading Co. Ltd. v Randolph Motors Ltd.*[82] In the instant case, the Court contended that one of the options open to an aggrieved purchaser in a contract of sale is to '... abide by the contract and

---

[80] Sale of Goods Act 1962, Act 137.

[81] [2016] CA, No. J4/9/2015 [5].

[82] [1982–1983] GLR 536 [543].

then bring an action to recover damages for the loss he has sustained …' due to the breach. This had also manifested in earlier case law predating the SGA 1962. For instance, in the matter of *Sackey v Fattal*,[83] the plaintiff brought an action for the claim of damages after accepting the entire consignment of goods on the basis that same were of inferior quality. It was held by the court that the plaintiff had acted well within her rights in so doing. In a similar earlier case of *Zakour v Pillsbury Mills Inc*,[84] it was stated by the court that a buyer should not be precluded from recovering damages where the goods are found to be inconsistent with the contract.

The above observations regarding the buyer's entitlement to claim damages where the seller is in breach of his implied obligation to supply the right quality of goods is in particular reference to the sale of goods. However, an equivalent requirement exists under the hire purchase realm for a consumer who is supplied with faulty goods to maintain an action for the claim of damages. Nevertheless, a distinction exists in terms of when a buyer may claim damages in the given case of hire purchase. Unlike in a contract for sale where a buyer may seek for damages regarding the implied quality and fitness of the goods, the right of the buyer to claim damages under hire-purchase is limited to the implied requirement for the fitness of the goods as highlighted earlier. The case of merchantable quality breach under the hire-purchase regime entitles the buyer to bring the contract to an end and to return the goods to the seller as previously examined in respect of the buyer's right to reject faulty goods.

The discussion here will, therefore, focus on the buyer's right to claim damages for the breach of the implied undertaking as to fitness within the realm of the hire-purchase law. Section 13 of the HPA, which stipulates the requirement for the fitness of goods, states in subsection 3 that: '[a] breach of a term specified in this section by the owner or seller gives the hirer or buyer a right to damages in respect of the breach, or to any other remedy that the Court thinks appropriate.'[85] Whilst the regime has not had the benefit of judicial consideration in recent times, reliance may be made on the Court's observation in the matter of *Kpeglo v SCOA Motors*,[86] which predated the 1974 regime, for guidance. In the instant case, the Supreme Court, in a categorical approval of the trial court's pronouncement, had stated *inter alia* that '… it was … open to him (the hirer) to affirm and keep the car in which case the company could give him legal title to it, and he could then sue for damages.' Drawing from this authority, it seems likely that a court faced with a similar question of law with respect to the import of the provision under the 1974 hire-purchase law may have no difficulty in making a similar determination. On this basis, it may be submitted that a hirer or buyer may be able to claim damages where the seller is in breach of his implied obligation as to the fitness of the goods.

[83] [1961] GLR 401 [405].

[84] [1961] GLR 720.

[85] Hire Purchase Decree 1974, NRCD 292.

[86] [1962] 2 GLR 82, [85] emphasis is added.

From above, it is clear that the buyer has a right to claim damages where the seller is in breach of his implied quality and fitness obligations with respect to the sale of goods contracts. In a hire-purchase transaction, the buyer's right to the claim of damages lies where the trader is in breach of his implied obligation as to the fitness of the goods. In the case of a breach as to the merchantable quality of the goods in a hire-purchase, the buyer's right is to reject the goods as earlier examined.

However, the critical question as to whether the award of damages to the consumer will be able to afford him with satisfactory redress remains broadly doubtful. It is important to point out that the criteria for the estimate of damages to a buyer who is supplied with faulty goods have been defined under section 56 of the SGA, 1962. The proviso states that: 'the measurement of damages in an action under section 55 of this Act is the loss which could reasonably have been foreseen by the seller at the time when the contract was made as likely to result from the breach of *the* contract'.[87] The courts have held this provision to be a restatement of the *Hadley v Baxendale*[88] *locus classicus* on the measurement of damages where a party to a contract is in breach.[89] Drawing from the *Hadley v Baxendale* case in particular, a plethora of case law has stated to the effect that the measure of damages to be awarded falls into two limbs. That is, damages naturally arising directly from the breach of the contract and damages which the parties would have had in contemplation as the likely outcome in the event of a breach of the contract.[90] Whilst damages which are presumed to flow naturally from the breach are said to be general damages, damages emanating from the contemplation of the parties in the event of the breach is considered special damages.[91] The buyer may only be able to claim special damages where he is able to demonstrate with sufficient 'degree of clarity and certainty' the specific lost he has incurred as a result of the breach otherwise he may be

[87] Section 56, Sale of Goods Act (1962), Act 137, emphasis added.

[88] (1854) 9 Ex. 342, 156 ER 145.

[89] This observation has been affirmed by the courts in a number cases. For details, see, *Glencore A. G. v Volta Aluminum Co. Ltd,* (2015), CA, No. J4/40/2013, [18]; See also, *Andreas Bschor GMBH v Birim Wood Complex Ltd and Birim Timbers Ltd* (2016), CA, No. J4/9/2015, [17]; See also, *Nartey-Tokoli and Others v Volta Aluminium Co. Ltd* (1989-90) 2 GLR, 341, [369]; See also, *Agbedor and Another v Yeboa* (1981) GLR 769, [775]–[776].

[90] *Andreas Bschor GMBH v Birim Wood Complex Ltd and Birim Timbers Ltd* (2016), CA, No. J4/9/2015, [17]; See also, *Glencore A. G. v Volta Aluminum Co. Ltd,* (2015), CA, No. J4/40/2013, [18]; See also, *G. A. Sarpong & Co. v Silver Star* Auto Ltd (2014) 72 G.M.J, [82]-[83]; (2014) CA Suit No. J4/43/2013, [12]; See also, *Delmas Agencies (Gh) Ltd. v Food Distributor Int. Ltd* [2007–2008] SCGLR 748, [754]; See also, *Attorney General v Faroe Atlantic Co. Ltd,* (2005 – 2006), SCGLR 271, [290]; See also, *Nartey-Tokoli and Others v Volta Aluminium Co. Ltd* (1989-90) 2 GLR, 341, [369]; See also, *Agbedor and Another v Yeboa* (1981) GLR 769, [775]–[776].

[91] *Andreas Bschor GMBH v Birim Wood Complex Ltd and Birim Timbers Ltd* (2016), CA, No. J4/9/2015, [16]; See also, *Glencore A. G. v Volta Aluminum Co. Ltd,* (2015), CA, No. J4/40/2013, [33]; See also, *Prah v Okai* [1966] GLR 560.

afforded nominal damages.[92] The courts have consistently maintained that special damages must be 'strictly proved' to give rise to a successful claim for damages.[93]

The overall essence of the buyer's entitlement to the claim of damages seems to be the restoration of the loss the buyer might have incurred as a result of the seller's breach of his implied quality obligation. In *Glencore A. G. v Volta Aluminum Co. Ltd*,[94] it was observed by the court that the purpose of the computation of how much money must be paid by the party in breach was basically 'to put the innocent party in nearly the same position that he would have been had the other party not breached the contract.' Also, in the matter of *Delmas Agencies (Gh) Ltd. v Food Distributor Int. Ltd*,[95] the court had equally maintained that: 'it is a well-established principle in law that in a claim for damages for breach of contract the party to the contract who is not guilty of such breach is to be placed financially, in the position he would have been *had* the contract not been breached.' A similar stance can be seen in earlier case law clearly pointing to the same direction that the overall goal of the award of damages to a party who is not in breach of the contract is to restore him to the same position he would have been if the breach had not occurred.[96] In *Borketey v Achinivu and Others*[97] for instance, it was held that 'the dominant rule of law is the principle of *resitutio in integrum' and* that '... the plaintiff is entitled to receive as damages such a sum of money as will place him in as good a position as he would have been if the (breach) ... had not occurred.' In the case of *Agyeibea v Fahim and Co.*,[98] the Court had held that the damages to which the hirer was entitled to were '... the damages measured by the loss of the instalments and deposits paid ....' Although the dominant rule from the above jurisprudence is the principle of *restitutio in integrum*, it has been maintained that too remote damages are not recoverable.[99] Generally, the effect of the authorities clearly point to the fact that the purpose of the grant of damages in the specific case of consumer matters is to ensure that the buyer is placed in the same position as if he was not supplied with faulty goods. The amount of damages to be paid is therefore targeted at ensuring that the aggrieved consumer is

[92] *Andreas Bschor GMBH v Birim Wood Complex Ltd and Birim Timbers Ltd* (2016), CA, No. J4/9/2015, [16]; See also, *Glencore A. G. v Volta Aluminum Co. Ltd*, (2015), CA, No. J4/40/2013, [33].

[93] *Andreas Bschor GMBH v Birim Wood Complex Ltd and Birim Timbers Ltd* (2016), CA, No. J4/9/2015, [16]; See also, *Glencore A. G. v Volta Aluminum Co. Ltd*, (2015), CA, No. J4/40/2013, [33]; See also, *Prah v. Okai* [1966] GLR 560.

[94] (2015), CA, No. J4/40/2013, [12].

[95] [2007-2008] SCGLR 748, [757] per Sophia Adinyira JSC, emphasis added.

[96] *Young Trading Agencies v Staveley and Co. Ltd* [1977] 1GLR 123, [136].

[97] (1966) GLR 92, [95] emphasis is mine; See also, the non-consumer case of *Royal Ducth Airlines (KLM) and Another v Farmex Ltd.* [1987–1988] 2 GLR 650 where the Supreme Court equally held that the principle of law in the measure of damages is restitution in integrum - mainly to restored to the position the party not in breach would have been if the breach had not occurred.

[98] (1968) GLR 463, p. 470.

[99] *West Africab Bakery v Mifzah* [1972] 1 GLR 78.

indemnified to the extent of the breach. This is particularly important to the goal of protecting the consumer.

In a nutshell, a buyer who is supplied with faulty goods may be entitled to claim damages. The available damages may either be general damages or special damages, with a strict duty on the buyer as a claimant to prove the loss to be able to succeed in his claim where the claim is for special damages. The overall goal of the award of damages is to restore the buyer to the position he would have been in if the breach had not occurred.

However, the critical concern is that the claim for damages may mostly not be able to afford the consumer a satisfactory redress. It is especially clear from the earlier discussion that the buyer may make a claim for damages where the non-conformity of the goods is not a condition of the contract but is seen as a trivial breach. The determination of the defects being trivial may consequently affect the degree of damages that may be awarded to the buyer. One leading commentator in the field of consumer law in Ghana observed that a consumer who is deprived of the right to reject the goods is unlikely to obtain damages that will be substantially useful to him. The author rightly held the conviction that the determination of the breach to be trivial may further convey the impression that the breach has not occasioned any significant prejudice to the rights of the buyer under the contract.[100] In particular, in the recent non-consumer case of *Andreas Bschor GMBH v Birim Wood Complex Ltd and another*,[101] the Supreme Court stated that: '[t]he settled position of the law is that … a court may award nominal damages under general damages where no real loss has been occasioned by the infringement of a right….'[102]

From the discussion, it is clear that the consumer may be able to claim damages as an alternative right to the remedy of rejection. However, in the instant case where the defects in the goods are taken not to go to the root of the contract, it may consequently result in the consumer being awarded damages that will be unsatisfactory and unhelpful to him. What might be useful to the consumer as an alternative to the claim for damages is to have the goods replaced or repaired for him. However, as noted previously, such remedies are not legal rights for consumers under the law in Ghana.

This clearly leaves consumers in Ghana with insufficient options to ensure that they are able to obtain satisfactory redress when faulty goods are supplied. Addressing this limitation of the law is therefore critical to ensure that consumers are better afforded the required alternative remedies which they may access when supplied with faulty goods. This is particularly important to ensure that consumers are better protected when they are supplied with faulty goods in Ghana.

[100] Dowuona-Hammond (1995).

[101] (2016), CA, No. J4/9/2015, [16].

[102] (2016), CA, No. J4/9/2015, [16] (emphasis is mine).

4.5 Conclusion

This Chapter addressed research question two of this book regarding whether the remedies available under the regime in Ghana are adequate to afford consumers with effective protection when they are supplied with faulty goods. The diagnosis of the regime found that consumers are only entitled to the remedies of rejection of faulty goods and the claim for damages when they are supplied with faulty goods in Ghana. The analysis further showed that the consumer right to reject faulty goods can only be exercised where there is a breach of a condition of the contract. On the other hand, the consumer right to the claim for damages may be activated where the breach is not a condition of the contract or the buyer choosing to keep the goods in a breach of a condition of the contract but maintain an action for damages in sales contracts. In the given instance of hire-purchase, the buyer's right to reject faulty goods is confined to breach of the merchantable quality, with the right to claim damages connected to the breach of the implied requirement for the fitness of the goods.

The analysis of the existing remedies identified a number of uncertainties and limitations which are not practically helpful in affording consumers with the needed remedies when they are supplied with faulty goods in Ghana. In particular, the consumer right to reject faulty goods as a primary remedy cannot be exercised where the defect in the goods is trivial and does not amount to a breach of a condition. The question of what amounts to trivial and not a condition of the contract is uncertain under the regime. The analysis of the right to reject faulty goods also revealed elements of uncertainty as to the precise timeframe a consumer may be able to exercise the right to reject faulty goods after the goods have been delivered to him. The discussion of the right to reject faulty goods further showed that a consumer who is rejecting faulty goods has no other alternative option but to terminate the contract and refuse to pay for the goods or demand a refund if the payment had been made. The analysis, therefore, found that this is unsatisfactory, especially where a consumer wishes to reject the goods but keeps the contract alive if he can obtain an alternative remedy such as identical replacement or repair or even replacement with close substitute goods. The desirable remedies were, however, discovered not to exist under the regime in Ghana as legal rights. This, therefore, leaves the regime with insufficient remedies that reflect the desired expectations of consumers in Ghana.

The discussion also found that the consumer's claim for damages as the alternative right may not always be adequate to the consumer whose principal desire is to have goods capable of meeting his intended purpose. Moreover, the discussion also noted that where the faulty goods are rendered as not amounting to a condition of the contract, the amount of damages may also not be satisfactory to the consumer. In view of the uncertainties and limitations of the remedies under the regime, it is submitted that the available remedies are not adequate to ensure that consumers are afforded with the required remedies when they are supplied with non-conforming quality and fitness of goods in Ghana.

The next chapter will focus on addressing the identified deficiencies of the consumer remedies for faulty goods. The discussion will especially analyse the deficiencies of the consumer remedies for faulty goods in comparison with English law and its EU influence while taking into consideration the domestic circumstances in Ghana. The result of the comparative analysis will provide an informed basis on which to put forward recommendations for legislative and judicial considerations in resolving the issues in Ghana.

References:

Ansa-Asare K (1981) Case for a comprehensive framework of consumer protection in Ghana. Rev Ghana Law 14(13):73–89

Dei-Anang KK (1967) Caveat venditor ghaniensis. Univ Ghana Law J 4:90. https://doi.org/10.1525/sp.2007.54.1.23

Dowuona-Hammond C (1995) Protecting the purchaser of goods under Ghanaian law. Rev Ghana Law 19:105

Dowuona-Hammond C (2018) Consumer law and policy in Ghana. J Consum Policy 41:333–354

Nsubuga LF, Naatu F, Kaaka DZ (2024) Consumer protection in hire purchase transactions: a case study of Ghana's legal framework. J Law Sustain Dev 12(10):e3972–e3972

Yidana N (2020) Enacting a consumer protection law in Ghana: possible lessons from the UK Consumer Rights Act 2015. Law Res Rev Quart 6(4):323–342

Chapter 5
Consumer Remedies for Faulty Goods Under English Law: Resolving the Shortfalls of the Law in Ghana

5.1 Introduction

The preceding Chapter analysed the adequacy of the consumer remedies for faulty goods in Ghana and highlighted a number of deficiencies of the regime. The present Chapter further seeks to examine the extent to which the approach of English law might be persuasive in addressing the concerns in Ghana while being mindful of the peculiar circumstances in Ghana. The analysis of the issues will particularly draw from the experience of English law and its EU influence on consumer remedies for faulty goods. This is mainly to address research question four of this book regarding whether the English law and its EU-influenced remedies for consumers could provide a template that may be useful in resolving the deficiencies of consumer remedies for faulty goods in Ghana. In particular, a number of uncertainties and limitations were especially highlighted in Chap. 3 earlier to militate against the degree of protection available under the present regime for consumers when they are supplied with faulty goods.

This chapter, therefore, seeks to identify possible solutions to the various uncertainties and limitations that were discovered to better advance the cause of consumers when they are supplied with faulty goods in Ghana. The analysis of the issues in this chapter will be carried out, particularly drawing from the experience of English law and its EU influence on matters of consumer remedies for faulty goods, as noted above.

Before analysing the main issues in Ghana in light of English law, however, it is first necessary to succinctly restate concisely the basis for the selection of English law as the litmus test for the comparison as earlier provided in Chap. 1 of this book. The choice of English law, as earlier observed in Chap. 1, is premised on a number of important grounds. First, the English regime has, over the years, undergone a

N. Yidana, *Consumer Law and Policy on Faulty Goods*, Ius Gentium: Comparative Perspectives on Law and Justice 134,
https://doi.org/10.1007/978-3-032-08700-3_5

series of reforms addressing matters of similar nature,[1] which presently confront the regime for the protection of consumers in Ghana. Within the domain of comparative scholarship, as shown in Chap. 1, it is proper to seek guidance from jurisdictions that have taken the lead in resolving similar problems and not reinvent the wheels, and this underlines the choice of English law for the present discourse. The analysis will nevertheless take into account the domestic realities in Ghana in the comparative process to mitigate possible failures on account of the socio-economic and cultural variations between the two jurisdictions. Legal actors in Ghana have also had an active interest in commonly resorting to English law for persuasive guidance, which scholars of comparative law similarly highlighted could be one of the convincing grounds for the choice of a regime for comparison as was set out in Chap. 1. One of the supporting rationales for the choice of English law for the comparative discourse is grounded on the common shared roots of the two jurisdictions on account of the historical colonial ties. As was shown in Chap. 1, a comparative analysis of deficiencies in domestic law with a foreign jurisdiction of shared common ties has the tendency to produce best-fit solutions to resolve domestic problems. Moreover, the degree of richness and maturity of English law, both in terms of jurisprudence and academic commentary, which has been advocated as one of the fundamentals for successful comparative experience as was demonstrated in Chap. 1, further informed the choice of English law for the comparative discourse.[2]

Following the above background on the basis of using the English law for the comparison, it is also worth restating concisely, as earlier noted, the background of the consumer remedies for faulty goods under the English law, which will provide the main yardstick for the analysis. Under English law, as highlighted in Chap. 1, the remedies of consumers for faulty goods reflect what has been termed as a short-term right to reject faulty goods, the remedy of repair or replacement, and the remedy of price reduction or the final right to reject. Consumers may also avail themselves of the common law remedies of specific performance, claim of damages, or seek an order for specific implement (in Scotland), among others. It was, therefore, concluded that the remedies for consumers under the English law for faulty goods are broadly shaped with a combination of the English traditional remedies with some modifications and heavy influences of the European Union Consumer Sales Directive 1999.[3] In view of the huge influence of the EU Consumer Sales remedies on English law, the English Courts may likely follow the decisions of the CJEU in determining matters put before them in relation to the remedies

[1] The various reforms will be highlighted in the course of the analysis in this Chapter.

[2] For a detailed and further underling justification of the use of the English law for the present comparative discourse, see, Chap. 1 of this book on: 'The rationale for the use of the English regime for the comparative analysis', para. 1.4.

[3] The EU Directive on Consumer Sales was first implemented into English law through the Sale and Supply of Goods Regulations 2002 and has now been repealed by the Consumer Rights Act 2015.

drawn from the EU Directive, as similarly noted in Chap. 4.[4] In carrying out the comparative analysis, therefore, the relevant case law of the CJEU may be drawn to support the understanding of any point of law being analysed. Also, important to note is that the rights of consumers under the CRA 2015 have a wider application throughout the UK. In view of this, case law from the Scottish Courts may be drawn in appropriate instances to create the required understanding of the various issues being discussed.

Broadly, the Chapter is structured in four main parts, including this introduction. The second part of this introduction addresses the uncertainties regarding the consumer right to reject faulty goods in Ghana, drawing from the experience of English law. This part is divided into two subsections. The first subsection addresses the uncertainties around trivial defects, for which a consumer may not be able to reject goods that are faulty under the law in Ghana. The second subsection addresses the uncertainty surrounding the reasonable time for the consumer to reject faulty goods under Ghana law in light of the English law. The third part will further analyse the issue of the limitation of consumers to the termination of the contract as the only option for a consumer who rejects faulty goods under the law in Ghana. This leads to the need to ensure effective integration of the proposed reforms with the existing regime for the larger benefit of serving the interest of consumers in Ghana. This part also examines other alternative remedies where the prevailing regime and the proposed remedies might afford the consumer the required protection. The final part will sum up the main conclusions reached in the various sections of the Chapter. Following this background is the analysis of the various issues in Ghana, drawing from the English law highlighted above.

5.2 Resolving the Uncertainties of the Consumer Right to Reject Faulty Goods in Ghana Through the Lens of English Law

This section discusses the uncertainties in the consumer's right to reject faulty goods in Ghana, drawing from the experience of the English law. In particular, it was noted in Chap. 3 that the buyer's remedy of rejection was only applicable where the defect amounts to a breach of a fundamental condition of the contract that is not trivial. The question of what constitutes a trivial defect for which the consumer may not be able to exercise the right of rejection of the faulty goods was, however, not defined.

[4] It is important to state that while the UK prepares itself to leave the EU, case law of both the ECJ and the UK Courts pertaining to EU derived laws will invariably continue to have application and may influence the determination of the retained EU laws until they are modified by an act of parliament or set aside by the Supreme Court or the High Court of Justiciary (sitting as a Court of Appeal) in a manner that is consistent with departing from a UK originated law as per the recent EU Withdrawal Act; For details, see, Section 6, UK, European Union (Withdrawal) Act 2018, Chapter 16.

Moreover, it was noted that a buyer's right to reject faulty goods may be lost if he has not rejected the goods after the passage of a reasonable time. The reasonable time during which a consumer may be able to reject faulty goods was, however, found to be a source of uncertainty and accounted for most disputes. The uncertainty of the time to reject was similarly found to be the case regarding the determination of acceptance of the goods by intimation of acceptance or by conduct. In particular, the buyer's intimation of acceptance could deny him the benefit of rejecting the goods whether or not he has examined the goods. The uncertainties were found unhelpful to the overall interest of consumers especially in exercising their rights to reject goods that are faulty. It was therefore argued that the concerns needed to be addressed so as to ensure that the regime better served the needs of consumers with more enhanced protection against the menace of faulty goods in Ghana. The discussion in this part of the present chapter, therefore, seeks to resolve the various uncertainties drawing from the experience of English law but considered within the context of the situation in Ghana. The detailed discussion is set out below, starting with the uncertainty regarding what degree of defects will be considered trivial or minor, for which the rejection right will not apply.

5.2.1 Resolving the Threshold of Trivial or Minor Defects for Which a Consumer Cannot Reject Faulty Goods

In Chap. 4 of this book, it was established, as restated above, that while the consumer has the right to reject faulty goods under the law in Ghana, the right is not applicable where the defect is not a condition of the contract but trivial in nature. The problem, as was noted, is that the question as to what constitutes trivial or minor defects, which will not be of a condition of the contract, was found not defined in the statutes and by the courts. This was argued to leave the regime with uncertainty as to what extent defective goods may be rendered as not of a condition of the contract but a trivial defect disentitling the consumer from the right to reject the goods. The uncertainty was found to be of great concern on account of the fact that although the defect may be held not to be a condition of the contract, it might nevertheless have a heavy impact on the particular purpose of the buyer. It was therefore submitted that the uncertainty leaves the regime not helpful in practice to consumers in Ghana. The need to address the uncertainty was further found to be heightened in view of the fact that the determination of the defects not being a condition of the contract might consequently affect the damages the consumer may obtain if he choices to resort to the claim for damages as the alternative remedy available to him under the regime. In effect, this may leave the consumer who has been supplied with the faulty goods without satisfactory redress as was noted there. There is therefore the need for a further legislative intervention directed at clarifying what might not be seen as a condition of the contract but trivial or minor in the specific case of consumer transactions to ensure that a more certain regime is defined to better serve the needs of consumers in Ghana. This is especially critical to ensure that consumers are able to avail themselves of the remedy of rejection where appropriate when supplied with goods that are of a defective quality, which was noted in Chap. 1 to prevail in the market in Ghana.

Drawing from the experience of the English law, the CRA 2015 has employed two approaches through which a consumer may exercise the right to reject faulty goods with which he has been supplied. The approaches notably include the short-term right to reject and the final right to reject goods which are faulty.[5] These two schemes of rights to reject faulty good which will be examined shortly entitle the consumer to reject the goods where the seller is in breach of his obligations as regards the standard of satisfactory quality and fitness of the goods. It appears that the consumers' right to reject faulty goods does not exclude minor defects especially where the defect is rendered a relevant factor in the assessment of the quality of the goods. The non-exclusion of minor defects from the right of consumers to reject faulty goods was particularly affirmed in the Law Commission's pre-2015 Act Report where it commented on section 14(2B) of the SGA, 1979 which has now been restated in section 9 of the CRA 2015 as observed earlier in Chap. 3 of this book regarding the trader's obligation to supply goods of satisfactory quality. The Commission had specifically noted that: 'once a consumer has shown that one of the implied terms of quality has been breached, they may exercise the right to reject, provided they have not accepted the goods. There is no exclusion for minor defects, such as imperfection in appearance, finish, or small malfunctions.'[6]

The underlining philosophy for the legal rights of a consumer to reject faulty goods which defects may be minor had long been argued to mainly lie in the quest of ensuring that the consumer obtain 'proper quality goods at the full price, not defective goods at a lower price.'[7] This observation further reflected the argument that: 'if a consumer purchases a new item, they are paying the price for something new, not second-hand, or repaired. The consumer, if given the option, would usually not have chosen to purchase the damaged item, even at a discount.'[8] This is because consumers mostly attached immeasurable importance to the appearances of goods,

[5] The short-term right to reject and the final right to reject are provided under section 22 and 24 of the CRA 2015 respectively.

[6] The Commission, *Consumer Remedies for Faulty Goods* (The Law Com No 317 & Scot Law No 216, 2009) para. 3.98.

[7] This was especially noted in the 1987 Law Commission's report which was initially implemented in 1994 into the SGA 1979 and now expressed under section 9 of the Consumer Rights Act 2015. For details see, The Law Commission, *Sale and Supply of Goods* (The Law Co, The Law Com No 160 and Scot Law Com No 104, 1987) para. 4.4.

[8] Law Commission, *Consumer remedies for faulty goods* (Law Com No 317 & Scot Law Com No. 216, 2009) para. 3.109.

and the presence of dents, scratches and blemishes on the goods although minor, may possibly undermine the position of the consumer without rejection rights.[9]

Another critical philosophical ground that seems to add weight to the rationale of consumers being entitled to reject goods with minor defects is the issue of the possible failure of related remedies to offer the consumer a satisfactory redress. In particular, it had long been argued that damages, which was initially the only alternative remedy to the right of rejection under the then English law, might also not be able to offer satisfactory redress to the consumer for minor defects in goods that rendered them unsatisfactory.[10] This was especially construed within the premise that what the consumer mostly prefers is to obtain quality goods but not defective goods at a lower price possibly as noted above. In a related commentary regarding the consumer obtaining satisfactory redress from alternative remedies, it has been observed that the remedy of repair or replacement or price reduction as will be discussed later in this chapter may not always be attractive to the consumer like the classic right to reject the goods.[11] In the pre-2015 Act it was similarly contended that the remedy of repair or replacement might as well not be able to provide the consumer with satisfactory redress.[12] This might especially be the case where the repair failed to correct the defect or the replaced goods equally show similar manifested defects.[13] Under such circumstances, it has been observed that the consumer may be able to avail himself of the remedy of final rejection of the goods as will be examined shortly.[14]

In sum, a consumer under the English law may be able to reject goods with minor defects where the consumer claim for damages, or repair or replacement or price reduction of the goods may not be able to afford the consumer with satisfactory redress as examined above. Essentially, a similar legislative measure in Ghana that expressly allows consumers the right to reject faulty goods where any other remedy will likely not be helpful to the consumer although the defects may be minor, will be viable to clarifying the uncertainty of the law regarding defects to which a consumer may be able to exercise the right of rejection. In particular, such a statutory requirement will bring clarity to defects which are not of a condition of the contract to which the consumer may not be able to reject the goods.

It is nevertheless important to state that where the defect is so minute to the extent of it being qualified as *de minimis*, it may still be fair to disallow rejection. For instance, suppose a car which the consumer bought refused to start days after purchase as a result of the battery terminal not being properly fitted. Such a problem

---

[9] Law Commission, *Consumer remedies for faulty goods* (Law Com No 317 & Scot Law Com No. 216, 2009) para. 3.101.

[10] The Law Commission, *Sale and Supply of Goods* (The Law Co, The Law Com No 160 and Scot Law Com No 104, 1987) Para. 4.4.

[11] Bridge (2017), para. 14.097.

[12] Law Commission, *Consumer remedies for faulty goods* (Law Com No 317 & Scot Law Com No. 216, 2009) para. 3.101.

[13] Section 24, CRA 2015.

[14] For details see, Barry et al. (2016), para. 3.124, a guide to Section 24, CRA 2015.

only requires a few minutes to fix and this should not give rise to the remedy of rejection. It is important to note, however, that such a requirement is well known under the English law as regards the consumer right to reject faulty goods with minor defects. For instance, to give effect to the right of the buyer to reject faulty goods with minor defects, it was observed in the pre-2015 Act in *Darren Egan v. Motor Services (Bath) Ltd*[15] by Lady Justice Smith that the buyer ought to be able to persuade the court that the minor defects had sufficient consequence on which basis a reasonable person would find the goods unsatisfactory. The minor defect which may lead to the consumer rejection of the goods should not, however, be quite negligible. Especially, it had been argued that while a breach in relation to the appearance and finish of the goods as well as freedom from minor defects may render the goods unsatisfactory, this may not be the situation where the defect is 'so minor as to render it *de minimis'*. Similarly, the Law Commission had also contended that the defects of the goods that should occasion the consumer's entitlement to reject the goods should not be so trifling as to be considered as falling within the *de minimis non curat lex* principle.[16]

As indicated above, qualifying minor defects such that the right to rejection may apply and so trivial minor defects particularly to the extent of being rendered *de minimis* where the right to reject may disapply will likely provide a more balanced and fairer regime for both traders and consumers in Ghana. This will especially ensure that in consumer matters, defects which will not be read as a condition of the contract will be confined to defects which are so minor as to fall within the remit of the general principle of *de minimis.* This will consequently address two major hurdles. First, it will be clear that the consumer's rejection right embraces minor defects except those within the remit of de minimis. Second, it will also bring clarity to the question of what might be termed as a trivial defect to which the consumer may not be able to exercise the right to reject faulty goods with minor defects.

It is worth stating that it might be useful for the legislative intervention to require that a consumer is constantly entitled to reject goods for minor defects which are not *de minimis* especially where the goods in question are new goods. This will be critical to forestall the arising of any dispute as to whether a consumer is entitled to exercise the right to reject faulty goods with minor defects which are not so minor. This will especially be consistent with the earlier argument in this chapter that the appearance and finish and freedom from minor defects as part of the aspect of quality known under the English law should be given a constant application in Ghana in order to avoid the tendency of any dispute as to whether these are relevant.

Nevertheless, this will similarly depart from the English law which only allows rejection where the minor defect is a relevant factor in the given case. In the pre-2015 Act, it was especially contended that the presence of defects of appearance and finish and freedom from minor defects 'will not necessarily render the goods

---

15 [2007] EWCA Civ 1002, [2008] 1 WLR 1589.

16 Law Commission, *Consumer remedies for faulty goods* (Law Com No 317 & Scot Law Com No. 216, 2009) para. 3.104.

unsatisfactory as they are only to be considered in appropriate cases as part of the overall assessment of the goods' quality.'[17] In the *Darren Egan v Motor Services (Bath) Ltd*[18] case, the Court confirmed that pointing to a minor defect in the goods was not sufficient to entitle a buyer to reject the goods. Also, in the recent case of *Peebles v Rembrand Builders Merchants Ltd,*[19] it was affirmed that '[a]ppearance and finish and durability, are aspect of quality in appropriate cases' and that '[a]ll these factors are in play in the present case.'[20] In short, the consumers' right to reject faulty goods with minor defects under the English law will only arise where the said minor defects are considered as a relevant factor in the particular case as observed above.

Essentially as noted, however, permitting a constant application of the right for the consumer to exercise a right of rejection unless a defect is so minor to the level of being regarded *de minimis* in Ghana will likely ensure that consumer disputes possibly get resolved with much ease leaving less need for court litigation. While the campaign for the rejection right for minor defects which are not *de minimis* is for new goods, it remains appropriate to require that minor defects in second hand goods should only give rise to the remedy of rejection where relevant as similarly observed under the English law above. This is especially critical on account of the fact that the degree of quality of second-hand goods is not similar to that of new goods. Moreover, various second-hand goods that are sold will have varied degrees of quality levels based on several factors such as the age of the goods and the degree of defects already in the goods at the time of the transaction among others. The application of the relevance theory in determining whether to allow the consumer to reject goods with minor defects in matters of second-hand goods may therefore allow the court to fairly weigh all the available evidence in coming to a decision. It is worth stating that the case for consumers to reject new goods with minor defects which are not *de minimis*, but requiring the right to reject second-hand goods with minor defects on the basis of the defects being a relevant factor would largely ensure that the remedies are consistent with the earlier proposal regarding the requirements for the quality of goods.[21] This would especially be the case if the recommendation of the quality regime earlier in Chap. 3 of this book and the remedy as observed here are given a legislative effect.

So far, the argument has been that the clear requirement in English law that the consumer may be able to reject goods with minor defects provided the defects are not *de minimis* will be viable in remedying the uncertainty of the undefined trivial

---

[17] Howells and Weatherill (2005), p. 178.

[18] [2007] EWCA Civ 1002; [2008] 1 WLR 1589.

[19] [2017] G.W.D. 15-236.

[20] [2017] SC Dun. 28, WL 01831372, Para. 53.

[21] In this chapter para. 5.2.2.1, this book proposed the adoption of the 'aspects of quality' as provided under the English law in Ghana. It was, however, noted that the quality criterion should be required constantly where the goods are new goods, but that, the application of the aspects of quality in the case of second-hand goods should be subjected to the test of each aspects of quality being a relevant factor in a case by case basis.

defects in Ghana which may possibly afford consumers with more enhanced protection in Ghana. The express clarity of the law in Ghana that trivial or minor defects which are *de minimis* in character is where the consumer will lose the right to reject the goods as above will likely advance the cause of consumers in Ghana especially when replicated. In particular, such a legislative requirement will ensure that consumers are not left with faulty goods where even an award of damages, which is presently the available legal right, may not be able to afford the consumer a satisfactory remedy.

However, while English law requires that the right to reject faulty goods with minor defects can only be exercised where the defect is a relevant factor on a case-by-case basis, it is submitted that the right to reject faulty goods should be made constant in the case of new goods in Ghana. The law in Ghana should further stipulate that where the goods are second-hand goods, the right to reject will be subject to the relevance theory as similarly pertained under English law. The legislative intervention in this way will likely ensure that a consumer who purchases a brand-new microwave oven, for example, which begins to show discolouration a few weeks after purchase, although minor, may nevertheless entitle the consumer to possibly reject the product. This is especially crucial to allow the consumer to obtain a similar, and of course, the right quality microwave oven for his intended use. This will significantly ensure that consumers in Ghana are better protected against being supplied with defective goods. This will consequently ensure that consumers are properly protected against the menace of substandard quality of goods, which were shown in Chap. 1 previously to dominate in the market in Ghana.

5.2.2 *Reasonable Time to Reject Faulty Goods in Ghana: Lessons from English Law*

In examining the rights of consumers in Ghana under Chap. 3 as noted above, it was ascertained that the buyer has a right to reject faulty goods under the Ghanaian law. The right of the buyer to reject faulty goods was however found inapplicable in certain instances. In particular, the buyer's right to reject faulty goods was discovered to be excluded where he is deemed to have accepted the goods. As noted earlier, one of the instances in which the buyer would be deemed to have accepted the goods and his right was extinguished was noted to be where he has not rejected the goods after the lapse of a reasonable time. The problem, however, was that the acceptable time frame within which the buyer may be allowed to exercise the right to reject non-conforming goods was left undefined. This constituted a source of uncertainty as to when a consumer rejection of faulty goods will be permitted. The uncertainty was particularly seen to manifest in the varied determination of the reasonable time during which rejection could be allowed by the Courts. The uncertainty was therefore argued as unhelpful to providing consumers with a very clear guidance to better afford them with the required protection against the menace of substandard quality of goods in the market in Ghana. This was noted to form an important ground requiring a further legislative intervention that particularly provides a clear guidance for the regulation of consumer transactions in Ghana. This was argued to be crucial to ensure that consumers are able to act within a clearly defined time frame when supplied with defective goods. This was found to be crucial so as to ensure that consumers in Ghana are properly protected against the prevalence of the substandard quality of goods in the market in Ghana, as evidenced in Chap. 1 of this book of which a consumer could be entrapped with.

In examining English law through a comparative lens, two sets of rights to reject faulty goods have been provided for the benefit of consumers under section 20 of the CRA 2015, as highlighted above.[22] As noted previously, the two schemes of rights to reject defective goods are mainly categorised as a short-term right to reject and a final right to reject. While the short-term right to reject faulty goods is a creature of the CRA 2015, essentially as a modified version of the traditional classic right to reject for breach of a condition known under the Sale of Goods Act 1979, the final right to reject is a product of the 1999 EU Directive[23] which had previously been implemented in the UK under the 1979 SGA through the Sale and Supply of Goods Regulations 2002.[24]

The description of the extent of the short-term right to reject and final right to reject are respectively provided in sections 22 and 24 of the CRA 2015. In considering the short-term right to reject first, section 22 explicitly provides a clear time limit during which a consumer in the UK can reject and return non-conforming goods to the trader. In particular, a time period of thirty days (30 days) is statutorily set out as a short-time right for a consumer to reject and return faulty goods.[25] The thirty (30) day period seems to be the period during which the consumer may be able to ascertain the conformity or otherwise of the goods in order to reject the goods if they are faulty. It was particularly related in the pre-2015 Act that: 'in most cases 30 days would give the consumer a reasonable opportunity to inspect the goods and test them for a short period in actual use.'[26] It was further contended that in the given case of clothes, '[t]he 30-day period is intended to allow enough time to wear the clothes and wash them and, if they fall apart in the wash, return them to the shop. For a washing machine, 30 days should provide enough time to install the

---

[22] The two sets of rights to reject have first been mentioned under section 19 of the CRA as part of other schemes of rights a consumer may exercise in the event that the goods purchased are found faulty.

[23] Directive 1999 Art 3 (5)-(6).

[24] The present provision in the CRA 2015 is mainly a combined restatement of the English law in a modified version and the EU Directive previously implemented into the UK SGA 1979.

[25] Section 22(3), the UK CRA 2015.

[26] Law Commission, *Consumer remedies for faulty goods* (Law Com No 317 & Scot Law Com No. 216, 2009) para. 3.51.

machine and use the main programmes. For a new computer, it enables the consumer to install the software they intend to use and to test it in practice.'[27]

However, where the goods are of a kind that are reasonably expected to perish earlier than the thirty day span, the period in question brings to an end the valid rejection period.[28] The Act's Explanatory Notes particularly state that for perishable goods, 'the period for exercising the short-term right to reject lasts only as long as it would be reasonable to expect those goods to last.'[29] Moreover, the parties may nevertheless agree to an alternatively longer time period but not less than the stipulated 30 days.[30] The time period particularly starts to run once the goods are delivered to the buyer or ownership of the goods is transferred to the buyer.[31] The buyer's rejection of the goods within this stipulated time period entitles him to a full refund of the price already paid or anything transferred to the trader in lieu of the price.[32] The short-term period of thirty days allowance for the right of rejection of faulty goods seems essentially to be meant to afford consumers and retailers an unambiguous regime to which they may be able to rely on in resolving matters of defects in goods based on possibly similar understanding of the requirement of the law. This especially reflects the observation of the Law Commission in the pre-2015 Act that: '[w]e know that it is very rare for consumers to take disputes to court; it is also very rare for consumers to employ lawyers to advise them. It is therefore imperative that the law is capable of being understood, remembered and asserted by consumers. On the balance, and in practical terms, we think that the introduction of a 30- day normal period for the right to reject will benefit the average consumer. It will also assist the retailers by providing a simple standard for their staff.'[33] This observation largely summarises the underlining philosophy of the short-term right to reject faulty goods.

As clearly seen above, the English law provides a very clear thirty day period during which goods that are detected to be defective could be rejected. Essentially, providing a similar legislative short-time period of thirty days during which consumers who are supplied with faulty may exercise the right of rejecting the said goods in Ghana will equally be helpful for consumers in Ghana. In particular, a similar clear time period will resolve the present ambiguity regarding the precise

---

[27] Law Commission, *Consumer remedies for faulty goods* (Law Com No 317 & Scot Law Com No. 216, 2009) para. 3.51.

[28] Section 22(4) of the CRA 2015.

[29] Explanatory Notes to the Consumer Rights Act 2015, para. 128 - commentary on section 22(4) of the Act; See also, Department for Business, Innovation and Skills, 'Consumer Rights Act: Goods, Guidance for Business' (September 2015) <https://www.businesscompanion.info/sites/default/files/CRA-Goods-Guidance-for-Business-Sep-2015.pdf>. para 5 [43], accessed on the 15/07/2025.

[30] Twigg-Flesner et al. (2016), p. 508.

[31] Section 22, the UK CRA 2015.

[32] Section 20 (7), UK CRA 2015; see also, Explanatory Notes to the CRA 2015, para. 110; See also, Denis Barry and others (n 14) para. 3.92.

[33] Law Commission, *Consumer remedies for faulty goods* (Law Com No 317 & Scot Law Com No. 216, 2009) para. 3.53.

time period during which a consumer may be permitted to reject non-conforming goods in Ghana.

Introducing a similar thirty-day period for consumers to reject non-conforming goods will broadly help consumers assess the quality conformance of the goods they purchased. In sum, replicating thirty day time period as a short-term right to reject faulty goods in Ghana will provide a very useful opportunity during which a consumer may be able to identify likely defects in the goods so as to form a decision of rejection of the goods or otherwise This will consequently ensure that consumers are not being left with goods which are defective without remedy.

However, the crucial question that remains central falls on what might be the plight of the consumer where the seller attempts to remedy a defective product during which time the 30-day period elapses? The issue is, will the buyer still be able to reject the goods if the attempted remedy fails or will s/he lose the right to reject the goods? Addressing this question is vital to ensure that in devising a legislative measure to resolve the problem relating to the length of time to effectively reject faulty goods in Ghana is carried out devoid of new uncertainties.

Highly appealing to note is that the English law seems to have introduced measures to deal with the state of the buyer as regards the seller's effort at a repair or replacement of the goods which may lead to the lapse of the 30-day short-term period. In particular, the English law requires the 30-day short-term right to reject faulty goods to stop running where the consumer requests a repair or replacement of the goods.[34] It has been observed that the repair or replacement may either be at the request of the consumer or the seller with the consumer agreement during which the 30 day time period stops running.[35] However, following the trader supply of the goods in response to the request, the time limit for the consumer to exercise the short-time right to reject is either seven (7) days or the waiting period before the repair or replacement request was made if that is longer.[36] This seems to imply that if the goods are repaired or different sets of goods are supplied by the trader as a replacement but the goods still failed to conform to the required quality, the consumer will have 7 days or the remaining period before the initial rejection to exercise the short-term right to reject the goods. For instance, it has been related that suppose:

> [a] consumer bought a watch which has stopped working. They want the trader to repair it but don't want to forfeit their short-term right to reject, should the repair not work. They take it back to the trader on the 25th day after the purchase and the trader agrees to fix the watch. The 30 day period therefore stops running on the 25 days – this is the start of the 'waiting period'. After two weeks, the trader has had the watch repaired and returns it to the consumer. The waiting period ends on the day the consumer receives the goods back.

---

[34] section 22(6), the UK CRA 2015.

[35] Bridge (2017). para 14.097; See also, Department for Business, Innovation and Skills, 'Consumer Rights Act: Goods, Guidance for Business' (September 2015) <https://www.businesscompanion.info/sites/default/files/CRA-Goods-Guidance-for-Business-Sep-2015.pdf>. para 5 [42], accessed on the 15/07/2025.

[36] Section 22 (7), the UK CRA 2015.

> The consumer has a further 7 days to exercise their short-time right to reject, because this is longer than the remainder of the 30 day period. Two days after the watch is returned to the consumer it stops working again. The consumer can exercise the short-term right to reject provided they do so in the following 5 days (as this is what remains of the 7 days after the 'waiting period').[37]

The illustration clearly explains how the provision might be applied in dealing with a situation in which a seller undertakes to repair defects in the goods and the extent to which the consumer might still reject the goods if the defects persist afterwards. This clearly addresses the question as to what the plight of a consumer might be if a remedy for the defect is being sought during which time the 30-day period elapses especially if the short-term right to reject is similarly transposed into the regime in Ghana. The English law guideline provides a very good template through which the anticipated uncertainty could be dealt with in adopting a similar measure of defining a time frame for the consumer rights to reject faulty goods in Ghana.

Besides the benefit of resolving the uncertainty about the length of time for a consumer to reject faulty goods, introduction of the short-term time right to reject in Ghana will as well offer the consumer the opportunity to possibly inspect or examine the goods' quality conformity within the short-time period. This will therefore resolve the barrier of consumers' right to reject faulty goods when they are deemed to have intimated acceptance of the goods even when they have not examined the goods as was noted earlier in Chap. 4 to presently be the case in Ghana.

Nevertheless, while the time duration of thirty days may be suitable for the consumer to detect possible defects in some categories of goods, this may not be possible with many other goods. This is particularly possible in the case of 'credence' or 'experience' goods where it takes a little while before a buyer can detect deficiencies in the goods.[38] This makes the thirty day period not ideal to resolve problems consumers of such goods may encounter in Ghana. It is however, important to note that the English law has further provided a window of opportunity for consumers of goods in which the thirty-day period will not be appropriate. Under section 24 of the CRA 2015, consumers under the English law are entitled to what has been described as a final right to reject goods that are faulty as mentioned earlier. The consumer entitlement to this final right to reject non-conforming goods is, however, subject to other conditions. That is to say, before a consumer can avail himself/herself of the final right to reject, there should have arisen a failure of conformity of the goods after either a repair or replacement; or the consumer non-entitlement to either repair or replacement due to such being impossible or disproportionate; or the trader failed to carry out the consumer's request for a repair or replacement within a reasonable

[37] Department for Business, Innovation and Skills, 'Consumer Rights Act: Goods, Guidance for Business' (September 2015) <https://www.businesscompanion.info/sites/default/files/CRA-Goods-Guidance-for-Business-Sep-2015.pdf>, accessed on the 15/07/2025. para 5 [43].

[38] Examples of 'experience' goods include; television set, radio set, and home appliances like fridges, microwaves, and blenders among others. For further details, see Leahy and William Howard (2005); See also, Benz (2007) [1] –[5].

time and without significant inconvenience to the consumer.[39] It must be noted that the remedy of repair and replacement will further be considered shortly taking into consideration the arising issues in the Ghanaian context as earlier highlighted. On the issue of the final right to reject non-conforming goods, the occurrence of any of the three instances entitles the buyer the final right to reject the goods under the English law.

While exercising the right to reject faulty goods within the initial thirty-day period noted earlier will entitle the consumer to a full refund of all money already paid, a consumer exercising the final right to reject will only be entitled to a full refund if the right is exercised before the six months has lapsed. This is because within the six months duration, it is presumed that the defects existed in the goods at the time the goods were delivered. In particular, the Explanatory notes of the CRA 2015 especially provide that: 'if a breach of the statutory rights—for example a fault—arises in the first 6 months from delivery, it is presumed to have been present at the time of delivery unless the trader proves otherwise or this presumption is incompatible with the nature of the goods or the particular breach or fault.'[40]

Rejection of the goods after the sixth month on the other hand, will attract a corresponding deduction of the money already paid to reflect the consumer usage of the goods over the period the goods remained in his possession.[41] In the Act's guidance for businesses in dealing with consumer complaints of faulty goods, it has particularly been related about a consumer who bought a product and uses it for about 14 months before complaining of a defect which the trader's repair failed to completely resolve. Under such scenarios, it has been suggested that the consumer's rejection should attract a reduction of the money the consumer had already paid to take account of the wear and tear of the product during its use in accordance with the trader's professional judgement.[42] In a commentary on the provision, it has been argued that: 'the calculation of any amount to take account of the use the consumer has had of the goods should focus on the prevention of the consumer's unjustified enrichment, and so reflect the benefit enjoyed in respect of the goods.'[43]

As indicated above, the seller is entitled to use his professional judgement in determining the amount to be reduced. Following the seller's determination of the amount to be reduced, however, it is open to the consumer to either accept or contest the amount of reduction of use if dissatisfied.[44] This, however, excludes the goods remaining in the possession of the consumer due to the failure of the seller to take custody of the goods prior to the lapse of the sixth month after the consumer took delivery of the goods.[45] The non-deduction during the six months rejection window

---

[39] Section 24 (5), the UK CRA 2015.

[40] Explanatory Notes to the Consumer Rights Act 2015, Para. 97.

[41] Section 24 (6), the UK CRA 2015.

[42] Department for Business (n 28) para 7, [51] – Example 30.

[43] Bridge (2017) para. 14.100, footnote – 627.

[44] Department for Business (n 28) para 7, [51] – Example 30.

[45] Section 24 (9), the UK CRA 2015.

excludes motor vehicles of which usage deduction may be carry out at any time even within the six months of the goods delivery.[46] It has especially been submitted that: '[t]he refund can be reduced to take account of the use that the consumer has had of the goods where the consumer exercises the right to reject in the first 6 months, if the goods they are rejecting consist of a motor vehicle.'[47]

There is no doubt that replicating a similar measure as expressed under the English law above will offer important guidance to both consumers and traders in the market in Ghana. Essentially, such a legislative measure will be practically useful to protecting consumers of goods that fall within 'credence' or 'experience' goods brackets where the defects in the goods manifest after the span of the initial thirty days short-term right to reject. More importantly, its adoption in Ghana will further enable consumers the window of opportunity to be protected against being trapped with unsuccessfully repaired or replaced goods.

In summary, the short-term right to reject faulty goods known under the English will be practically useful in resolving the lack of clarity of the length of time during which a consumer may be able to reject faulty goods if replicated in Ghana. Moreover, where the defects are not the type that can be revealed during the 30-day period, the consumer may still be able to reject the goods through the final right to reject if similarly adopted in Ghana. The adoption of similar legislative measures will bring certainty into the regime in Ghana. This will practically be helpful to consumers in addressing the problem of faulty goods when supplied to them. This will possibly inspire the confidence of consumers especially if they act quickly with the knowledge that they can get a refund when sold defective goods. This will further ensure that they are able to buy from other traders who might offer them what they had wished to buy in the first instance.

5.3 Resolving the Limitations of the Consumer Remedies for Faulty Goods in Ghana

This part of the chapter seeks to address the limitations of the remedies for consumers in Ghana drawing guidance from the English law and its EU-motivated consumer remedies for faulty goods whilst taking the local situation in Ghana into account. In examining the remedies for consumers in Ghana under Chap. 4 of this book, it was revealed that where a consumer rejects faulty goods, the only alternative option he has is to terminate the contract. This was found to be unsatisfactory especially where the consumer requires the goods for his particular purpose which cannot be accomplished without the goods. This was further noted to be worrisome

[46] Section 24 (10), the UK CRA 2015.

[47] Department for Business, Innovation and Skills, 'Consumer Rights Act: Goods, Guidance for Business' (September 2015) <https://www.businesscompanion.info/sites/default/files/CRA-Goods-Guidance-for-Business-Sep-2015.pdf>, accessed on the 15/07/2025, para 7, [51]; See also, Twigg-Flesner (2017), p. 128 [136]; See also, Twigg-Flesner et al. (2016) p. 512.

particularly in the instant case where the consumer, though rejecting the goods, would wish to keep the contract alive if he could get a cure. The consumer, however, has no legal rights to any cure under the law in Ghana. This was therefore highlighted as unsatisfactory as noted above. The present part of this Chapter therefore seeks to address this limitation of the law in Ghana taking inspirations from the English law which itself has been inspired by the EU sales regime as pointed out above. This discussion will however be tailored to the domestic needs of consumers in Ghana. The discussion commences with first resolving the limitation of options a consumer could pursue when rejecting faulty goods below.

5.3.1 Terminating the Contract After the Rejection of Faulty Goods in Ghana: Lessons from English Law and Its EU Experience

In examining the rights of consumers in Ghana in Chap. 3, it was observed as noted above that the buyer's option following the right of rejection of faulty goods was to bring the sales agreement or contract to an end. While this was noted as an important means of possibly enabling the consumer to avail himself of acquiring the right quality of goods from other traders in the same category of goods, the consumer may nevertheless confront insurmountable difficulty where the seller is the only dealer in the kind of goods in question. The case of the consumer rejection of the goods and bringing the contract to an end without other suppliers of the goods in the market to which the consumer could obtain the right quality of goods, will likely mean that the consumer's particular requirements for the goods will be left unfulfilled. This was found to be further complicated as there is no alternative option under the regime for the consumer except to claim damages which itself may still not address the consumer's particular need for the goods for the intended purpose. The combined elements of rejection and termination of the contract without alternative remedies particularly in situations where the seller has monopoly over the goods in question may be detrimental to the overall interest of the consumer in meeting his requirement as was argued. It was therefore further submitted that a further legislative response was critical in order to ensure that consumers are provided with alternative measures they could resort to while rejecting faulty goods. This was particularly noted to be crucial so as to avoid the tendency of consumers being deprived of a remedy that allows them to have their need for the goods met through alternative remedies while rejecting the faulty goods.

In perusing the experience of the English law and its EU influence, the regime appears to employ other alternative remedies to which a consumer could access in addition to treating the contract as being at an end when rejecting goods which are faulty. These remedies mainly include the remedy of repair and replacement of the faulty goods as alternative options to terminating the contract upon rejection of the defective goods. Section 19(3) particularly provides for the entitlement of consumers to have non-conforming goods supplied to them repaired or replaced.[48] This is further reinforced by section 23 which maintained that the moment the buyer opts for the right of repair or replacement, the trader is under a duty to carry out the requested remedy within a reasonable time frame and without significant inconvenience to the consumer.[49] As stated by the Act's Explanatory Notes moreover, '[o]nce the consumer has opted for a repair or replacement of the goods, he or she may not ask for the other of these or exercise the short-term right to reject, without first allowing the trader a reasonable time to complete that chosen remedy. However, if waiting a reasonable time would cause the consumer significant inconvenience then the consumer can pursue an alternative remedy without doing so.'[50] It has further been observed that: '[a] replacement would usually need to be identical, that is of the same make and model and if the goods were bought new then the replacement would need to be new.'[51] The remedies of repair and replacement are broadly construed as providing consumers with the opportunity to choose 'from a more elaborate menu of remedies which places more emphasis on repair and replacement, and rather less on rejection and termination.'[52]

The adoption of the remedies of repair and replacement in Ghana as similarly provided under the English law could possibly resolve the problem where the consumer rejection and termination (presently being the only option available) may lead to the difficulty in obtaining similar goods from other suppliers especially where the trader has monopoly in the supply of the goods in question. The remedies of repair and replacement appear to be appropriate measures that could effectively assist consumers if replicated in Ghana for the resolution of disputes about substandard quality of goods when delivered to them in the course of a contract. In particular, the consumer getting the goods repaired or replaced will save him from the fear of not getting similar goods from other traders where the goods are monopolised by a single trader. Moreover, the repair or replacement of the goods will further save the consumer the trouble of looking elsewhere for similar goods to meet his requirements. It has equally been observed that replacement or cure of the defective goods may better serve the interests of both parties by giving the seller the opportunity to retender the goods and the buyer the chance of receiving the goods he had wished to acquire.[53]

However, the critical question is what circumstances should trigger repair and what should inform the demand for replacement of the goods? Addressing this important question is especially vital to prevent possible conflict when adopted in Ghana. For instance, in a situation where the consumer prefers a replacement of the

[48] The UK CRA 2015.

[49] Subsection 2, the UK CRA 2015.

[50] Explanatory Notes to the CRA 2015, para. 133.

[51] Explanatory Notes to the CRA 2015, para. 132.

[52] Goode and McKendrick (2016), para 14.68.

[53] Dowuona-Hammond (1995) [126].

defective goods and the trader insists on providing a repair of the defective goods and vice visa. This could possibly arise where the trader feels that his interest will greatly be affected in offering a replacement. On the other hand, the consumer may also feel that the repair may not properly restore the goods to a desirable state.[54]

Drawing further from the English law and its EU influence, it broadly seems that the English law has left the choice freely open to the consumer to determine as to whether to seek for repair or replacement. It has especially been argued that 'the decision as to whether to elect for repair or replacement is one for the consumer and not the seller.'[55] Nevertheless, the consumer entitlement to freely decide as to whether to request for a repair or replacement is subject to the caveat of its not being impossible or disproportionate 'to the other of those remedies' comparatively.[56] The determination of whether the remedy requested would be disproportionate is particularly expected to take into account: '(a) the value which the goods would have if they conformed to the contract, (b) the significance of the lack of conformity, and (c) whether the other remedy could be effected without significant inconvenience to the consumer.'[57] In the Act's Guidance for business operators on goods, it has been observed that although the consumer may opt for either a repair or a replacement, if the remedy the consumer chooses is disproportionately costly compared to the other or if it is impossible, the consumer will have to accept the other option.[58] It has been argued that the question for the court is to determine whether repair of the goods in question will be disproportionate when compared with replacement and vice versa but not comparing repair or replacement to price reduction or rejection.[59] The overall essence of the remedy of repair or replacement which a consumer is open to choose under the English law is directly aimed at ensuring that non-conforming goods are brought into conformity.[60]

---

[54] The case of *A. G. Sarpong v Silver Star Auto* (2014) GMJ appears to provide a closer illustration of this. In the instant case in particular, the trader wanted to repair the broken-down car installing a new engine, but the customer wanted a replacement of the car as per the manufacturing warranty.

[55] Baskind et al. (2016), p. 440; see also, Twigg-Flesner et al. (2016), p. 510; See also in the pre-2015 Act in, Howells and Weatherill (2005), p. 200; See also, Dobson and Stokes (2012), para 13-015.

[56] Section 23(3), the UK CRA 2015.

[57] Section 23 (4), the UK CRA 2015.

[58] Department for Business, Innovation and Skills, 'Consumer Rights Act: Goods, Guidance for Business' (September 2015) <https://www.businesscompanion.info/sites/default/files/CRA-Goods-Guidance-for-Business-Sep-2015.pdf>, accessed on the 15/07/2025, para 6 [44].

[59] Goode and McKendrick (2016), para 14.69.

[60] Repair has been defined under section 23 (8) to mean making goods that do not conform to a contract conform. While replacement has not been defined under the Act, Bradgate and Twigg-Flesner had argued in the pre-2015 Act that it relates to the '… direct replacement of the non-conforming goods with goods which do conform to the contract.' – Bradgate and Twigg-Flesner (2003), p. 88.

The implementation of this part of the regime can be seen in the recent Scottish case of *Peebles v Rembrand Builders Merchants Ltd.*[61] which was decided under the pre-2015 regime. In the instant case, the consumer had purchased roof tiles from the trader for their retirement home. The tiles, however, became patchy and discoloured after 5 years of usage. Recoating was subsequently carried out by the manufacturer but failed to resolve the problem due to poor work. The buyers thereafter refused a second recoating offer and demanded the replacement of the tiles. The court found that if the claimant had granted the second request and the work was properly carried out, it could have rectified the defects. The Court therefore held that the demand for the replacement was disproportionate and unreasonable on account of the cost involved at the expense of the cheaper alternative.

So, as clearly observed above, the point of the law is that the consumer's right to request repair or replacement is open to the consumer to decide. However, the choice the consumer settles on should not be to the extent of imposing unreasonable cost on the trader. The choice of either repair or replacement should be one that takes into consideration the nature of the goods, the cost of the remedy sought and the convenience of both parties in a balanced manner. This is mainly on account of the fact that the overall goal of the remedies of repair and replacement are to bring the non-conforming goods into conformity. This should therefore be done without causing significant inconvenience to both the consumer and the trader.

The consumer being open to choose either the remedy of repair or replacement of the non-conforming goods if replicated in Ghana will enable an affected consumer to select the remedy that best suits his/her needs without causing inconvenience in terms of unreasonable added cost to the trader. This will ideally be suitable to meeting the needs of consumers in Ghana particularly in having a say on what is redelivered to him as either a repaired or a replaced goods. As mentioned above, the underscored spirit of the remedy of repair or replacement under the English law is mainly to ensure that goods that do not conform to the contract are brought into conformity. This is apparently vital to meeting the expectation of consumers in Ghana if similarly provided in Ghana.

Moreover, introducing the remedies of repair and replacement into the Ghanaian law may further be appropriate to ensure that consumers are able especially to demand the remedy of repair or replacement when supplied with substandard quality goods. The market in Ghana was shown in Chap. 1 of this book to be inundated with the incidence of substandard goods. This was argued to increase the chances of consumers buying goods that may fail to function. A consumer buying substandard goods with defects will, therefore, need to have the defect rectified, which, unfortunately, is not provided by law in Ghana, as was noted in Chap. 4. Therefore, introducing a similar remedy in Ghana as expressed under the English law will practically

[61] [2017] G.W.D. 15-236; See also the ECJ in the joined cases C-65/09 and C- 87/09 *Gebr Weber GmbH v Wittmer Putz v Medianess Electronics GmbH* [2011] WLR (D) 210 where it was also observed that disproportionate should exclusively be viewed in relation to the other remedy as the Directive made reference to two remedies of repair or replacement where the goods supplied are not in conformity.

enable consumers in Ghana who purchased non-conforming goods to have the right to require the goods to be repaired or replaced. Essentially, the primary object of the consumer is to have his need for the goods met.[62] The replication of the repair and replacement legislative measure in Ghana, as similarly provided under the English law, will therefore reflect the consumer desire to have a defective good rectified. This is because the repair of the faulty goods or their replacement will ensure that the consumer requirements are satisfied.

One other important element of the English provision which is of significant value and worthy of consideration in Ghana is that the trader repair or replacement of the goods comes with no added cost to the buyer. As mentioned earlier, the English law implemented the EU Directive as regards the consumer right to have non-conforming goods repaired or replaced without any cost for the use of the goods before the defect detection. In a matter before the CJEU, a company had replaced defective goods to the consumer but demanded that the consumer pay for the use of the goods he had before the replacement. It was, however, held by the CJEU that a consumer must not be made to pay for the use of goods that turn out to be defective.[63] The decision of the CJEU is similarly expected in matters of similar questions being placed before the English Courts. This is especially the case, as the CJEU decisions at the moment are binding on the English courts, and it seems that this will continue after Brexit under the terms of the EU Withdrawal Act 2018 as was noted previously in this chapter, unless and until determined otherwise by Parliament.

The doctrine of no cost to the buyer in his request for repair or replacement of the goods similarly in Ghana will encourage consumers who have problems with their purchases to take advantage of getting their desire needs of the goods fulfilled. A similar requirement will especially inspire consumer confidence to demand for repair or replacement of non-conforming goods. Consumers will particularly draw inspiration from the doctrine of no cost to assert their rights to demand the repair or replacement of the goods when established to be faulty. This will be a positive instrument if adopted to ensure that consumers who encounter defective or substandard goods can get either the defect rectified or the substandard goods replaced.

---

[62] Ansa-Asare (1981).

[63] Case C-404/06 *Quelle AG v Bundesverba'nd der Verbraucherzentralen und Verbraucherverbände* [2008] ECR 1-2685; see also, the joined cases C-65/09 and C-87/09 *Gebr Weber GmbH v Wittmer Putz v Medianess Electronics GmbH* [2011] WLR (D) 210 where the seller was held to be liable to bear the cost of removal and installation of goods that were found defective and replaced. It is worth restating that the CJEU decisions at the moment are binding on the English courts, and it seems that this will continue after Brexit under Section 6(2) of the EU Withdrawal Act 2018, unless and until determined otherwise by Parliament.

5.3.2 Integrating the Proposed Remedies of Repair and Replacement Into the Existing Remedy of Rejection and Termination in Ghana

The immediately preceding section addressed the problem regarding the lack of alternative measures for consumers when rejecting faulty goods except to terminate the contract under the present law in Ghana. In drawing from the experience of the English law and its EU influence, it is argued there that the remedies of repair and replacement are fundamental alternatives that should be given legislative attention in Ghana as alternative remedies for consumers alongside the option of rejection and termination of the contract. The critical question that remains unresolved is the extent to which these proposed remedies of repair and replacement might properly be integrated into the existing remedy of rejection and termination as presently found under the law in Ghana as highlighted above. This present subsection therefore seeks to provide the path through which a successful integration might be achieved for the overall benefits of consumers in Ghana.

As indicated above, the preceding discussion was mainly focused on the remedies of repair and replacement as additional options, the introduction of which into the regime in Ghana could better afford consumers the opportunity to seek the repair or replacement of faulty goods, and to further allow the parties to keep alive their transactional agreements. The implementation of the remedies of repair and replacement in Ghana will seem to mean that the consumer rejection of faulty goods will entitle him not only to the remedy of repair or replacement of the goods but also to the option of terminating the contract which is already part of the regime in Ghana as earlier mentioned.

However, the important issue that warrants redress is the manner in which these remedies might operate for the benefit of consumers without creating confusion. In particular, providing guidance as regards how these proposed legislative measures might properly be integrated into the regime is significant to ensure that the remedies regime is very well simplified for the broader benefit of consumers in Ghana.

In Chap. 3 as briefly restated above, it was made clear that the consumer upon rejection of faulty goods is further entitled to terminate the contract under the law in Ghana. While the rights of the consumer to reject faulty goods and to terminate the contract appear to require to be exercised together, they are nevertheless at different stages—the consumer first rejects the goods and second terminates the contract as this is the only option available under the regime. With the above proposal for the adoption of the remedies of repair and replacement, a consumer seeking the remedy of repair or replacement if they are implemented by the legislature will possibly mean that he is as well rejecting the goods but not terminating the contract. There is therefore the need to clarify the manner in which the implementation of these proposed remedies could better integrate with the present regime of rejection and termination.

In considering the experience of the English law and its EU influence, the consumer's right to reject non-conforming goods embraces the short-term right to reject and the final right to reject as previously discussed in this Chapter. Under each of these rights to reject, the consumer is entitled to 'reject the goods and treat the contract as at an end'.[64] The consumer rejection of the goods and treating the contract as being at an end is to be effected by the consumer making this known to the trader.[65] Before the present regime under the 2015 Act, the English Court had long observed that 'a right to reject is, after all, only a particular form of the right to rescind the contract.'[66] Also, in the pre-2015 regime, it was held by the Scottish Court that where there is a material breach in a consumer contract, the buyer is entitled to reject the goods and treat the contract as repudiated.[67] The observations of the Courts in the pre-2015 regime is likely to be followed in a similar manner under the present regime especially regarding the effect of the right to reject and to treat the contract as at an end. Following the consumer rejection of the goods, the trader has a corresponding duty to refund the money already paid by the consumer or anything in lieu of the money that was transferred.[68]

Broadly speaking, the English law position on the remedy of rejection and termination as observed above seems not different from the buyer's right to reject and terminate the contract under the law in Ghana as briefly mentioned earlier drawing from the previous discussion in Chap. 4 of this book. The remedy of rejection and termination under the English law nevertheless appears to operate alongside the remedies of repair and replacement as discussed earlier. This seems to mean that the English law does not deem it necessary to explicitly clarify that the consumer rejection of faulty goods should openly be a condition preceding termination, repair, and replacement as rights to which the consumer could choose from.

However, in implementing the rights of consumers to seek the remedies of repair and replacement of defective goods in Ghana as recommended earlier, it may be more helpful to clarify that the buyer's right to reject faulty goods further entitles him to three optional remedies including, the right to have the defects repaired, the right to have the goods replaced and the right to terminate the contract. This will possibly ensure that the remedy of repair and replacement integrates appropriately with the existing remedy of rejection and termination. This is especially critical in

---

[64] The right to reject and treat the contract as at an end is, however, subject to severable contracts rules provided under section 20(20) and (21). In sum, section 20(2) stipulates that the right to reject and treat the contract as at an end do not apply to the final right to reject where the contract is severable in relation to goods contract to which the defects arise from instalment delivery as per section 26 (3) (in which the consumer is entitled to exercise the short-time right to reject in respect of the whole contract or to reject the goods in an instalment). Also, as per section 20(21), in a severable obligation, the consumer is entitled to reject the goods and treat that obligation as at an end or to exercise any of the stipulated rights in respect of the whole contract depending on the terms of the contract and the circumstances of the case.

[65] Section 20 (5), the UK CRA 2015.

[66] Devlin J. in *Kwei Tek Chao v British Traders and Shippers Ltd* [1954] 2 Q.B. 459 [480].

[67] *Lamarra v Capital Bank Plc* [2007] S.C. 95; 2006 S.L.T. 1053; 2007 S.C.L.R. 719; 2006 G.W.D. 33-686; para. 70 & 82.

[68] Section 20 (7) and (11)-(12), UK CRA 2015. Subsection 15 further requires that the refund be carried out within the time span of 14 days from when the trader agreed to the refund.

that if a consumer is seeking for a repair or replacement of the goods as a right, if the proposal in this book is adopted into the legal framework in Ghana, it will imply that the consumer is rejecting the goods until the defect in them is rectified by either the repair or replacement as earlier noted. The clarification will especially be important to avoid the possibility of confusion as to whether a consumer who is supplied with defective goods will be entitled to seek rejection and termination or repair or replacement of the goods if the proposal earlier for the introduction of the remedies of repair and replacement is given effect.[69]

In short, the separate ambits of first rejection and then termination, repair and replacement as options, will be particularly important to bring certainty into the regime in terms of a consumer being able to reject defective goods while being open to other alternative remedies including the option of repair, replacement, or termination of the contract depending on the consumer preference and availability of the preferred option. In light of this, a consumer who wishes to resort to the remedy of repair, or replacement (if they are adopted), or termination, will have the statutory clearance to do so. This will clear the regime of any ambiguities for the benefit of consumers in Ghana. Essentially, it seems to be an ideal practice for consumers who are supplied with defective goods to more often than not, contact the seller for a redress, and it is only when there is a fallout that the idea of termination of the contract becomes an option. The clarity will therefore be more relevant to consumers as it will directly reflect the expectations of consumers in Ghana.

It is, however, important to note that similar recommendations had been made by the English Law Commissions mainly to achieve an effective integration of the UK law and the EU remedial schemes. In particular, the English Law Commission had proposed that the right to reject non-conforming goods should be provided as a standalone right of the consumer. This was further to entitle the consumer to three immediate options of termination, repair, or replacement of which the consumer could exercise any.[70] This was nevertheless rejected at the implementation stage. The failure to see the proposed layout of the right to reject faulty goods with three optional remedies at first instance implemented has nevertheless been criticised to be regrettable.[71] It has further been argued that such implementation would not only have resulted in a proper integration of the English law with the EU law, but also, would have simplified the law for the benefit of consumers in the UK.[72]

Although the proposal for the right to reject at first instance to be followed up with the options of repair, replacement or termination was not successful at the implementation level as noted above, the regime nevertheless seems to have the remedy of rejection running through rejection and termination (short-term right to reject), repair and replacement. This therefore appears to further leave the option to

[69] For details of the proposal for the adoption of the remedies of repair and replacement, see para. 6.3.1 earlier in this Chapter.

[70] Law Commission, *Consumer remedies for faulty goods* (Law Com No 317 & Scot Law Com No. 216, 2009) para.3.111 to 115.

[71] Twigg-Flesner et al. (2016), p. 508.

[72] Twigg-Flesner et al. (2016), p. 508.

the consumer to decide whether to terminate the contract or to make (or accept) a request for the remedy of repair or replacement. It had particularly been argued in the pre-2015 Act that while the right to reject similarly gives the right to the consumer to treat the contract as terminated, the consumer is nevertheless open to reject the goods while accepting a cure to keep the contract alive.[73] The cure the consumer in rejecting the goods may resort to instead of termination is to request for the remedy of repair or replacement as previously discussed.

As clearly pointed out above in the case of implementing the remedies of repair and replacement into the regime in Ghana, rejection and termination to separately operate in Ghana without being exercised together, it will be of great benefit to both consumers and traders in terms of clarity of the regime in Ghana. Essentially, consumers will easily understand that while rejecting the goods for their non-conformity, they are not restricted to the limits of only termination of the contract but entitled to other more preferred options if provided as mentioned earlier. On the part of the trader, it may be more satisfying to offer other alternative remedies than to have the consumer returned the goods and demand repayment as currently pertains. It is therefore worth noting that separating the right to reject and the right to terminate the contract under the law in Ghana will be practically useful to the cause of consumers. This will enable consumers with problems of substandard or defective goods purchases to seek appropriate cures from sellers where more appropriate and desirable.

5.3.3 Next Steps Where the Remedies of Repair, Replacement and the Right to Reject do Not Work

Drawing from the experience of the English law and its EU influence, the previous sections specifically advanced a number of possible solutions to the deficiencies of the consumer remedies for faulty goods in Ghana that were identified in Chap. 3 earlier. In particular, the analysis so far argued that there is the need to clarify that goods with minor defects can be rejected except where the defects are *de minimis* in character. The analysis also stressed the need to introduce a clear short-term period of thirty days during which a consumer should be able reject goods which are faulty in response to the uncertainty of when to exercise the right to reject. More importantly, the point has been made for introduction of the remedies of repair and replacement and a clear mention that these remedies together with termination of the contract should function as the alternative options for consumers to resort to while rejecting faulty goods. The needs for a longer time right to reject faulty goods

[73] Howells and Weatherill (2005), p. 191. This observation was made in the pre-2015 regime.

outside the initial short-term right of 30 days have also been advanced in respect of where repair or replacement fails to resolve the defects.

While the above proposed reforms are broadly critical to provide consumers in Ghana with a more enhanced scheme of remedies as regards faulty goods, the unresolved question that continues to linger is where rejection is not appealing to the consumer and repair or replacement (if the proposals in this book are adopted as discussed) fails to remedy the defect. In particular, where it emerged that the defects cannot be rectified, and there are no identical goods for the seller to replace the defective goods and the buyer's rejection of the goods will not also serve his interest. The proposed reforms noted above have not dealt with this. Addressing what might be the plight of the consumer is important so as to ensure that he is guaranteed with being offered a more comparable remedy under every given circumstance.

In examining the experience of the English law and its EU influence further, it has in place a remedial scheme where the consumer may request for the reduction of the price of the goods. This remedy originates from the EU Sale Directive which was first implemented into the SGA 1979 through Regulation 2002 but has now been transposed into the CRA 2015.[74] Section 24 contains the remedy of price reduction and likewise, the final right to reject as discussed earlier in this Chapter. The provision particularly states that: '[t]he right to a price reduction is the right— (a) to require the trader to reduce by an appropriate amount the price the consumer is required to pay under the contract, or anything else the consumer is required to transfer under the contract, and (b) to receive a refund from the trader for anything already paid or otherwise transferred by the consumer above the reduced amount.'[75] As indicated above, the right to price reduction is contained in the same provision with the final right to reject non-conforming goods under the English law which has already been examined earlier. A consumer is, however, permitted to exercise one but not both together.[76] This has been reaffirmed in the Blackstone's Guide to the Act where it has been observed that 'the consumer must choose whether to exercise his right to a price reduction or the final right to reject, but not both.'[77] As similarly indicated earlier under the final right to reject, the consumer right to request for a price reduction can only be triggered subject to either a failed success of a repair or replacement to correct the defect at first instance, or its being impossible or disproportionate to require repair or replacement from the seller, or the trader's failure to carry out a requested repair or replacement within a reasonable time and without significant inconvenience to the consumer.

A similar provision in Ghana could be very useful to ensure that consumers are able to avail themselves of the remedy of price reduction of the goods instead of rejection especially where repair or replacement are unavailable or failed to resolve

[74] Section 48E (3) of the SGA 1979 which provided for the consumer right to price reduction has since been brought under section 24 of the CRA 2015.

[75] The UK CRA 2015.

[76] Section 24(5), the UK CRA 2015.

[77] Barry et al. (2016), para. 3.126.

the problem. The replication of a similar remedy in Ghana will possibly ensure that consumers who are unable to find successful repair or replacement of a defective good may still manage with the goods, but at a reduced price commensurate with the value of the goods he has received. In effect, the remedy of price reduction may resolve to some extent the issue of the consumer not being able to obtain a satisfactory redress in relying on the earlier proposed remedial reforms.

It might be argued that damages to which consumers in Ghana are presently entitled may procure the same objective. However, whereas the primary function of damages is relative to consequences flowing from a contractual breach, price reduction seeks a fundamentally different rational. The rationale of the price reduction remedy had been argued to mainly constitute the price that needs to be reduced to reflect the value of the goods the consumer actually received.[78] This essentially takes into account the extent of the defect detected.

The introduction of price reduction as a consumer remedy in Ghana as similarly contained under the English law will therefore ensure that a consumer who is supplied faulty goods that cannot be replaced, or for which repair cannot completely address is able to seek a price reduction to take account of the actual value of the goods as noted above. This is extremely important taking into account the proven existence of substandard and defective goods in the market in Ghana as previously highlighted in Chap. 1 of this book. The stated records of instances of substandard and defective goods in the market increase the tendency of consumers to buy goods that are faulty or defective and for which repair or replacement, if adopted or offered on a goodwill basis, may not resolve the problem. Moreover, the impossibility of the goods' replacement may also be possible in the case of second-hand goods, for example. Given that many of the goods consumed in the country are imports, the impossibility of a defective replacement may also arise when the particular brand of goods runs out of stock, and it is not clear when the trader may be able to import similar kinds of goods for which replacement could be offered. In all these instances, the availability of price reduction to which a consumer could resort to is essential. In such circumstances, the consumer will not be left with goods that failed to reflect the value for which he has paid for, but he will have the price reduced commensurate with the degree of quality of the goods through the benefit of price reduction legislation in Ghana if adopted.

One important issue of concern that needs to be given the required attention in considering replicating a similar legislative measure in Ghana is the extent to which the reduction may be made. This is particularly vital so as to ensure that the reduction is made fairly without prejudice to the parties. Taking guidance from the English law commentary, the circumstance of each case seems to be the yardstick for the price reduction determination. For example, the Explanatory Notes of the CRA 2015 require that: 'If the consumer opts to keep the goods and require a reduction in price the question of what is an appropriate amount will depend on the circumstances and the remaining functionality of the goods. It is intended that the

[78] Howells and Weatherill (2005), p. 201.

reduction in price should reflect the difference in value between what the consumer paid and the value of what they actually receive, and could be as much as a full refund or the full amount already paid.'[79] In addressing the extent to which businesses may apply the provision on the price reduction, the Act's guidance for businesses similarly observed that the reduction they 'offer must be an appropriate amount. This should usually reflect the difference between the value of the goods as they were sold (with the issue) and their value if there had been no fault (i.e. the amount that the consumer paid originally).'[80] The above commentary clearly provides a very clear and balanced guidance which might be useful in replicating a similar measure in Ghana.

Another important element that needs addressing in introducing the remedy of price reduction for the benefit of consumers when they buy faulty goods in Ghana relates to where the defects with the goods do not completely affect the usage of the goods for the consumer purpose. However, where the goods are not fit for their purpose, price reduction may similarly not be a worthy remedy as well. This seems to be the expectation under the English law. It was especially observed in a commentary in the pre-2015 Act on the equivalent SGA provision that: 'the remedy of price reduction will not be "appropriate" … if the goods are unable to perform the main function or purpose for which the buyer acquired them. In the case of defective quality, a price reduction is likely to be appropriate when the defect in the quality of the goods relates to an aspect of the goods which does not impede their use as intended by the buyer.'[81]

A price reduction will likely provide the consumer with a preferable remedy where the goods are able to help him accomplish his primary basis of acquiring them. In the case of more serious defects, which directly affect the use of the goods, it had been further argued under the English pre-2015 regime that the buyer may be well-off seeking a replacement or termination (rescission) of the contract.[82] The difficulty however is where the consumer rejection and termination of the agreement involve goods for which the trader is the sole dealer in that kind of goods as previously observed. A similar difficulty may as well arise where the replacement, which is basically about identical goods as previously observed, is not possible. The important question then is, what should be the plight of the consumer under such circumstances.

The English law as examined above provides for the remedies of rejection (short-term and final right to reject), or replacement or repair with the alternative being price reduction. Other remedies the consumer could avail himself of are the common law remedies of specific performance, damages, specific implement, relying

[79] Explanatory Notes to the CRA 2015, para. 139; *Kynaston-Mainwaring v GVE London Ltd*, 2022 WL 10712475 (2022).

[80] Department for Business, Innovation and Skills (2015) Consumer Rights Act: Goods, Guidance for Business, <https://www.businesscompanion.info/sites/default/files/CRA-Goods-Guidance-for-Business-Sep-2015.pdf>. accessed on the 15/07/2025, para 7 [54].

[81] Bridge (2017), para 12.093; See also, Barry et al. (2016), para. 3.131.

[82] Bridge (2017), para 12.093.

on the breach against a claim by the trader for the price and treating the contract as being at an end on the basis of the traders' breach of an express term as previously highlighted in Chap. 2 of this book.[83] The common law remedies are similarly available for consumers in Ghana. As noted above, however, these options may sometimes fall short of affording the consumer with the required remedy especially where the seller is the sole supplier of the particular goods in question as mentioned earlier. The crucial question is what might be more acceptable to the consumer where repair or replacement or price reduction or rejection will not address his concern satisfactorily?

It may be argued that the consumer having the option of requesting comparable goods as a replacement, if available, may be more beneficial to the consumer. For example, a consumer who was supplied with a Dell computer that is faulty may be better off if an HP Computer is delivered to him as a close substitute especially if identical brand replacement is not possible and the other remedial options discussed above are not satisfactory enough. This could especially avoid the tendency of the consumer being left with the option of exercising the final right of rejection with the likely consequential effect of not getting the goods for his intended need particularly where there is only one sole trader in the said goods as noted earlier. Introducing such an alternative remedy in Ghana may particularly ensure that consumers are not left without a satisfactory remedy where identical goods have run-out of stock and the other remedies may not satisfy the intended object of the consumer. This will particularly check instances where it might take months for the traders to have a new consignment of similar goods imported into the country.

The options of price reduction or replacement with comparable goods if adopted in the regime in Ghana will likely offer consumers with an enhanced remedies regime. Broadly, the remedy of price reduction and the remedy of replacement with non-identical goods particularly where replacement with identical goods is not possible within a convenient time frame may appropriately complement the remedies of repair, replacement with identical goods, and rejection if given legislative effect in Ghana. This will generally ensure that consumers have a wide range of remedies they could rely on in dealing with faulty goods in Ghana. This will be helpful for consumers particularly taking into account the alleged prevalence of substandard goods in the markets in Ghana as was noted in Chap. 1 of this book.

5.4 Conclusion

This Chapter was mainly to address the uncertainties and limitations of consumer remedies for faulty goods in Ghana that were identified earlier in Chap. 4 of this book. The Chapter especially addressed the deficiencies of the consumer's remedies in Ghana drawing from the experience of the English law and its European Union

[83] Section 19 (11), the UK CRA 2015.

influence. As can be seen, whilst the English law and its EU experience provides important guidelines that are practically useful to addressing the uncertainties and limitations of the consumer remedies for faulty goods in Ghana, some aspects nevertheless need to be modified to reflect the circumstances in the domestic setting in Ghana. In particular, it is clear from the analysis that the English law clarification that the right to reject faulty goods includes minor defects except defects which are so trivial to the extent of being rendered *de minimis* will similarly be very helpful to resolving the question of what constitute trivial or minor defects for which consumers may be deprived of the remedy of rejection in Ghana. Nevertheless, whilst the English law requires that the consumer may only assert his right to reject where the defect, which is not *de minimis,* is a relevant factor, this may only be appropriate for second hand goods in Ghana but needs to be modified in the case of new goods to the effect of allowing the right to reject in defects which are not *de minimis*.

The analysis also revealed that the thirty day short-term period during which consumers may reject faulty goods provided under the English law will be helpful in resolving the uncertainty regarding the length of time during which consumers may be successful in rejecting faulty goods in Ghana if similarly adopted. The short-time period if adopted will further ensure that the consumer is given an ample time to examine the goods thereby addressing the concern of the lack of regard for the consumer examination of the goods in the determination of the buyer intimation of acceptance in Ghana.

Through the influence of the European Union Consumer Sales Directive moreover, the English law provides for the remedy of repair or replacement which consumers could request or accept from a trader where the goods that are delivered to them are faulty. The adoption of similar legislative measures entitling consumers in Ghana to the remedy of repair or replacement could as well address the issue of the consumer being limited to the option of only terminating the contract after rejection. However, the regime in Ghana needs to be modified to the effect that upon rejection of faulty goods, the consumer will immediately have three options of repair, replacement or termination to choose from. Though, the outcome might be the same, this will nevertheless, depart from the arrangement of the English law where the buyer is to either reject and treat the contract as being at an end, or request for repair or replacement of the goods with the various instances having the elements of rejection as was demonstrated in the discussion. Clarifying that following rejection of the faulty goods, the consumer may opt for termination or repair or replacement will help ensure that an effective integration is achieved between the remedies of repair and replacement with the existing consumer remedy of rejection and termination in Ghana as was shown in the analysis.

Moreover, the English law and its EU motivated remedy of price reduction, which allows a consumer with faulty goods where repair fails, or replacement is not possible to seek for the reduction of the price of the goods to commensurate with the actual value of the goods. This will equally resolve the concern of what might be the plight of the consumer if repair does not address the defect and it is also not possible to replace the goods if they are introduced into the regime in Ghana. It has also been argued that where the goods' replacement is impossible coupled with the other proposed remedies being not satisfactory, it might be useful if the consumer is able to seek for the replacement of the goods with closed substitute goods.

In sum, while some of the remedies contained under the English law and its EU influence will be directly valuable to responding to the uncertainties and limitations of the consumer remedies for faulty goods in Ghana, a number of aspects will need to be modified to reflect the circumstances in the domestic setting in Ghana as highlighted in the discussion. This, in effect, will make the law more practically beneficial to consumers in Ghana.

The next chapter will examine the means of enforcement of the remedies in Ghana with highlight of issues of concern for further discussion in Chap. 7 later.

References

Ansa-Asare K (1981) Case for a comprehensive framework of consumer protection in Ghana. Rev Ghana Law 14(13):73–89

Barry D, Jenkins E, Lloyd D, Douglas-Jones B, Sumnall C (2016) Blackstone's guide to the consumer rights act 2015. Oxford University Press

Baskind E, Osborne G, Rach L (2016) Commercial law, 2nd edn. Oxford University Press

Benz MA (2007) 'Experience and credence goods: an introduction', Strategies in markets for experience and credence goods. Springer, [1]–[5]

Bradgate R, Twigg-Flesner C (2003) Blackstone's guide to consumer guarantees: a guide to the new provisions of consumer sales law. Oxford University Press

Bridge MG (2017) Benjamin's sale of goods, 10th edn. Sweet & Maxwell

Department for Business, Innovation and Skills (2015) Consumer Rights Act: Goods, Guidance for Business. https://www.businesscompanion.info/sites/default/files/CRA-Goods-Guidance-for-Business-Sep-2015.pdf. Accessed 15 July 2025

Dobson P, Stokes R (2012) Commercial law. Sweet & Maxwell

Dowuona-Hammond C (1995) Protecting the purchaser of goods under Ghanaian law. Rev Ghana Law 19:105

Explanatory Notes to the Consumer Rights Act 2015

Goode R, McKendrick E (2016) Goode on commercial law, 5th edn. Penguin Books

Howells G, Weatherill S (2005) Consumer protection law, 2nd edn. Ashgate

Leahy AS, William Howard W (2005) Search and experience goods: evidence from the 1960's and 70's. Journal of Applied Business Research 21(1):45

The Commission, Consumer Remedies for Faulty Goods (The Law Com No 317 & Scot Law No 216, 2009)

The Law Commission, Sale and Supply of Goods (The Law Co, The Law Com No 160 and Scot Law Com No 104, 1987).

Twigg-Flesner C (2017) Consumer sales law in the United Kingdom. In: Howells G et al. (eds) Comparative consumer sales law. Routledge, p 128

Twigg-Flesner C et al (2016) Atiyah and Adams' sale of goods, 13th edn. Pearson

Chapter 6
Mechanisms for the Enforcement of Consumer Remedies for Faulty Goods in Ghana

6.1 Introduction

The present Chapter examines the adequacy of the available mechanisms for the enforcement of consumer law in Ghana. This is critical to ensure that potential bottlenecks that may impede the application of the law for the benefit of consumers are addressed to enable consumers to derive the maximum protection devised for them under the regime. This is broadly in response to research question three regarding whether the prevailing mechanisms for the enforcement of consumer remedies for defective goods are adequate to meet the needs of consumers in Ghana. Addressing this important question is crucial to ensure that potential concerns are addressed for the overall benefit of consumers in Ghana, as indicated above.

Broadly, the available channel for consumers to resort to in resolving disputes about faulty goods remains the courts or the use of Alternative Dispute Resolution (ADR) mechanisms. Before reviewing the forms for the redress of consumer disputes, however, it is worth noting that a consumer's first port of call when supplied with faulty goods is usually to approach the seller who sold the goods to him for informal redress. This might result in the consumer being offered a repair or replacement of the goods on a goodwill basis. It has been observed that a seller may only offer such a remedy where the consumer is a known customer of the seller and is very likely to return for subsequent purchases, but new customers are likely not to get the seller to repair or replace the goods on such goodwill grounds.[1] In effect, a consumer who is denied the repair or replacement of the goods within the remit of a goodwill basis may be left stranded with the option to either take them or leave them. So, where the consumer failed to get the defective goods rectified, he may be left with the option of resorting to the Court or the ADR route for redress if possible.

[1] Nkansah et al. (2016), p. 295.

N. Yidana, *Consumer Law and Policy on Faulty Goods*, Ius Gentium: Comparative Perspectives on Law and Justice 134,
https://doi.org/10.1007/978-3-032-08700-3_6

Before examining the courts system and the ADR redress procedure, the public means of enforcement of consumer legislation will need to be considered.

The chapter is divided into five main sections. The first section is this introductory outline. The second part examines the case of consumer claims before the courts in Ghana primarily to find out the degree to which the system takes into account the tailored issues of consumer claims being mostly small claims. In light of this, the discussion in this section will concentrate on the procedure for a consumer to invoke the jurisdiction of the courts with particular focus on the District court where most small consumer claims may occur. The third part reviews the Alternative Dispute Resolution (ADR) mechanisms in Ghana with the primary object being to ascertain the extent to which the ADR system supports the resolution of consumer disputes in Ghana. This part also discusses customary arbitration to discover the extent to which customary arbitration assist in helping consumers find redress when supplied with faulty goods. The fourth part examines the extent to which education and information for consumers have been integrated into the regime as a source of empowerment of consumers to seek redress when supplied with non-conforming goods. The fifth part provides a conclusion to this Chapter. This section mainly highlights the various issues that need to be addressed in order to ensure that consumers are afforded an effective redress mechanism. Below is a review of the enforcement measures of public institutions with particular focus as to whether the measures could lead to remedies for consumers.

6.2 Making a Consumer Claim in a Court of Law in Ghana

As observed above, a consumer who has an issue with faulty goods often contacts the seller first for redress, and where attempt at redress fails, he may resort to the Court of law for a possible resolution. In particular, a consumer may pursue a claim before the District Court or the Circuit Court or the High Court depending on the value of the claim as will be seen shortly. However, a party who is unsatisfied with a trial court decision has a right of appeal with or without leave, depending on the court of instance to the High Court, Court of Appeal and to the Supreme Court as the final appellate court in Ghana.[2]

It is important to state that there is no procedure specifically and exclusively designed for making and hearing a claim of a consumer in a court of law in Ghana. There is, however, a clearly defined civil procedure that every civil case is expected to follow. Essentially, the applicable rules of civil procedure for instituting and

[2] The Court of Appeal has an appellate authority to hear and determine matters from the High Court and the Circuit Court per section 11 of the Courts Act 1993, Act 459. However, a subsequent appeal thereafter would be entertained by the Supreme Court which will pronounce a final and binding verdict as provided under section 4 of the Courts Act 1993, Act 459. The provisions of the Courts Act gave effect to Article 131 of the Constitution of the fourth Republic of Ghana 1992 which provide the Supreme Court as the final appellate court of the land.

maintaining a claim before a court of law are governed by the District Court Rules[3] and the High Court (Civil Procedure) Rules[4] respectively for matters before the District Court and the Circuit Court/High Court. It is also important to point out that the High Court civil procedure rules apply in similar manner to matters that are placed before either the Circuit Courts or the High Court but with the possibility for modifications in the Circuit Court *mutatis mutandis*.[5] Equally important to state is that, whilst the High Court (Civil Procedure) Rules follow a more heavily formalised procedure, the District Court Rules may operate flexibly in certain instances as will be seen shortly in the discussion. As most consumer claims are usually small claims and may often fall for determination before the District Court, the present discussion will focus on the civil procedure applied in making a claim before the District Court. It is critical to state that the discussion is not meant to provide an exhaustive account of the procedure but only to highlight critical concerns regarding initiating and maintaining a consumer claim before the District Court. The purpose is mainly to contribute to addressing underlying concerns to better respond to the plight of consumers in seeking redress in Ghana.

Before the analysis, however, it is important to underline that the District Court is bound by the decisions of the superior courts in determining matters that are placed before the court as a question of law. As such, authorities of the Superior Courts on matters that relate to the application of the District Court Rules and on general points of law in respect of the procedures will be drawn upon to better appreciate the extent to which the rules may be applied. Set out below is the procedure of bringing a claim before the District Court and the arising concerns in respect of small claims.

6.2.1 *Making Consumer Claims Before the District Courts in Ghana*

The present subsection seeks to appraise the process of making a consumer claim in the courts in Ghana. The analysis will be directed at identifying issues that need addressing to better enhance the mechanisms for the effective enforcement of consumer remedies in Ghana. Essentially, the procedure for making a claim before a District Court commences with 'a writ of summons issued by the Registrar on oral or written application and filled out and signed or marked by the plaintiff.'[6] The writ of summons briefly states the exact cause of the plaintiff's action, the relief sought and supported with a general form.[7] Aside from the writ of summons, the plaintiff is

---

[3] District Court Rules 2009, C. I. 59.

[4] C. I. 47, (2004).

[5] Order 1, Rule 1, the High Court (Civil Procedure) Rules 2004, C. I. 47.

[6] Order 2, Rule 3 (5), District Court Rules 2009, C.I. 59.

[7] Order 2, Rule 3(7) and Order 3, Rule 1(1), District Court Rules 2009, C. I. 59.

required to further accompany the writ of summons with a written affidavit of the particulars and supporting documents, if any, to provide a reasonable amount of information to the defendant regarding the claim.[8] The particulars of the plaintiff's claims are required to be delivered to the Registrar before the writ of summons is issued and to be attached to the writ of summons and summons for service to the defendant.[9] In the case of an illiterate plaintiff, he may narrate his story to have the particulars of his claims reduced into writing by a literate person.[10] It had been stated that the statement of the particulars is necessary to prevent surprises and to acquaint the other party with the burden he has to discharge.[11]

Whilst the writ of summons and statement of particulars of the claim may appear simpler to a lawyer, these may seem arcane or esoteric to the ordinary consumer who has no prior idea about the court processes. The particularization of the claims of the plaintiff is especially fundamental to the court's determination of the matter. Without the particulars, the plaintiff could be deprived of the remedies he may be entitled to. It was stated in *Akati v Nartey*[12] that the District Court 'has no power to make any award, be it equitable or legal if a claim for (the award) has not been stated in the particulars of the claim.'[13] Similarly, it had also been stated that failure to set out particulars of a claim could be fatal to the success of the claim.[14] In effect, a consumer seeking to make a claim before the District Court needs to ensure that the particulars are clearly expressed to avoid having an unsuccessful claim. This clearly may not be easy for the majority of consumers without the assistance of lawyers in Ghana.

Upon issuing the writ of summons, a hearing notice is served on the defendant or his agent at the instance of the Registrar.[15] On receiving the writ of summons and affidavit, the defendant may file an affidavit stating clearly whether he is contesting a part or the entire claim accompanied with his supporting documents not less than five days before the date set for the hearing.[16] Following the defendant's affidavit, however, the Court has the authority to determine whether the defendant has shown a good defence to the claim to warrant the court's admission or rejection of the defence. In effect, where the defence 'does not amount in law to a defence of the plaintiff's claim,' the court may discontinue further proceedings and deliver judgement for the plaintiff.[17] Similarly, where the defendant fails to file an affidavit in defence of the plaintiff's claim, the court may as well treat the plaintiff's 'suit as an

[8] Order 3, Rule 1(1), District Court Rules 2009, C.I. 59.

[9] Order 3, Rule 1 (3 & 7), District Court Rules 2009, C.I. 59.

[10] Order 3, Rule 1 (4), District Court Rules 2009, C. I. 59.

[11] *Mensah v Appiah and Another* [1964] GLR 248 [250].

[12] [1980] GLR 218.

[13] *Akati v Nartey* [1980] GLR 218, p233 (emphasis added).

[14] *Mensah v Appiah and another* [1964] GLR 248.

[15] Order 2, Rule 3(13), District Court Rules 2009, C. I. 59.

[16] Order 8, Rule 3, District Court Rules 2009, C.I. 59.

[17] Order 8, Rule 4, District Court Rules 2009, C.I. 59.

undefended suit' and proceed thereon to give its judgement without requiring the plaintiff to summon witnesses to prove his case.[18]

It is important to note that in both the cases of an undefended suit and a defence which misses the standard of a defence, the claimant will still require to apply to the court for a summary determination to be made in his favour but with proof that there are no further questions to answer. Moreover, the court is generally to determine matters that are put before it in a summary manner.[19] This is to give effect to the requirement of the District Court rules 'to be interpreted and applied in a manner that helps to (a) achieve speedy and effective justice, (b) avoid delays and unnecessary expense….'[20]

Clearly from the above, the claimant may obtain final judgment where the suit is undefended or where the trader's defence does not amount to a defence in law in the opinion of the Court. The possibility for a summary determination to be made promptly seems helpful especially in consumer matters. This will be viable in ensuring that the consumer is offered the required redress in a timely fashion. But, as indicated above, the consumer navigating through the initial hurdle of filing the case with the appropriate particulars before the court, may not be easy for the majority of consumers in Ghana.

Moreover, a further critical concern may also arise where the court admits the defendant's defence and the matter is adjudged by the court to warrant trial. In particular, it has been stated that 'summary procedure is only appropriate to cases which are plain and obvious'.[21] So, where there are unresolved questions in the parties' submissions, the case will ordinarily proceed to trial. Essentially, the plaintiff will be required to open his case when the case is called for trial.[22] He may have to support his oral submissions with evidence and may also call on his witnesses to testify. The plaintiff and his witness, if any, precede their testimony by taking an oath or making an affirmation to speak the truth and may be cross-examined by the defendant or the lawyer for the defendant. The plaintiff may, if s/he had been cross-examined, be re-examined by his/her counsel before his/her case is closed.[23] It is during the testimonies that the plaintiff has to prove what s/he claims against the defendant.[24] However, the evidence led at trial should not be completely at variance with the pleadings, otherwise, 'it cannot be held that the party has proved the case set out in his pleadings.'[25] It is important to note that in the case of an illiterate and unrepresented party, the court may only rely on positive admissions of facts on the

[18] Order 8, Rule 7, District Court Rules 2009, C.I. 59.

[19] Order 18, Rule 1, District Court Rules 2009, C.I. 59.

[20] Order 1, rule 1(2) (a) and (b), District Court Rules 2009, C. I. 59.

[21] *Sam Jonah v Richmond Aggrey and others* [19th July, 2013] C.A., No. J4/10/2013, [10].

[22] Order 25, Rule 4(1), District Court Rules 2009, C.I. 59.

[23] Order 25, Rule 4(2) – (4), District Court Rules 2009, C.I. 59.

[24] *Adjetey Agbosu v Kotey* [2003/04] 1 SCGLR 420 [465].

[25] *Ababio and Another v Adusei* [2018] GHASC 19, CA, NO. J4/19/2014, [13].

issue before it rather than implied admission *sub silentio*.[26] It is arguable that the majority of consumers will be uncomfortable having to going through this rigorous process in seeking redress.[27] This is particularly likely to be the case where the claim is of a small value and the claimant is uncertain of the outcome.

Following the plaintiff submissions, the defendant will similarly open his case and adduce his evidence and call his witnesses, if any, who may also be cross-examined by the plaintiff or his representative.[28] The court has affirmed that the defendant has a duty to adduce those facts or evidence that will induce the determination to be made in his favour.[29] Following the testimonies of both parties, the lawyers representing them may be allowed to address the court before the court delivers its judgement on the matter, but the case may be adjourned to a later date for the court to deliver its judgement where the parties have no counsel.[30]

It is important to state that the trial will ordinarily be conducted without the need for the parties to file written statements of their case before the District Court.[31] It was recently affirmed by the Court of Appeal that filing of a statement of defence, is not a mandatory requirement under the District Court Rules.[32] However, there are instances where the parties may be required to file their written statements of claims, defence and counterclaims where the court deems it necessary in the interests of justice. The Court's order to the parties to file written statements of claims can be issued at any time in the course of the case. [33] The District Court Rules provide that: 'where it appears to the Court (for reasons recorded in the minutes) that the nature and circumstances of a case make it expedient in the interest of justice to have written statements, the (Court) may order (a) the plaintiff to file a written statement of claim, and (b) the defendant to file a written answer or statement of defence'.[34]

The above provision seems to imply that the parties and more especially the consumer-claimant for the present purpose, will have an increased burden to discharge and this may further require due diligence. The Rules emphasised that the parties will be required to state their written statements of facts 'directly, precisely, distinctly, and as briefly as is consistent with clarity' when the Court request their written statements.[35] It has been observed that where the statement of claim fails to disclose any reasonable cause of action, the court has the ample powers 'to prevent the prosecution of actions which are manifestly groundless and devoid of any cause

---

[26] *Mante v Botwe* [1989/90] 1 GLR 479 [492]; See also, *Osei Kwaku v Opanin Kofi Marfo and Another* [2013] CA, H1/34/2013 [9].

[27] It is a common knowledge that most lay persons both literate and non-literate get worry when the idea of taking a matter to court come out as an option to the resolution of a matter.

[28] Order 25, Rule 4(5) –(8) , District Court Rules 2009, C.I. 59.

[29] *Adjetey Agbosu v Kotey* [2003/04] 1 SCGLR 420, p. 465.

[30] Order 25, Rule 4(9) &(10), District Court Rules 2009, C.I. 59.

[31] Order 18, Rule 1, District Court Rules 2009, CI 59.

[32] *Osei Kwaku v Opanin Kofi Marfo and Another* [2013], Ca, H1/34/2013, [8].

[33] Order 18, Rule 1 (2), District Court Rules 2009, CI 59.

[34] Order 18, Rule 1 (1), District Court Rules 2009, CI 59 (emphasis added).

[35] Order 18, Rule 4, District Court Rules 2009, CI 59.

of action.'[36] The court further stressed that: 'the efficient conduct of a case includes the drafting of correct pleadings, the marshalling and adducing of the relevant evidence during the trial and the invocation of the correct principle of law,' and that lack of attention to these details could result in the inevitable loss of a claim.[37] This will clearly increase the degree of complexity which a consumer will be required to go through.

Drawing from the discussion, it is clear that the overall process of instituting and maintaining a claim in the District court is a complex procedure. As already noted earlier, the average consumer may obviously not be able to work through the intricacies of the court process in seeking redress. This certainly requires a prior mastery of the procedural requirements to sustain the trial process which the average consumer, who is not a lawyer, may not have knowledge of. It is therefore clear that a consumer will definitely require the assistance of a lawyer to help him to navigate through the complexities. This perfectly mirrors the observation made in the light of the procedural complexities, that: 'a consumer will need to deploy the whole of the civil process to prosecute the claim' and that this will invariably require the technical assistance of a lawyer.[38] As will be seen shortly, however, the cost implications of engaging the service of a lawyer may consequently discourage the average consumer from seeking redress in Ghana.

It is important to mention that commentators have so far put forward suggestions to assist in dealing with the situation of consumer claims. In particular, calls have been made for the adoption of a small claims court to specifically deal with matters relative to small claims.[39] Nkansah *et al* especially suggested to the effect that the introduction of the Small Claims Court should operate as a division within the District Court. The authors further suggested that the adoption of such a division should be made to operate with informal procedures. They argued that the use of informal procedures in the proposed small claims division of the District Court will possibly make the system very attractive to consumers with faulty goods to institute and maintain claims in the court over the goods.[40]

The proposal for the establishment of a small claims court as a division of the District Court with less formalised procedures is indeed, a welcome suggestion. The problematic aspect of the proposal however lies with the authors' further suggestion that the small claims court division of the District Court when implemented by the legislature and established should also make room for pre-settlement negotiations and mediation. Whilst the idea of pre-settlement negotiation and mediation itself is a great idea, the proposed manner in which they intend it to be handled raises critical questions. The view they held is that the pre-settlement negotiation and

[36] *Sam Jonah v Richmond Aggrey and others* [19th July 2013] C.A., No. J4/10/2013, [12].

[37] *Ambrose Dotse Klah v Phoenix Insurance Co.* [30th May 2012] CA, J4/19/2011, [1].

[38] Nkansah (2016), p. 295 [302]; See also, Dowuona-hammond and Atuguba (2006); See also, Ansa-Asare (1981).

[39] Nkansah (2016), p. 295 [308]; see also, Dowuona-Hammond and Atuguba (2006), para. 6.1 [70].

[40] Nkansah et al. (2016), p. 295.

mediation should be undertaken by the designated officials of the small claims court and only proceed to formal proceedings when settlement fails. The worry is that such a practice may introduce elements of bias in breach of the rules of natural justice especially the principle of *Nemo judex in causa sua* and may lead to distrust in the small claims court when introduced as suggested. This may arise, especially, where the pre-settlement fails and the same designated staff who presided over or officiated the pre-settlement proceedings turn round to preside over the same matter in the proposed small claims court.

It is therefore important that the potential conflict likely to be brought about by the proposal for the pre-negotiated settlement and mediation to be run by designated staff who will turn round to officiate over the claim in the court is addressed. This is critical to guarantee that when the proposed small claims court with the less cumbersome procedures is established, the role conflict which is likely to undermine the rules of natural justice is eliminated. This will be useful in ensuring that the envisioned small claims court when given effect with the less taxing procedures will be viable to resolving the present complex procedures of the court.

6.2.2 *Cost of Litigation in Consumer Claims in Ghana*

As observed above, the District Court is the lowest court in Ghana where most small claims of consumers regarding faulty goods may be brought. In bringing a claim before the court, the claimant (the consumer) will have to pay the prescribed statutory filing fee to invoke the jurisdiction of the court. The filing fee to pay is relative to the values and nature of the claim.[41] The Court of Appeal had observed that where the appropriate filing fee is not paid, the issuance of writ of summons will be improper and the court will have no jurisdiction to entertain the action that is brought before it.[42] In effect, the claimant will have to pay the filing fee to access the audience of the court. Also intriguing to note is that a claimant usually has to meet other unapproved payments mostly to court officials and private bailiffs in an attempt to file a claim.[43] It has therefore been argued that instituting and maintaining a legal action in a District Court on average costs litigants in the region of Gh¢3,000.00 (about £450), and costs about Gh¢5000 (about £750) in the Circuit Court.[44] It is quite evident that a consumer who bought a faulty microwave at a cost of Gh¢500.00 (about £75) for example, may likely find it an unworthy venture to contemplate initiating an action in the District Court taking into account the high legal fees reflecting the filing fees and the unofficial charges. So, whilst most consumers may

[41] The payable fees to the various courts in Ghana are set out in the Civil Proceedings (Fees and Allowances) (Amendment) Rules 2014.

[42] *AC International v Edlund Mining Ltd* [2004] HI/176/2004, [22].

[43] Owusu-Dapaa and Bediako (2015), Anomah and Amoah (2024).

[44] Owusu-Dapaa and Bediako (2015), See also, Brobbey (2011).

be disinterested in pursuing a claim due to the high filing fees, the majority of consumers in Ghana may simply not be able to afford the fees even if they wished to seek redress. As Atuguba puts it '...many people do not sue because of the fees' and this is a 'denial of access to justice for those people.'[45]

Moreover as previously examined, whilst a consumer may be able to obtain a summary judgement in an undefended suit or where the defence is not a defence in law, the process of initiating a claim in the District Court with the prospect of obtaining a summary determination may appear complex to the ordinary consumer. In effect, a consumer may need to employ the services of a lawyer to help him in making a claim before the court. Essentially, the general state of affairs has been that one will have to engage the service of a lawyer to even kick start correspondences that will eventually result in the claim being lodged in the Court. The consumer's use of a lawyer will imply that he will have to pay for the services of the lawyer. Generally, the Scale of Fees (SoF) which the Ghana Bar Association (GBA) sets from time to time is what lawyers are expected to use as the basis in negotiating with clients on the amount to charge for the legal service. In the case of the District Court, the SoF requires that the brief fees to charge should not be more than 50% of the brief fees of the High Court and Circuit Courts which are 10–20% of the value of the case.[46] The legal fees for the service of a lawyer the consumer will have to pay add up to the bill he has to be prepared to meet in pursuing a claim in the court. This may further distance the majority of average citizens from the confines of the law court particularly taking into account the cost of the goods. This may be attributable to the high legal fees or to the issue of affordability.

It is important, however, to note that a claimant does not necessarily need a lawyer to represent him in filing a case before the District Court,[47] and in both the Circuit Court and the High Court in civil matters.[48] The concern, however, is that a consumer who has no legal representation to help in directing him to make the appropriate claims may be unable to advance the right arguments to obtain the remedies he is entitled. In *Cubagee v Asare and others,*[49] the court noted that the plaintiff was unable to assist the court to determine the matter because he was not a lawyer but had filed the case on his own. The issue is that the District Court has no authority to grant either equitable or legal award if a claim for it has not been stated by the claimant in his particulars of the claim.[50] It has been observed that lay claimants who file their own cases relying on the guidance of courts bailiffs, commissioners of oath and clerks in drafting their particulars of claims turn out most often to be

[45] Atuguba (2017).

[46] Ghana Bar Association, 'Scale of Fees Adopted at the Mid-Year Review Conference on 20th April 2022 at Labadi Beach Hotel in Accra Intr' 1., para. E & F.

[47] Order 3, Rule 1(5), District Court Rules 2009 C. I. 59.

[48] Order 4, Rule 1(1), The High Court (Civil Procedure) Rules 2004, C. I. 47.

[49] *Cubagee v Asare and Others* (2018) GHASC, C.A. J6/04/2017 [6].

[50] *Akati v Nartey* (1980) GLR 218 [233].

affected greatly in their versions of the case due to legal lapses.[51] In effect, a consumer who is unable to afford the services of a lawyer under the present regime may miss rights he has not been able to claim before the court due to his lack of legal representation but to which rights he is entitled under the law.

It is, however, important to note that claimants may be able to pursue claims through a representative action.[52] This is especially where the claimants have similar issues regarding the same subject matter.[53] Significant to note is that where a suit is pending before the court, persons who are affected or likely to be affected may be able to apply to join the existing suit.[54] Moreover, the court also has the power to order for the consolidation of similar claims for uniform management[55] and may also issue a notice for persons who are affected by a pending suit to join the suit before proceeding to hear the claim.[56] Representative actions basically ensure that a multiplicity of actions on the same subject matter is averted whilst providing the parties with effective justice.[57] For the present purpose, a representative action has the benefit of ensuring that the claimants are able to share cost in maintaining the action. Whilst the representative action will certainly ensure that the claimants are able to share the cost of maintaining the action, this is only limited to where the claimants have similar concerns regarding the same subject matter. In effect, parties with claims regarding different goods against the same trader will not be able to benefit from the representative action. Moreover, consumers with faulty goods which is not a shared problem with other consumers, will still be faced with high cost of litigation as a barrier to seeking redress.

It is, however, desirable to acknowledge the existence of the Legal Aid Scheme in Ghana with the core mandate of providing the required legal assistance to persons who cannot afford the cost of legal services. However, the scope of issues covered under the Legal Aid Scheme does not appear to include instances where consumers wish to pursue claims in respect of faulty goods.[58] Consequently, consumers who purchased faulty goods and wish to seek redress cannot obtain the service of the Legal Aid Scheme.

---

[51] Owusu-Dapaa and Bediako (2015).

[52] Rule 1, Order 9, District Court Rules 2009, C. I. 59.

[53] Rule 1, Order 9, District Court Rules 2009, C. I. 59.

[54] Rule 5(3), Order 9, District Court Rules 2009, C.I. 59.

[55] Rule 11, Order 9, District Court Rules 2009, C.I. 59.

[56] Rule 5 (1 -2), Order 9, District Court Rules 2009, C.I. 59.

[57] *Marian Awuni v West African Examination Council* [21st July 2004], No. 9/2003; *Ghana Muslim Representative Council v Salifu* [1975] 2 GLR 246; *Dove v Wuta offei* [1966] GLR 299.

[58] Legal Aid Scheme Act 1997., Section 2 provide the civil matters that can receive legal aid under the Scheme. It reads 'a person is entitled to legal aid (a) If that person earns the government minimum wage or less and desires legal representation in (ii) a civil matter relating to landlord and tenant, insurance, inheritance with particular reference to the Intestate Succession Act, 1985(2), maintenance of children and any other civil matters as prescribed by Parliament.'

Furthermore, recent development in Ghana has witnessed the growth of consumer advocacy groups mainly in their infant stages.[59] The primary activities of the various consumer societies are largely advocacy on general consumer issues in Ghana.[60] They do not attend to individual consumers who wish to seek for redress in a court of law.

As mentioned earlier, suggestions have been made by commentators for the adoption of small claims courts in Ghana. In line with this, Nkansah *et al* went further to suggest that the establishment of the small claims courts as divisions of the existing District Courts should be made to operate without requiring the filing of statutory fees.[61] This is a welcome suggestion. This will ensure that consumers are not unmotivated from making claims on the basis of constraints of fees. It will likely motivate consumers with faulty goods to institute and maintain claims in the small claims court when given the needed approval. What remains unresolved is the issue of the unofficial payments which litigants are often made to pay before having their cases processed. This will need to be addressed to ensure that if it is free to file a case, it is truly free.

Moreover, the authors proposed that the adoption of the small claims court should come with the opportunity for consumers to confidently represent themselves before the court without the need for legal representation.[62] This seems to reinforce the existing requirement of the civil procedure rules which already do not make it mandatory for a party to be represented by a legal counsel as noted previously. As observed earlier, however, the question of what might be done to ensure that a consumer who pleads without legal representation is granted all the claims he or she is entitled to remains unresolved under the proposal for the adoption of a small claims court. There is the need to address this important concern to ensure that a consumer who is seeking redress without the services of a lawyer is able to obtain the remedies under the law.

In sum, the issue of exorbitant legal fees possibly deterring consumers from seeking redress will need to be addressed completely. This is necessary to spare claimants the unofficial charges which often visit persons initiating actions with added hardships. Similarly, the extent to which consumers may be able to claim the remedies they are entitled to even where they do not have legal representation will need to be addressed. Resolving these concerns is crucial to ensure that access to redress is not limited to only consumers who are capable of paying both the court fees and for hiring the services of lawyers. Instead, resolving the issues will ensure that consumers are able to seek for redress when they are supplied with faulty goods irrespective of their financial resources.

[59] The Consumer Protection Agency, The Consumer Advocacy Centre, Consumer Watch, etc. Most of the consumer advocacy groups were formed in 2008 except the Consumer Association of Ghana which was formed since 1991.

[60] Dowuona-Hammond (2007) p. 337.

[61] Nkansah and others (n 1).

[62] Ibid 295.

6.2.3 Monetary Jurisdiction of the District Court and Consumer Claims in Ghana

This subsection examines the monetary jurisdiction of the courts in Ghana in respect of where a consumer may seek redress when supplied with faulty goods. As mentioned above, the court in which a consumer may seek redress is broadly dependent on the value of the claim. In the case of the District court, a consumer may be able to bring a claim before the court if the claim is not more than GH¢20,000.00 (about £1370).[63] A claim which is above GH¢20,000.00 but not beyond GH¢50,000.00 (about £3424) may only be made at the Circuit Court.[64] Where the value of the subject matter of the claim is more than GH¢50,000.00, the claim can only be pursued in the High Court.[65]

Taking the monetary ceiling of the District Court into consideration, it is clear that consumers with claims below GH¢20,000,00 will have no problem being able to seek redress before the District Court, which is the lowest court of the land. Further commentary on the monetary jurisdiction will need to be contrasted with the applicable procedures before the District Court and the Circuit Court. It is these two courts for which there are limitations in respect of the monetary jurisdictions. As already noted above, whilst the High Court Rules, which operate with highly formalised strict rules, are the applicable procedures in the Circuit Court, the District Court Rules, which may be applied flexibly in some instances, are the applicable rules in the District Court. In particular, it is worth restating that a consumer may be able to benefit from summary judgment where the claim is undefended or where the defence failed to meet a defence to warrant full trial.

In effect, a consumer claim in which the value of the subject matter exceeds Gh¢20,000.00, as mentioned above, will not be able to benefit from the possible summary determination as the District Court will lack the jurisdiction to entertain the matter. This further implies that most consumer disputes involving the purchase of cars for private use will fall outside the scope of the District Court and even the Circuit Court. This will be the case even for second-hand cars, which the majority of consumers in Ghana buy from second-hand goods traders. This is because the average second-hand cars, which are predominantly on sale by traders in the Ghanaian market, exceed the monetary limits assigned to the Circuit Court. It is worth pointing out that the present monetary jurisdictions were the result of the 2015 amendments. Prior to this, the jurisdictional limits were Gh¢5000 (about £342) and Gh¢10,000.00 (about £685) for the District Court and the Circuit Court, respectively. The amendment was therefore an important milestone. However, it is

---

[63] https://www.bog.gov.gh/treasury-and-the-markets/daily-interbank-fx-rates/, accessed, 18/08/2025.

[64] Ibid.

[65] The Courts Act 1993, Act 459, Sections 42 & 47 (as amended by L.I. 2211, 18th December 2014/5th March 2015).

evident that many consumer claims will have to be filed in the High Court due to the lack of jurisdiction of the courts below.

Although the Cedi significantly appreciated between late April and July 2025, it had experienced consistent depreciation at unprecedented levels since 2022 until its recent gains.[66] Despite it performance improvements, substantial amount of consumer goods remains beyond the monetary jurisdictional limit of the District Court. Moreover, there is still considerable uncertainty about the sustainability of the current Cedi gains.[67] This further shows that most consumer claims can only be made at the High Court in Ghana.

The interests of consumers in Ghana could be better protected if the monetary limit of the District Court, where less formalised rules may apply, is revised to better reflect the value of most consumer goods. This would help ensure that buyers of second-hand cars, for instance, can seek redress in Ghana's District Courts. Additionally, it would support the development of a more customised consumer redress scheme, especially if the proposals advocated in this book receive legislative approval.

6.3 Alternative Dispute Resolution (ADR) as a Mechanism for the Settlement of Consumer Disputes in Ghana

Aside from resorting to the courts for the redress of civil disputes, as observed above, there are Alternative Dispute Resolution (ADR) mechanisms through which disputes may be brought to an end. The use of ADR mechanisms may be viewed from three angles. First, the resort to ADR mechanism may originate from the courts referral of the parties to have the matter resolved which may then be adopted as the court's decision.[68] Secondly, the use of ADR mechanisms may also be the result of the parties' prior agreement to resolve any dispute that may arise in the course of their dealings through arbitration.[69] The third instance is where upon the occurrence of the dispute, the parties voluntarily submit the dispute to a third party to have the matter determined impartially but on its merit under the practice of customary

---

[66] For details, see Business & Financial Times (02/08/2025) Cedi depreciation and its ripple effects available online at <https://thebftonline.com/2025/08/05/cedi-depreciation-and-its-ripple-effects/> accessed 04 August 2025. See also, Joy Business, (March 4, 2025) Cedi depreciation stood above 19% between 2022 and 2024 – Report available at <https://www.myjoyonline.com/cedi-depreciation-stood-above-19-between-2022-and-2024-report/> accessed on the 04/08/2025.

[67] Ghanaweb (28 May 2025) 'How sustainable will the cedi gains be', available online at <https://www.ghanaweb.com/GhanaHomePage/business/How-sustainable-will-the-cedi-gains-be-Professor-Bokpin-explains-1985728>, accessed on 18/08/2025.

[68] The Courts may do this relying on the Courts Act, 1993 and the High Court (Civil Procedure) Rules, 2004 (C.I. 47).

[69] This is governed by the Alternative Dispute Resolution Act 2010, Act 798.

arbitration.[70] These are discussed shortly. It is however, important to mention that awards given in any of the ADR mechanisms in Ghana are enforceable by the courts where due process was strictly observed in arriving at the awards. The extent to which the ADR mechanisms might offer consumers the required means of redress and the issues arising are discussed below. The discussion starts with the court-connected ADR and where the parties has a prior agreement to refer arising matters to arbitration.

6.3.1 Court-Connected ADR, the Prior Agreement of the Parties' to Arbitrate and Issues Arising in Respect of Small Claims of Consumers

As indicated above, the use of ADR mechanisms for the resolution of disputes is a common practice in Ghana. The practice where the courts encourage parties to resolve disputes through ADR and where the parties' prior agreement binds them to have the matter determined through arbitration is the focus of the examination here. This discussion will seek to ascertain the extent to which any of these processes might be suitable to sufficiently deal with consumer matters in respect of small claims in Ghana. The review starts with court-connected ADR and then follows up with parties' prior agreement.

Essentially, the courts in Ghana are enjoined by law to promote the amicable out of court settlement of civil matters that are placed before them. In particular, it has been provided that where there is a suit or proceeding pending before a court, the court may 'promote reconciliation among the parties, and encourage and facilitate the amicable settlement of the suit or proceeding.'[71] Similarly, Order 58 of the High Court (Civil Procedure) Rules requires the Commercial Division of the High Court in Ghana to always subject parties in a civil dispute to a pre-trial settlement before allowing a full-scale trial to commence where there is no agreed settlement.[72] The quest of the Judiciary to give an enhancement to the use of various ADR methods in line with the Courts Act, 1993 and Order 58 of the High Court (Civil Procedure) Rules further introduced what has been termed as the Uniform Practice Manual on Court-Connected ADR practice.[73] The Court-connected ADR is to give effect to methods such as negotiation, mediation, conciliation, arbitration, customary arbitration, mediation-arbitration (Med-Arb) and Natural case evaluation.[74] The scheme

[70] This is usually a process of customary mediation and negotiation for the settlement of the dispute between the parties. This has been given a legislative force under the ADR Act 2010.

[71] The Courts Act 1993, Act 459., section 72.

[72] The High Court (Civil Procedure) Rules 2004, Order 58, Rule 4.

[73] Judicial Service of Ghana (2010).

[74] Ibid. para. 1.2.

particularly contends that 'Judges and Magistrates have a duty to facilitate, promote, and refer cases to ADR where appropriate'.[75]

The period of formulation of the court-connected ADR manual also witnessed the enactment of the Alternative Dispute Resolution Act.[76] The Act equally requires the courts in Ghana to promote the use of arbitration, mediation and customary arbitration in the resolution of civil disputes between parties. Under the Act, the courts may refer parties to arbitration[77] or to mediation[78] or to customary arbitration[79] subject to the agreement of the parties. In commenting on the effect of the provision in respect of arbitration, the Supreme Court recently noted that the court may only make a referral to arbitration 'on the condition that both parties agree to the court making the referral.'[80] It is worth stating that a similar reading may be made in respect of the parties consent for a referral as the primary pre-condition to give force to mediation and customary arbitration.

Before a case is submitted to any of these forums for resolution under the court connected regime, however, the case should have first been filed before a court of law for the referral to be made based on the parties' agreement.[81] The parties whose case is placed before the ADR committee are to compensate the committee in line with the committee's determination, which takes into account the complex nature of the matter, the qualification, and level of expertise of the neutrals.[82] The committee may demand full payment of their fees to precede the delivering of the award.[83]

In can be seen from the above that, the application of the Court-connected ADR mechanisms on any matter is subject to the case being filed first in the court by the parties before the court can have the opportunity to make the referral of the matter to have it resolved through any of the highlighted ADR mechanisms. In effect, a consumer dispute can only be referred to the ADR process where the matter has been filed before the court under the court-connected ADR mechanisms. As noted earlier, however, the technicalities involved in the pleadings process may still imply that the consumer can only navigate through the court processes with the support of a lawyer, who will most probably charge legal fees. Moreover, the cost of filling the case before the court may also not permit the average consumer to think of bringing the matter before the court for the referral to be made. The parties as also noted above will have a fee to pay depending on the complexity of the dispute, qualification, and degree of experiences of the presiding committee in the ADR model. Whilst the court-connected ADR models may be more attuned to non-consumer

---

[75] Ibid. para. 4.4.

[76] Alternative Dispute Resolution Act 2010, Act 798.

[77] Ibid., section 7.

[78] Ibid., section 64.

[79] Ibid., section 91.

[80] *De Simone Ltd v Olam Ghana Ltd* (2018) NO. J4/03/2018 [9].

[81] Judicial Service of Ghana (2010). para. 2.1.2.

[82] Ibid. para. 4.3.3.

[83] Ibid. para 5.7.2. (i).

matters, it is doubtful if this will be helpful for consumers with problems of small claims. For example, a consumer who buys a faulty mobile phone at a cost of Gh¢ 300.00 may certainly find the process he has to go through in seeking redress unhelpful.

Following closely to the court-connected ADR practice is where the parties had a prior agreement to refer any arising dispute to arbitrators for a resolution. In particular, the Alternative Dispute Resolution (ADR) Act[84] stipulates that parties to an agreement may introduced a clause into their agreements at the time of reaching the agreement that where there is a dispute, they will refer the matter to arbitrators to have the dispute determined on its merits.[85] So, here, the parties' use of ADR is not a referral by the court, but it is based on the parties' agreement made at the start of the contract to refer any arising issues to arbitration. In effect, any dispute that occurs and falls within the ambit of what the parties had agreed to be a subject of arbitration will first be submitted to arbitration for a determination. The court recently confirmed that where a party commences an action in a court whilst there was a provision in their agreement for arbitration, the court is enjoined to stay the proceedings and rather refer the parties to the arbitration.[86]

The instance in which the parties agree at the time of forming the contract to refer a dispute about the agreement to arbitration seems to be more of a common practice in non-consumer transactions. In the sale and supply of the majority of consumer goods, it is very rare to have parties agreeing at the time of the transaction to refer disputes over the goods to arbitration. It has particularly been observed that arbitration is largely not an attractive avenue for the resolution of many consumer disputes.[87]

Moreover, following the reference of any arising disputes to arbitration in response to their prior agreement, the parties and the arbitrators will have to agree on the fees the parties are to pay for the services of the arbitrators. This is expected to take into consideration the value of the subject matter, the case complexity, and hourly rate which the parties may deem appropriate.[88] The fees may subsequently be reviewed if the need arises based on the parties' negotiated agreement or with the assistance of the Court. Taking the fees into consideration, it may end up being expensive addressing especially a consumer case. This will be the case where the parties are unable to reach a compromise and the case is to be placed before the court again for determination. This will consequently hike the cost of resolving the dispute making arbitration ill-suited to deal with small claims such as a GH¢200.00 worth of a faulty mobile phone. This reinforces the above observation that the use of arbitration is not suitable for most small claims of consumers.

---

[84] Alternative Dispute Resolution Act 2010, Act 798.

[85] Ibid., section 6.

[86] *Republic v High Court (Comm Division, Accra) Exparte Chacem Ltd* (2018) GHASC 34, (No J5/29/2018) [2018], P11.

[87] Nkansah and others (n 1). 295.

[88] Alternative Dispute Resolution Act 2010, Act 798, section 22.

In summary, the court-connected ADR regime only arises where a case has been filed before a court of law. However, the cost of initiating courtroom litigation, which includes legal fees and filing fees, the expense of travelling to and from the court each court date and the fees for the ADR provider will collectively render the total cost of resolving the matter a bit expensive for the purpose of consumer dispute settlement especially where the claims are small. The cost might even spiral upwards where the parties failed to reach a resolution and the dispute is relayed before the courts for determination. Given the unsuitability of the existing court-connected regime to most small claims of consumers as noted earlier, the critical question that arises is, to what extent can consumers' benefit from ADR practice in Ghana without cost being a barrier. Addressing this vital question is crucial to ensure that consumers are able to seek the needed redress when they are supplied with faulty goods in Ghana.

6.3.2 Customary Arbitration and Consumer Claims

As indicated earlier, one important medium through which disputes between parties may be resolved is through customary arbitration. Customary arbitration is mainly a practice whereby parties to a dispute refer the matter to an impartial person for the purpose of having the matter resolved informally, but on its merits. The referral is often made to a traditional authority or a chief of the community, or a highly respected person such as an Imam (an Islamic cleric), or a pastor in the community for customary arbitration encompassing customary arbitration as explained, and customary mediation referred to as negotiation for settlement.[89] The Court of Appeal has observed recently that: 'It is pertinent to state that the practice of customary arbitration has long been recognized as one of the means for resolving civil disputes in the traditional Ghanaian society. This practice has evolved over the years and our legal literature is replete with decisions confirming the efficacy of the process of customary arbitration.'[90] The question is, to what extent can the customary arbitration system of redressing disputes be helpful in resolving consumer disputes in Ghana? Answering this question will require a review of the regime.

It is significant to state that the ADR Act 2010 (Act 798) reinforces the operation of customary arbitration in Ghana. In the first place, section 92 provides that a person may only act as an arbitrator where parties to a dispute agree to willingly submit their dispute to him to have it determined. The provision went further to note that ADR Centres,[91] for which the Act provides for the establishment of, as mentioned earlier, are to keep a list of persons within the centres who may be able to act as

[89] Ibid, section 113.

[90] *Madam Adwoa Frema v Abusuapanin Sarfo Boakye* [2014] C.A., H1/5, para. 9.; see also, Nolan-Haley and Annor-Ohene (2014); See also, Nkansah et al. (2016) 295.

[91] Alternative Dispute Resolution Act 2010, Act 798, Sections 114–124.

arbitrators where possible.[92] For this, section 90 sets out the procedure that should be followed in invoking customary arbitration. First, it is required that a party to the dispute should submit the dispute to the arbitrator and request for his intervention to resolve the matter. Second, the arbitrator is then required to inform the other party of the submission of the dispute to him or her for his or her intervention in the dispute and request both parties to pay a fee or a token for the arbitration to commence. Payment of the fee or token by both parties constitutes the parties' voluntary submission of the dispute to and appointment of the arbitrator.[93] It is, however, worth noting that, a party's failure to pay the fee or the token indicates a rejection of the customary arbitration procedure by that party and cannot be forced into having the issue determined by that mechanism.[94] This mechanism therefore fails and cannot be used to resolve the dispute despite the fact that the other party may accede to the mechanism and pay the fee. The determination of disputes in customary arbitration is basically premised on the rules of natural justice and fairness without the need to follow any formal legal rules or procedure as it pertains in the judicial structure.[95]

The provisions of Act 798 reflects the observations of the Courts that the validity of a customary arbitration lies on: 'a voluntary submission of the dispute by the parties to arbitrators for the purpose of having the dispute decided informally, but on its merits; a prior agreement by both parties to accept the award of the arbitrators; and publication of the award."[96] The Courts went further to add that 'the award of the arbitration must not be arbitrary but must be arrived at after hearing both parties in a judicial manner and the practice and procedure for the time being followed in the Native Court or Tribunal of the area must be followed as nearly as possible.'[97]

As observed above, customary arbitration is deeply rooted as an important part of settling disputes among the members in the various communities in Ghana. The parties' resort to a customary mechanism for the redress of their disputes is however required to be premised on voluntary submission of the dispute by the parties to the arbitrator coupled with the desire to accept the award to bring finality to the dispute. Consequently, parties who submit their dispute to be determined under customary arbitration are bound by the award. The Courts have observed that: 'once there has been a valid customary arbitration the parties are estopped from raising the same issue subsequently by action in court.'[98]

---

[92] Ibid.

[93] Ibid, section 9 (1–3).

[94] Ibid., section 90 (4 – 6).

[95] Ibid., section 93.

[96] *Budu II v Caesar* (1959) GLR 410 [414]; See also, *Madam Adwoa Frema v Abusuapanin Sarfo* Boakye [2014] C.A., H1/5, para. 9; see also, *Akunor v Okan* (1977) 1 GLR 173.; See also, *Mansa and Others v Adutwumwaa and Others* [2012] J4/25/2012.; See also, *Manu v Kontre* [1965] 375.; See also, *Asano v Taku & Another* [1973] 2 312.

[97] *Budu II v. Caesar* [1959] 410 [414]; *Madam Adwoa Frema v Abusuapanin Sarfo* Boakye [2014] C.A., H1/5, para. 10.

[98] *Madam Adwoa Frema v Abusuapanin Sarfo* Boakye [2014] C.A., H1/5, para 10.

Nkansah *et al* have argued, and rightly so, that consumers are more likely to find it more convenient to resolve their consumer disputes through customary arbitration on account of the fact that the transactions are conducted within the various town and village markets.[99] It must be added that every community in these villages and towns where most of these transactions occur, has a traditional authority or authorities who are very much willing to have arising disputes addressed for the continuous communal living of their members. This, therefore, places customary arbitration as a very useful mechanism that could effectively support in dealing with disputes that arise in relation to consumer matters about defective goods.

The problem, however, is that the extent to which remedies that are well thought out and provided under the law may influence the remedies a consumer may obtain in a customary arbitration, remain uncertain. The uncertainty is further heightened by virtue of the fact that most of the revered persons who act as customary arbitrators are usually the traditional rulers. The majority of these traditional rulers do not have an academic background and may likely have limited appreciation of the competing rights of the parties under the law in Ghana, which they present before his/her outfit for resolution. It is important to note that the significance of the customary arbitrator to have some degree of information of the law underlying the parties' dispute is not necessarily to interpret the law *per se*, but to better understand the crux of the dispute. This may be more helpful to allow the impartial customary arbitrator to make determinations that reinforce the rules of natural justice and fairness. There is, however, uncertainty regarding how the law may help in the determination of consumer disputes.

Resolving this key concern is significant for two underlying reasons. First, addressing the issue will help ensure that the redress consumers obtain is comparatively close to what they may obtain when they go to the small claims court when this is established. In addition, it will also guarantee a reduction in the number of appeals against customary arbitration awards. There is therefore the need to resolve the uncertainty regarding the extent to which customary arbitrators' determination of disputes may possibly draw guidance from the remedies for consumers in delivering awards.

6.4 Consumer Education and Awareness

In addition to the mechanisms of redress as discussed above, the extent to which consumers may benefit from the redress schemes also needs to be examined. This is important in that the degree of enhancement of the mechanisms for the redress of consumer disputes alone is not a sufficient guarantee of an effective enforcement of consumer remedies. Especially, there is the need for any possible enhancement of the schemes of redress to be properly complemented with appropriate awareness

[99] Nkansah et al. (2016), pp. 295, 305; see also, Nolan-Haley and Annor-Ohene (2014), p. 3.

and education of consumers to adequately empower them to be prepared to assert their rights when breached.

Essentially, there is no clearly defined scheme in place for the empowerment of consumers to be better informed to be able to assert their rights when there is a breach of their rights in Ghana. It is, however, fair to indicate that there is the National Commission for Civic Education (NCCE) which has been mandated 'to create and sustain' awareness of the public on matters relative to civic rights and obligations.[100] Clearly, its functions do not appear to encapsulate consumer education and awareness.

To fill this gap, the Draft Consumer Protection Policy (CPP) as noted earlier in Chap. 1 proposes for the enactment of consumer protection legislation. The proposed legislation as captured under the CPP is to enjoin the NCCE with the primary responsibility of sensitisation and education of consumers in Ghana.[101] This is to give effect to the CPP policy objective which is to empower consumers through education and provision of information to be able to assert their rights in the market environment.[102] The CPP also proposes for the establishment of a Consumer Protection Authority (CPA) which is to have as part of its role the function of implementing programmes for the educational benefit of consumers and providers of goods and services.[103]

The significance of providing consumers with relevant information and education as captured under the Policy document reflects both earlier and recent observations by leading campaigners for the reform of the regime. Especially, observations have been made that: '[t]he impacts of consumer legislation in any society depends to a great extent on the awareness of consumers and their willingness to enforce their rights. Consumer education should … be a significant part of any attempt to enhance consumer welfare.'[104]

Clearly, the meaningfulness of the redress system broadly depends on consumers being adequately empowered to assert their rights to the claim of remedies for faulty goods when supplied to them. This further implies that consumers may be better empowered if they have access to sufficient amount of information and education about their rights and the possible means through which they could find redress. This therefore renders the proposal for the NCCE and the proposed establishment of the CPA to take up the responsibility of affording consumers with the needed information and education a well sounded proposition.

The problem, however, is that it seems uncertain as to whether under the projected arrangement, the proposed information, and education to consumers extend to cover the provision of advice to individual consumers when they are in dispute

---

[100] National Commission for Civic Education Act 1993, Act 452., section 3.

[101] Ministry of Trade and Industry (2014), p. 49.

[102] Ibid., pp. 7–8.

[103] Ibid. p 48.

[104] Dowuona-Hammond and Atuguba (2006), p. 10; see also, Dowuona-Hammond (1995); See also, Dowuona-Hammond (2018).

with a trader over defective goods. Whilst general consumer education and information is an important measure to awaken the consciousness of consumers to be willing to use the mechanisms as a source of seeking redress as observed above, advice to individual consumers who are directly affected is crucial in boosting the confidence of consumers. It is therefore important to address this uncertainty so as to ensure that consumers are offered not only universal information and education but also has the opportunity to be individually advised when the need arises.

6.5 Conclusion

This Chapter mainly assessed the adequacy of the existing mechanisms for the redress of disputes between traders and consumers regarding defects in the quality of goods in Ghana. The discussion was designed to address research question three of this book, as noted in Chap. 1 and restated in the introductory part of this Chapter. The research question is whether the present mechanisms of enforcement of consumer remedies are sufficient to provide consumers with the needed platform to obtain redress on matters of faulty goods. The discussion identified a number of mechanisms through which consumers may be able to seek redress in times of disputes over the quality of goods. However, a number of factors appear to leave the various mechanisms with very limited chances of affording consumers with the needed assistance in obtaining redress.

As established in the analysis, the possible complexities of the procedures in the courts where a case is not summarily determined may deter most consumers from bringing actions against traders for the supply of faulty goods. In response to ensuring that the complexities do not prevent a consumer from seeking redress, commentators have suggested the adoption of small claims courts to operate with simplified procedures as a division of the District Court structure in Ghana. The problem as observed in the analysis is the suggestion that the introduction of the small claims court should have the effect of allowing the designated staff to hold a pre-settlement negotiation and mediation conference with the parties prior to a trial if the parties fail to accept a proposed remedy. As clearly argued in the discussion, such a practice could lead to mistrust in the degree of fairness in the trial process by the designated staff due to the likelihood of bias. The possible conflict that may arise in such a practice will need to be resolved before its introduction to ensure that the regime directly serves the needs of consumers.

The discussion also identified the high cost of litigation as another important element that may grind the consumer quest to seek redress to a halt. However, the proposals for the adoption of the small claims courts have been made with further suggestion that when given the force of law, parties should be permitted to file their small claims at no cost. Involving the service of lawyers has also been suggested not to be a part of the small claims court when given the light of day. Although, a consumer may be able to bring an action without the aid of a lawyer, the question as to whether the court can award the consumer remedies which he has not pleaded in his action due to the lack of technical guidance of a lawyer has not been addressed.

Moreover, the courts in Ghana are enjoined by law to refer disputing parties to an ADR regime subject to the parties' prior agreement or consent and the amenability of the dispute to an ADR mechanism, with room for litigation only where there is a failure to reach a compromise. In the case of consumer disputes, as shown in the analysis, the court-connected ADR measures are not ideal for most consumer matters. The extent to which this could be modified to better suit the case of consumers is critical so as to ensure that consumers are able to benefit from the ADR schemes. It is also clear from the analysis that customary arbitration has shown to be a more convenient regime that may be harnessed to afford consumers the needed forum for redressing consumer related disputes. Nevertheless, the extent to which customary arbitrators may draw guidance from the relevant statutes, not necessarily for purposes of interpretation but for a better appreciation of the basis and resolution of the dispute of the parties has not been addressed.

The values of information and education to consumers as tools of empowerment to enable them to assert their rights through the redress mechanisms have received significant support from existing academic literature and the Draft Consumer Protection Policy. However, the extent to which the supply of the prescribed information and education to consumers may cover or include the provision of advice to individual consumers remains unclear.

The above concerns need to be addressed in order to ensure that consumers in Ghana are guaranteed a more effective and accessible mechanism for the pursuit of claims for defective goods. This will be critical to ensure that the mechanisms available are able to assist consumers in obtaining the defined remedies under the law in Ghana. The next chapter will further explore the extent to which the deficiencies of the mechanisms of redress in Ghana could be resolved through the lens of the law in England and Wales whilst bearing in mind the local circumstances in Ghana.

References

Anomah S, Amoah EK (2024) Balancing Justice in Pixels: legal and constitutional implications of virtual court sessions in Ghana. EHASS 5(3):271–283

Ansa-Asare K (1981) The case for a comprehensive framework of consumer protection in Ghana. Rev Ghana Law 14:13, 73

Atuguba RA (2017) Reform of civil litigation in Ghana. Annual Conference of the Ghana Bar Association

Brobbey SA (2011) Practice and procedure in the trial courts and tribunals of Ghana, 2nd edn. Black Mask

Business & Financial Times (2 Feb 2025) Cedi depreciation and its ripple effects available online at <https://thebftonline.com/2025/02/05/cedi-depreciation-and-its-ripple-effects/> Accessed 4 Aug 2025

Constitution of the Fourth Republic of Ghana 1992

Dowuona-Hammond C (1995) Protecting the purchaser of goods under Ghanaian law. Rev Ghana Law 19:105

Dowuona-Hammond C (2007) Evolution of consumer protection law in Ghana - developments from independence to date. In: Josiah-Aryeh NA, Fowa Hammond Mensa-Bonsu A, Henrietta JAN, Dowuona-Hammond C, Appiagyei-Atua K (eds) Ghana law since independence: history, development and prospects. Black Mask Ltd., p 337

Dowuona-Hammond C (2018) Consumer law and policy in Ghana. J Consum Policy 41(4):333–354

Dowuona-Hammond C, Atuguba R (2006) The policy and legal framework for consumer protection in Ghana. Friedrich Ebert Foundation (FES)

Ghana Bar Association (2015) Scale of Fees Adopted at the Mid-Year Review Conference on 9th April 2015 at La Palm Royal Beach Hotel in Accra Introduction' 1

Ghanaweb (28 May 2025) How sustainable will the cedi gains be. Available online at <https://www.ghanaweb.com/GhanaHomePage/business/How-sustainable-will-the-cedi-gains-be-Professor-Bokpin-explains-1985728>. Accessed 18 Aug 2025

Joy Business (March 4, 2025) Cedi depreciation stood above 19% between 2022 and 2024 – Report available online at <https://www.myjoyonline.com/cedi-depreciation-stood-above-19-between-2022-and-2024-report/> Accessed 4 Aug 2025

Judicial Service of Ghana (2010) Uniform Practice Manual: On Court-Connected Alternative Dispute Resolution (ADR) Practice

Ministry of Trade and Industry (2014) Draft Consumer Protection Policy. Government of Ghana.

Nolan-Haley J M and Annor-Ohene J K (2014) Procedural justice beyond borders: mediation in Ghana. Harv Negot Law Rev

Owusu-Dapaa E, Bediako EA (2015) Austerity in civil procedure: a critical assessment of the impact of global economic downturn on civil justice in Ghana. Erasmus Law Rev 8:10

Nkansah et al (2016) Dispute resolution and consumer protection in Ghana in Oppong R F & Agyebeng K (eds), A commitment to law, development and public policy: a Festschrift in Honour of Nana Dr. Samuel Kwadwo Boaten Asante, Wildy Simmonds and Hill Publishing.

Chapter 7
Mechanisms for the Enforcement of Consumer Remedies Under English Law: Resolving the Shortfalls of the Law in Ghana

7.1 Introduction

The preceding Chapter examined the adequacy of the redress mechanisms for the enforcement of consumer remedies in Ghana with respect to a consumer purchase of faulty goods. The current Chapter is meant to further resolve the concerns relating to enforcing the remedies for faulty goods in Ghana, taking persuasive guidance from English law. This is especially in response to the central question regarding whether the English law's measures of enforcement of consumer remedies will be helpful in resolving the limitations for the enforcement of consumer remedies in Ghana. As indicated earlier in Chap. 6, the appropriateness of the remedies will be of little value without the opportunity for consumers to be able to enforce them when confronted with faulty goods. A number of concerns were especially identified to render the present redress mechanisms ill-suited to the enforcement of consumer remedies in respect of most consumer claims in Ghana. The courts as the primary source of redress were found to present express challenges to consumers with respect to high costs of litigation, difficulty in attaining justice without legal representation, complexities of the court proceedings with reform proposals being beset with likely role-conflict, and the low monetary jurisdiction of the lower courts. Moreover, the court-connected ADR schemes were also found to be unsuitable for dealing with most consumer claims. Similarly, whilst the customary redress scheme was found to be more accessible, there were uncertainties as to the extent to which customary arbitrators were informed about the statutory remedies for the purpose of drawing guidance where necessary. The current chapter, as indicated above, seeks to address these concerns. The discourse will particularly take possible guidance from the English law whilst being mindful of the domestic setting in Ghana where necessary.

Before addressing the substantive concerns about the enforcement mechanisms, taking guidance from the English law, a succinct restatement of the underlining

N. Yidana, *Consumer Law and Policy on Faulty Goods*, Ius Gentium: Comparative Perspectives on Law and Justice 134,
https://doi.org/10.1007/978-3-032-08700-3_7

rationale for the resort to the English law appears necessary to refresh the minds of readers. The choice of the English law for this comparative discussion is anchored on a number of solid grounds within the sphere of comparative law as stated in Chap. 1. One of the bases lies with the fact that the English law has benefitted from several years of reforms responding to concerns which presently confront Ghana. And as was noted in Chap. 1, it is acceptable to take guidance from pioneers without necessarily reinventing the wheel. Furthermore, Ghana historically has colonial ties with the English law to which comparative scholars have given solid credence in selecting a jurisdiction for comparison. Other recounted rationales which support the choice of the English law are the degree of maturity of the regime and its existing persuasive character to both the courts and lawyers in Ghana.[1]

Having provided a succinct recap of the rationale for the choice of the English law for the comparative analysis, it is important to state here that analysis in this chapter which is largely concerned about redress mechanisms does not engage much case law. However, leading commentators on the various aspects of the mechanisms for the enforcement of consumer remedies including reports of the English law Commission are drawn to support the analysis where appropriate.

The Chapter is divided into five main parts or sections. The first part is this introduction. The second part addresses the issue regarding high cost of litigation, complex proceedings, monetary jurisdiction, and consumer access to justice. The third part further focuses on resolving the issue about the ADR measures. This particularly looks at the issues surrounding the court-connected ADR mechanisms and the customary arbitration scheme. The fourth part addresses the uncertainty about the extent of education and awareness required under the proposed Consumer Protection Policy 2014. The fifth part provides a conclusion by highlighting the findings of the Chapter analysis.

7.2 The Settlement of Consumer Disputes in the Courts in Ghana: Lessons from the English Law

This section discusses the concerns regarding the settlement of consumer disputes in the courts. The analysis in this section reflects four main subsections. The first subsection seeks to address the issues regarding the high cost of litigation as an obstacle to the making of consumer claims in Ghana. The second subsection addresses the likely role conflict in the proposed small claims mandate of pre-trial settlement and negotiation and actual trial. The third subsection resolves the concerns about the limitation of the lower courts in respect of their power to award

[1] For detailed justification for the use of the English law for the present comparative discourse, see, Chap. 1 of this book on: 'The rationale for the use of the English regime for the comparative analysis', para. 1.4.

remedies outside what the consumer sought. The fourth subsection addresses the problem pertaining to the monetary jurisdiction of the District Court. The issue about the high cost of litigation as a barrier to consumer access to the courts is analysed below.

7.2.1 *Cost of Litigation as a Barrier to Consumer Claims in Ghana*

Another important issue that was identified in Chap. 6 as having the tendency to frustrate a consumer's quest for redress in court in respect of a dispute over faulty goods was the issue of the high cost of litigation. It was noted in the first instance that a consumer will have to bring a claim in accordance with the District Court Rules, 2009 before the District Court or the High Court (Civil Procedure) Rules 2004 in the circuit Court and High Court as was noted in Chap. 6.[2] A succinct review of the relevant parts of the Rules in Chap. 6 of this book, however, showed that the procedures are sophisticated and may require the methodical expertise of a trained lawyer to properly manoeuvre through the complexities of the courts. This was noted to automatically require the payment of legal service fees. It was also pointed out that the claimant will have to meet the various court charges. Other unofficial payment to court officials was also highlighted to add to the cost claimants have to meet.

It was especially found that a consumer may be discouraged from initiating an action before a court of law on account of the high cost of litigation. As was noted in Chap. 6 in particular, the overall cost of seeking redress in the courts may far outweigh the cost of the goods. These could consequently lead to the consumer dropping the idea of seeking redress in the courts. This will result in the consumer being left without redress. The crucial question regarding the extent to which issues of litigation cost may not dispossess consumers of the benefit of the protection under the regime was therefore found to need addressing. Resolving this was especially noted to be critical in order to ensure that consumers are able to seek redress when they are supplied with faulty goods.[3]

In examining the English law for possible guidance, it is found that the regime employs a number of measures that encouraged consumers to bring or make claims in court on matters of disputes over faulty goods without being deterred by the high cost of litigation.[4] One important measure under the English law that seeks to limit the cost of litigation impact on the consumer for the present purpose is Money

[2] For details, see para. 6.2.

[3] For details, see para. 6.2.

[4] Money Claim Online, Collective actions, Group Litigation Order; Representation action. For details, see, Howells (2009) p. 329 [343].; See also Bridge (2017), paras 14.252–14.253.

Claim Online (MCOL). This was first introduced in 2002[5] and mainly employs the Civil Procedure Rules but with Practice Direction specifically tailored to online claims.[6] The MCOL allow claimants to file their cases online for the claim of money worth not more than £100,000 without the need for direct contact with court officials.[7] The defendant can also acknowledge receipt of service of the claim and may file his defence online.[8] In the absence of a defence, or where the defendant admits to the claims, the claimant will be entitled to request for a judgement.[9] Lord Justice Briggs reaffirmed that 'where the claim is unopposed the claimant may request both judgment and (if unsatisfied) a warrant of control online.'[10] It is worth stating that the use of the online means of seeking redress is confined to where the claimant has a fixed amount of money relating to the dispute in question.[11] Also important to note is that the claimant's claims, the defendant's defence or admission and the claimant request for judgement are all done online for the court's evaluation of the substance of the case in reaching its decision. However, where the defendant completely denies the claim, the court may then require the appearance of the parties for a hearing.[12]

It has been observed that the system provides an opportunity for the courts to provide parties with a final settlement of a consumer dispute but with the option for a displeased party to appeal.[13] It is also worth noting that the HM Courts and Tribunals Services responsible for handling claims which are filed through the online route further set out very clear guidelines as a guide to consumers who wish to make claims for the recovery of money from traders or service providers.[14] The cost savings of the MCOL have accounted for a large number of users, amounting to 80% being litigants in person (LIPs).[15]

A similar measure in Ghana, but in a modified manner, will be very helpful to consumers in seeking redress. In particular, while the operation of MCOL is confined to where the claim is about a fixed amount of money not exceeding £100,000,

---

[5] It is important to note that this is being updated constantly to reflect changing circumstances and the latest changes being in 2019. The recent change is particularly to enable claimants to notify the courts where there is a settlement after he/she had filed the claim. The notification is to be done online which the court could then pick on that to stay proceedings unless the defendant objects. For details see, the Practice Direction Amendments (PD 10A.) of the 106th Updates to the Civil Procedure Rules 1998—to be effective from the 18th March 2019.

[6] Civil Procedure Rules (as amended) – Rules and Directions 1998.

[7] The application process can be found at HM Courts and Tribunals Services, 'Money Claim Online (MCOL) – User Guide for Claimants' accessed on 15/03/2025.

[8] Ibid [12].

[9] Ibid [15].

[10] Briggs (2015), para. 2.28.

[11] Twigg-Flesner (2017), p. 128; Riefa and Willett (2018), p. 673.

[12] HM Courts and Tribunals Services (n 7), p. 4.

[13] Reifa and Willett (2018), p. 128.

[14] HM Courts and Tribunals Services (n 7).

[15] Lord Justice Briggs (2015) 2.28.

it is submitted that this will need to be modified to permit consumers with faulty goods to file claims virtually as it pertains to the MCOL. Providing the opportunity for consumers to make claims online will be significant in ensuring that consumers are able to avoid the many expenses which are often associated with seeking redress in the courts in Ghana. In particular, as noted in Chap. 6, the idea of consumers being required to pay unofficial charges will be avoided.[16] Moreover, the cost of travelling to attend to the business of the court at every sitting will be eliminated if the court finds the online submissions of the parties sufficient enough to decide on the matter. Another important benefit in support of introducing the filing of claims online is that the consumer's other daily work commitment will not be sacrificed for the purpose of coming to court to file a claim. Similarly, the sophistication of the court proceedings, which function as a barrier to consumer access to the court, will be eliminated.

In spite of the benefit of replicating the MCOL model in Ghana in the form of pursuing claims online, it is important to point out that calls for its introduction may raise questions about the majority of consumers who cannot read or write in English in terms of their ability to use the online platform procedure. Whilst this will be a genuine concern, it remains a settled practice that our law in Ghana encourages illiterate litigants who do not have legal representation to seek assistance from the educated elite to help in drafting the particulars of their claims.[17] In the same vein, a party who has a claim should be able to seek the help of the literate to file the case online if the MCOL model is introduced in Ghana. Indeed, in Ghana, the literate members of the society are most often very willing to give a helping hand to their neighbours who may need such assistance. This culture of being more prepared to assist neighbours and relatives will, therefore, ensure that the illiterate population will be able to seek the assistance of the educated elite in society to go through the process of filing a case if the online money claim scheme is introduced.

It is very important to note that Ghana is not alien to the use of virtual systems for court proceedings. In 2023, in particular, the Chief Justice of Ghana issued for the first time directions that provided for virtual court hearings during the courts' legal vacation.[18] While the initial Practice Direction permitted only lawyers in the jurisdiction to participate in the proceedings, this has recently been amended to allow lawyers who travel abroad to participate in virtual court proceedings from any part of the world.[19] More significantly, the virtual court proceedings have equally been extended to cover cases outside the legal vacation periods, including matters

[16] For details, see para. 4. 2.2.

[17] See Order 3, rule 1(4), District Court Rules 2009, C. I. 59 as discussed in para. 3.1 earlier in Chap. 6 of this book.

[18] Ghana Judiciary (2023) Practice Direction on Virtual Court Sessions, Practice Direction PD/CC/RCH/01/2023. In his earlier conference presentation, Atuguba (2017) argued that it was long overdue for the courts to shift to the use of electronic means of filing cases and delivery of court services, among others.

[19] Templars (2024) Dispute Resolution Digest available online at https://www.templars-law.com/app/uploads/2024/09/Dispute-Digest-Transcript-SEPT-24.pdf accessed on 05/07/2025.

before the Appeals Court in Tamale and court cases in Bolgatanga, Adenta and Tema.[20] Although the current practice of the virtual court system is a commendable novelty in the justice delivery system in Ghana, its operation presently does not cover the District court system where most small claims are made. Moreover, the operation of the prevailing virtual court system departs slightly from the claims online being advocated herein. Nevertheless, the virtual court system is a clear demonstration of the potential acceptability of online claims for faulty goods if adopted in Ghana. Introducing the online claim system in Ghana will potentially minimise the cost of seeking redress and significantly encourage consumers not to leave their claims uncontested.

However, the filing fee is another aspect of the MCOL model under English law that may need further modification in Ghana. Essentially, claimants are required to pay a court filing fee through the online service, and until a claimant pays the filing fee, his/her claim will not be worked on under the English law MCOL.[21] It is first worth acknowledging that the English law approach of requiring claimants to pay the court filing fee before the issue could be attended to, is consistent with the current practice of the courts in Ghana. However, this has contributed to leaving the courts beyond the reach of ordinary Ghanaian consumers. As noted in Chap. 6 earlier, the main obstacle that most consumers confront relates to being able to afford the cost of bringing a claim, including the filing fees before a court of law in Ghana.[22] Others are also discouraged from seeking redress for fear of paying court fees without being certain of the outcome in respect of what the court will say is the law. Modifying the approach to the court fees payment in adapting the MCOL (online filing and processing of consumer small claims) in the context of Ghana will, therefore, be helpful in addressing the court filing fees functioning as a barrier to consumer access to justice. In particular, the problem might be addressed better by making it possible for consumers to file small claims online, with the filing fee being deferred to when they are successful in the claim. It is worth noting that giving effect to the deferred conditional payment of court filing fees will especially reflect the already common practice in Ghanaian society where an act of good done to a person is mostly reciprocated with a thank you gift in either kind or cash payment.

It is important to, however, acknowledge that the essence of the court fees is to help the courts meet their daily administrative expenses.[23] The deferment of the filing fee payment to when successful should, therefore, be made available to consumers who will practically be unable to seek redress. For example, guidelines could be designed to ensure that persons whose monthly income is within a given range are qualified to access the deferred payment of the court filing fee regime if given

[20] Ghana Judiciary (undated) LINKS FOR VIRTUAL COURT SITTINGS, available online at https://judicial.gov.gh/index.php/virtualcourt accessed on 05/07/2025.

[21] For details see, https://www.gov.uk/make-court-claim-for-money/court-fees accessed on 13/05/2025.

[22] For details, see, para. 4.2.2.

[23] Lord Justice Briggs (2015) paras. 3.10.

approval. This is necessary to ensure that access to justice is brought to the doorsteps of the average Ghanaian consumer. This will be critical to ensure that the average Ghanaian is able to access redress when in a dispute over faulty goods. The overall effect will ensure that consumers are encouraged to pursue claims in respect of disputes over faulty goods. This will similarly have the tendency of ensuring that traders take the required steps to resolve disputes which arise without allowing them to escalate to the courts.

Another critical measure that the courts under English law are empowered to undertake is the power to deliver judgements based on the recorded submissions of the parties without requiring their appearance for an oral hearing. Part 27 of the Civil Procedure Rules, which governs the small claims track in particular, states that the court may dispose of the matter without hearing the parties by relying on the evidence they laid before the court subject to the agreement of the parties.[24] In the event of the evidence not being sufficient for the court to arrive at a decision, it is further required that the court may hold a preliminary hearing with the parties and this may be treated 'as the final hearing of the claim if all the parties agree.'[25] The essence of the preliminary hearing has been argued to be meant to aid the parties in reaching a settlement agreement, or to facilitate the progress of matters capable of enhancing the effectiveness of the actual trial process.[26]

Essentially, the practice of the English courts to rely on the recorded evidence of the parties to deliver judgment will equally be helpful to consumers if replicated in Ghana. First, it will save a lot of costs, which consumers may have to incur in travelling to the court whenever there is a hearing. Moreover, it will save the consumer the cost of paying legal fees to counsel for legal services. This will, therefore, contribute significantly to reducing the cost of litigation to the average consumer in Ghana when the MCOL model of filing claims online is adopted and effectively implemented in Ghana. Alternatively, the possibility of the courts to hold only a preliminary hearing and to treat the hearing as a final hearing subject to the parties' consent will be a welcome practice in Ghana if given legislative effect. This practice will ensure that consumers are able to obtain a swift determination of the matter which they submit before the court in Ghana. This will clearly cut down on the cost of seeking redress if a similar requirement is made available for the benefit of consumers in Ghana.

In short, the introduction of the modified MCOL scheme with the deferment of the court filing fee to the success of the consumer claim and empowering the courts to make determinations based on the recorded evidence if the issue in dispute is obvious will be practically beneficial to consumers. Adapting such measures will further encourage consumers to bring claims before the courts when given legislative approval in Ghana.

---

[24] CPR (amendments)- Small Claims Track, part 27.10.

[25] Ibid., Part 27.6 (4).

[26] Howells and Weatherill (2005), p. 616.

7.2.2 *Small Claims Division of the District Court and Pre-Trial Settlement Negotiations in Consumer Claims in Ghana*

In Chap. 6, it was found that the available civil procedure rules that are used in the courts are sophisticated to the lay consumer and may require the methodical expertise of a trained lawyer to properly manoeuvre through the complexities of proceedings in the courts. It was also observed that the cost of engaging the service of a lawyer may far outweigh the cost of the goods and the claims of the consumer and could consequently lead to the consumer dropping the idea of seeking redress in the courts. Existing proposals were further found to call for the establishment of a small claims court as a division of the District Court which proceedings should be informal to allow parties to represent themselves. Whilst this was found appropriate to deal with the present complexities, the problematic aspect was the suggestion for the designated officials of the small claims court to always engage the parties in a pre-settlement negotiation and arbitration and only proceed to trial where these procedures failed to resolve the difference. This was found to have the tendency of undermining the rules of natural justice in respect of *nemo judex in causa sua* especially if the suggestion of the designated staff at the pre-trial negotiation fails and he then turned out to preside over the same issue he had dealt with in a different capacity. It was therefore argued that the potential conflict that may arise needs to be resolved in introducing the small claims court in Ghana to avoid the chances of mistrust in the system when the small claims court is given legislative approval.[27]

In examining the English law as already noted, consumers may be able to file for a claim through the small claims track or using the Money Claims Online (MCOL) where the consumer is claiming for a fixed sum of money. Parties who filed their cases for determination under the small claims track or through MCOL are often received first at the Northampton County Court Business Centre in the whole of England and Wales. In both instances, the Centre engages the parties in a free mediation service in an attempt to reach an agreement via telephone interaction with the parties. However, where this fails, the matter is referred to a County Court Centre where parties will appear for a hearing. This is especially evident in Lord Briggs' report on the civil court structure. In particular, he highlighted that claims in both small claims and MCOL are 'handled, initially, in Northampton but then (only if disputed) being transferred to an appropriate County Court hearing centre in accordance with protocols which pay attention to, but which are not bound by, claimant choice or party preference.'[28] So, the crux of the matter is that the pre-trial attempt to reach a resolution is conducted by different persons and centres on where the court hearing will eventually take place.

[27] For details, see Chap. 6, para 6. 2.1.

[28] Briggs (2016), para. 8.7; See also Briggs (2015), paras. 2.26–2.29.

This is critical in introducing the small claims system in Ghana. Having impartial persons to handle the pre-hearing negotiation and mediation services distinct from the actual hearing of the matter in the small claims division of the District Court when given a legislative consideration is fundamental to help in ensuring that the potential of conflict of interest does not arise in dealing with a consumer claim. A similar path as pertained in making both the MCOL and the small claims under the English law will therefore resolve the concerns of the likely conflict of interest that will arise in having the designated staff handling both the pre-trial and actual trial of the matter advanced by proponents as noted in Chap. 6.

It is important to note that having different personalities handling the pre-trial negotiation and the court hearing as observed under the English law will be consistent with the prevailing practice before the courts in Ghana. In particular, under the current practice in Ghana, whenever a pre-trial settlement breaks down before a judge, the Registrar of the Court transfers the case from the court where the pre-trial settlement was held to another court of the same jurisdiction to be presided over by a different judge. In the specific case of the District Court for instance, where pre-trial settlement has failed in a particular District Court, the supervising High Court Judge will direct the Registrar to transfer the case from that District Court to another District Court for the purposes of avoiding the tendency of undermining the rules of natural justice.[29] It is therefore submitted that it will be appropriate as noted above to ensure that in establishing the small claims division of the District Court, different setups with different personalities are mandated to perform the separate functions of pre-trial hearings and small claims hearings.

7.2.3 *Resolving the Issue of the Courts' Limits to Award Remedies*

As highlighted above, the review of the procedure for making a claim before a court of law in Ghana in Chap. 6 revealed that there is no tailored procedure specifically, solely and purposely designed for the pursuit of consumer claims in court. In effect, the applicable rules which a consumer may follow are the District Court Rules and the High Court (civil procedure) Rules in making claims before the District Court and the Circuit Court/High Court respectively as was noted in Chap. 6. In bringing a matter before the court, it was observed that whilst a consumer may employ the services of a lawyer, he may nevertheless opt to pursue the matter without the assistance of a lawyer. The problem was, however, discovered that whilst a consumer may choose to bring an action in person, the courts' power to award remedies is only limited to what the claimant claims in his statement of particulars. This was

[29] District Court Rules 2009, Order 5 (Rule 2).

therefore argued to have the tendency of hurting lay consumers who go to court without legal assistance and cannot properly frame the statement of particulars to clearly bring out his claims for the court's determination. It was also discovered that proposals have been made by commentators for the adoption of small claims as a division of the District Court in Ghana. Similar to the present problem, whilst the proposal for the adoption of the small claims Court contends that such a Division of the District Court should enable consumers to institute actions without the support of lawyers, the proposal did not as well address the question regarding the issue of the courts' power to grant a party's reliefs being circumscribed, unless the reliefs are incidental to or directly flow from the party's claim, by the claims made by the party in his statement of particulars. Addressing this critical concern is especially important to ensure that a consumer who musters the courage to go to the court or use the small claims court (if established) in person, does not unduly suffer for want of a proper prayer for the appropriate remedies he would have possibly pleaded with the aid of a lawyer.[30]

Under the English law, the court has the vested power to determine the remedy that may be appropriate for the consumer and this may differ from what the consumer originally seeks.[31] In particular, it has been provided that 'the court may make an order under this section unconditionally or on such terms and conditions as to damages, payment, or the price and otherwise as it thinks just.'[32] It has especially been observed that the court takes an active role in the small claims court and may directly question witnesses in an effort at affording the parties a fair trial.[33] In relation to a contract for the supply of goods, the Explanatory Notes of the CRA particularly contend that a court may eventually 'order price reduction when the consumer had requested repair, if repair and replacement were impossible.'[34]

This vested authority for the courts to afford the consumer remedies which he did not anticipate has the tendency of ensuring that a consumer who is to be awarded remedies under such an instance will be able to obtain remedies he would not have gotten. This will similarly be helpful if considered in Ghana. This will particularly be useful in matters where the consumer is appearing before the court without legal representation. This will ensure that the remedies he would have been entitled to do not surpass him as a result of his inability to engage the service of a lawyer to help in better framing his particulars of claim.

Another important aspect of the English law that may enhance the position of consumers without legal representation if given the necessary attention in Ghana is the issue of the court taking into consideration unfair terms in the contractual transaction which the consumer is not able to bring to the attention of the court. In particular, the English Courts are empowered in consumer contracts to 'consider

---

[30] For details, see para. 4.2.1.

[31] Consumer Rights Act 2015, section 58(1).

[32] Consumer Rights Act 2015, section 58(7).

[33] Twigg-Flesner (2017) 128 [131].

[34] Explanatory Notes to the Consumer Rights Act 2015:, para. 285.

whether the term is fair even if none of the parties to the proceedings has raised that issue or indicated that it intends to raise it'.[35] The underlying philosophy of this provision is said to be linked to the EU conception of the 'nature and importance of public interest' protection in its Directive which a national court is 'required to assess of its own motion whether a contractual term is unfair'.[36] It has been observed that this has increased the authority of the court to consider the fairness of terms in consumer contracts even if the issue is not brought up by any of the parties.[37] It is important, however, to indicate that the obligation of the courts to determine the fairness of the term is keen where there is 'sufficient legal and factual material to enable the courts to consider the fairness of the term.'[38]

The authority of the courts to decide as to the fairness or unfairness of the terms of a contract especially where the court has a legal and factual basis to do so will enhance the position of consumers in Ghana when adopted in Ghana. This will be a welcome incentive to a consumer who is representing himself before the court and lacks the technical competence to clearly point the unfair term(s) to the court. The courts own voluntary assessment of the fairness of the term in the contract will help ensure that remedies that the consumer may be entitled to as a result of that unfair term are granted to him.

In a nutshell, introducing the measures aimed at empowering the courts to make determination of remedies that may enhance the position of the consumer where the court thinks fit, whether or not the consumer made a claim for such remedies or not will help address the fear of the consumer being deprived of essential remedies where he sues without legal representation. Similarly, giving authority to the court to deal with terms the court finds unfair will as well be useful in addressing the concern of the consumer not obtaining the redress he should be entitled to for being unable without a lawyer to point to the unfairness of the terms.

7.2.4 *Resolving the Issues of the Monetary Jurisdiction for the Making of Consumer Claims in the District Court in Ghana*

As recalled above, one of the issues of concern that was identified in Chap. 6 earlier regarding a consumer seeking redress in a court of law in Ghana was the monetary jurisdiction of the courts. As was shown there, the District Court, the Circuit Court

---

[35] Consumer Rights Act 2015, section 71 (2).

[36] The Consumer Rights Act 2015: Explanatory Notes, para. 340 citing the CJEU in Case C-168/05 *Mostaza Claro* (2006) ECRI-10421 at para. 38.

[37] Pupil Robin Kingham, 'The Consumer Rights Act 2015: A Summary Of Key Changes' <https://goughsq.co.uk/wp-content/uploads/2015/04/Consumer-Rights-Act-2015-Summary.pdf> accessed on 12/03/2025 [2]; see also, The Consumer Rights Act 2015: Explanatory Notes, para 339.

[38] Consumer Rights Act 2015, section 71 (3), emphasis added.

and the High Court are the trial courts in Ghana. The court in which a claimant will be able to bring a claim is dependent on the value of the claim and the monetary jurisdiction of the court. In particular, whilst the High Court was found not to have monetary limitation, the monetary jurisdiction of the Circuit Court and the District Court were pegged at Gh¢50,000 and Gh¢20,000 respectively as was revealed in Chap. 6. It was similarly shown that whilst the highly formalised High Court (Civil Procedure) Rules, 2004 are the applicable rules in the Circuit Court, the District Court applies the District Court Rules 2009 where some flexibility may be permitted in respect of the opportunity for a summary determination in an undefended suit or where the defence did not amount to a defence in law. So, the crux of the matter as was noted in Chap. 6 is that the monetary jurisdiction of Gh¢20,000.00 (about £3000) for a case to be determined in the District Court will not cover consumer goods in respect of motor vehicles. It was therefore argued that the monetary ceiling will need to be reviewed in order to ensure that the average motor vehicle consumers are able to seek redress in the District Court where some flexibility is permitted, and the cost of the claim may as well be low. It was further found to be critical to ensure that the average consumer is able to benefit from the proposals this book seeks to put forward regarding providing a more effective system of redress for consumers if given a legislative blessing.[39]

Before examining the monetary jurisdiction of the English law for guidance, it is first appropriate to mention that the County Court is the lowest court in the structure of the civil courts under the English law. The County Court however has three divisions including the small claims track,[40] the fast track[41] and the multi-track.[42] So, where a claim is filed before the County Court, the track the case will be allocated to is dependent on the value of the case. Claims which are not more than £10,000 are usually assigned to the small claims track of the court which is of importance to the present discussion. So, in effect, the monetary threshold of small claims under the English law is pegged at £10,000. It is worth mentioning that claims which exceed the limits of £10,000 but not more than £100,000 which mostly involve personal injury are often placed before the fast track and the multi-track divisions of the County Court.[43]

The primary focus as already mentioned is the small claims with the reserved monetary jurisdiction of the small claims track set at £10,000. It can be seen that this monetary ceiling of the small claims track under the English law is a higher figure, which is capable of covering most consumer goods. This will allow most consumers with claims of not more than £10,000 to be able to seek redress before the small claims track of the County Court. In commenting on the rationale for the assigned

[39] For details see, para. 4.2.3.

[40] Civil Procedure Rules (as amended) - Rules and Directions 1998, part 27.

[41] Ibid., part 28.

[42] Ibid., part 29.

[43] High Court and County Court Jurisdiction Order 1991 (SI 1991/724) as amended severally, with the latest being SI 2015/1641. For details, see, Bridge (2017), p. 14.251.

higher figure for small claims, *Benjamin's Sale of Goods* submitted that the limit is intentionally made high to ensure that the majority of consumer claims, which do not involve personal injuries, are covered.[44]

The philosophy behind fixing a higher figure likely to cover most consumer claims under English law is equally relevant in the case of Ghana. Providing a higher monetary limit for small claims that can cover most goods within the average consumer in Ghana will be vital in ensuring they can seek redress when supplied with defective goods. For instance, the average cost of most second-hand vehicles, which are within the means of the average Ghanaian, should be covered under such a ceiling amount which the small claims court should have the jurisdiction to hear and determine.

It is, however, important to acknowledge the possible argument that the higher monetary threshold for small claims in the UK is relative to its standard of living which is completely different from the case of Ghana, and for which a higher monetary ceiling for small claims (in the District Court or any tribunal set up for that purpose) in Ghana may not be necessary. Admittedly, whilst Ghana is a middle-income economy, the UK is an advanced economy with a high standard of living. This naturally requires that for the law to afford the needed protection to consumers in the UK, it should be measured against the purchasing power of the average consumer in the market. In effect, the English law ceiling amount for small claims at the value of £10,000 could be argued rightly to be in relation to a measure of the purchasing power of the average consumer. Whilst this might be one of the underlying bases, it is, however, important to note that the forces of globalisation have made it possible today for many of the goods which are consumed in the UK to be available for consumers in Ghana.

In particular, the present cost of a motor vehicle for an average Ghanaian in the market for example, is presently around the monetary limit (Gh¢50,000.00) of the Circuit Court in Ghana. In the Circuit Court as previously noted in Chap. 6, the High Court (Civil Procedure) Rules which are highly formalised rules of procedure are applicable. In effect, a consumer who purchased a faulty second-hand car at a cost of Gh¢50,000.00 for example, will be required to go through the strict rules of civil proceedings before the Circuit Court. This is because, such a case is above the threshold of the District court's monetary jurisdiction. Similarly, where the said cost of the vehicle is Gh¢55,000.00, such a case could only be entertained before the High Court with its strict rules of proceedings. As already shown in Chap. 6, however, the complexity of the court proceedings will demand that the consumer engages the services of a lawyer to pursue the claim whose cost may discourage him from seeking redress. It will therefore be useful to have a review of the monetary limits to ensure that cost in seeking redress does not act as a barrier to redress of consumer disputes in Ghana. This therefore underlined the argument for the monetary limitations of the District Court which presently stands at Gh¢20,000.00 to be reviewed upward to take into account of the purchasing power of the average

[44] Bridge (2017), para. 14.250.

consumer in Ghana. This is important to ensure that the average consumer is given the needed impetus to seek redress when supplied with faulty goods.

It might be argued that consumer goods with higher monetary values may raise complex legal questions and should not be left to be determined by the lowest courts in Ghana in respect of the above proposal for an upward review of the monetary jurisdiction. Whilst such an argument will be well placed, it remains a clear possibility that a claim within the present monetary threshold of the lowest courts may similarly raise complex legal questions. However, in both the existing and the proposed increment of the monetary jurisdiction of the lowest court, a party who is not satisfied with a decision of the court will have the door open to seek an appeal. With the upward adjustment of the monetary jurisdictional limit, the majority of consumers will have the opportunity to seek redress before the lowest courts in Ghana, where they stand the chance of benefiting from a flexible procedure. It is important to further note that every new change will always attract questions of fear of the unknown, and it is therefore in order for such legitimate questions to emerge. As noted already, where a party has a firm view that a complex question of fact or law has not been properly addressed, which could produce a more favourable outcome for him/her in a raised monetary jurisdiction of the lower court, an appeal could be sought.

In short, it remains crucial for the monetary jurisdiction to be aligned with the purchasing power of the average consumer in the country, considering the variety of goods available in the markets for consumers in Ghana. The key question then is what constitutes the realm of an average consumer, particularly regarding motor vehicles, in relation to the range of goods accessible to consumers in Ghana. While the average cost of a second-hand vehicle for an ordinary consumer is currently around Gh¢100,000.00, the persistent depreciation of the cedi makes it challenging to set a stable threshold that would remain reasonable in the future. Consequently, it is appropriate for the determination of a more comprehensive monetary threshold to be reviewed every two years. However, such a review should always account for the need to protect the average consumer in relation to their purchasing power when establishing a reasonable threshold. This is vital to prevent the risk of any proposed figure losing its relevance before the legislature has a chance to formalise the recommendations this text aims to propose.

7.3 The Use of Alternative Disputes Resolution (ADR) Mechanisms as a Means of Enforcing Consumer Claims for Remedies

This section considers the extent to which the arising issues about the use of ADR mechanisms for redress of consumer disputes in Ghana could be resolved by drawing guidance from the English law. The discussion is divided into two sub-sections. The first part seeks to address the issues arising about the unsuitability of the court-connected ADR schemes for claims which are small in Ghana. The second part also addresses the concerns regarding the extent to which determinations of matters in a customary arbitration scheme might be made while having regard to the statutory protection for the consumer. The discussion will be carried out in the light of the experiences of the English law as previously noted. The issue concerning the court-connected ADR scheme is first addressed below.

7.3.1 Addressing the Problem of ADR as a Means of Resolving Consumer Disputes in Ghana

As highlighted above, this subsection addresses the subject concerning the unsuitability of using the current court-connected ADR scheme as a means of resolving most small claims in Ghana. Essentially, one of the schemes for the redress of disputes in Ghana was identified in Chap. 6 to be the use of court-connected ADR mechanisms. Under this scheme of redress, the court refers the parties to an ADR mechanism such as mediation, reconciliation, or arbitration to have the matter determined so as to avoid litigation. The practice was, however, found to be unsuitable for the handling of most consumer cases involving small claims. This was especially linked to the fact that cases will need to be properly filed before the courts, which procedures may require the technical expertise of lawyers to be able to circumnavigate through the intricacies of pleadings to avoid procedural failures with the attended legal fees for both filing and for the services of the lawyer. The referral of cases to the ADR forums was also found to come with added costs in a form of fees determinable by the ADR practitioners taking into account their degree of experience, the nature of the problem and so on. The prevailing ADR practices were therefore found to be unsuitable for most small claims of consumers in Ghana. The critical question is to what extent can consumer matters benefit from ADR practices in Ghana without cost and complexity acting as a barrier to obtaining justice? As was highlighted previously it is important to resolve this crucial question so as to ensure that consumers are able to benefit from the ADR system of redress in Ghana.[45]

In reviewing the English law, the ADR mechanism for the redress of consumer matters is the resort to the Ombudsmen. This forum is especially regulated under the Alternative Dispute Resolution for Consumer Disputes Regulations 2015.[46] The 2015 ADR Regulations mainly implemented the EU ADR Directive for the resolution of consumer disputes[47] and places emphasis on the need to establish and certify

[45] For details see, Chap. 4, para 4.3.1.

[46] Regulations 2015 S.I. 2015/542.

[47] Council Directive 2013/11/EU of the European Parliament and of the Council of 21 May 2013 on Alternative Dispute Resolution for Consumer Disputes and amending Regulation (EC) No 2006/2004 and Directive 2009/22/EC.

ADR Schemes in the UK.[48] It is however important to note that before the 2015 ADR Regulations, some trade associations had put in place ADR schemes for the purposes of resolving consumer disputes with their members.[49] This is especially where the trader's use of its internal redress mechanism failed to afford satisfactory resolution of the consumer issue.[50]

The pre-2015 self-regulatory ADR schemes have been enhanced by the 2015 Regulations requiring them to be registered while new ones are established in sectors where there are none. The Chartered Trading Standard Institute is the competent authority that audits and approves ADR Bodies in accordance with the 2015 ADR Regulations.[51] Although it is not mandatory for businesses to participate in the Association's ADR schemes, they are nevertheless under an obligation to inform consumers of their rights to ADR services and possibly show the available schemes within the business industry which a consumer could rely on.[52]

The ADR redress mechanisms may take the form of mediation or adjudication.[53] Whilst the dispute may also be resolved through arbitration where this was part of the contract, the CRA 2015 amendment to the Arbitration Act 1996 prohibits such clauses in consumer contracts as unfair terms where the amount does not exceed £5000.[54] It has, therefore, been submitted that clauses in consumer contracts for the reference of disputes to arbitration, the amount of which is not in excess of the threshold, will have no outright binding effect on the consumer.[55]

For the purposes of illustration, some of the Ombudsmen ADR schemes notably include among others, the Ombudsman Service,[56] the Financial Ombudsman Service,[57] the Property Ombudsman,[58] and Parliamentary and Health Service Ombudsman.[59] Whilst the primary focus of these ombudsmen are beyond the scope of the present discussion, it suffices to mention that they carry similar functions in their respective sectors for the purpose of resolving conflicts between consumers and their registered members. For instance, the Ombudsman Service operations

---

48 Regulations 4 and 10; See also, Reifa and Willett (2018), p. 673 [685].

49 Bridge (2017) para. 14.249; Twigg-Flesner (2017), p. 128 [130].

50 Twigg-Flesner (2017), p. 128 [130].

51 CTSI, ADR approval, available online at <https://www.tradingstandards.uk/business-hub/adr-approval/adr-approval/>, accessed on 18/08/2025.

52 Alternative Dispute Resolution for Consumer Disputes (Competent Authorities and Information) Regulations 2015 S.I. 2015/542 implementing Directive 2013/11/EU on Alternative Dispute Resolution for Consumer Disputes, Regulation 19.

53 Reifa and Willett (2018), p. 673 [685].; see also, Hodges (2009), p. 151 [156].

54 Section 89–91 of the Arbitration Act 1996 as amended by Part II, Schedule 4 of the Consumer Rights Act, 2015, para. 30–32.

55 Bridge (2017) para. 14.248.

56 https://www.ombudsman-services.org/ accessed on 16/05/2025.

57 Financial Services and Markets Act 2000; See also, the FOS, Our aims and values <https://www.financial-ombudsman.org.uk/about/aims.htm> accessed on 02/04/2025.

58 https://www.tpos.co.uk/ accessed on 16/05/202025.

59 https://www.ombudsman.org.uk/.

embrace telecommunications, energy and other sectors relating to home improvement.[60] The Ombudsman Service mainly affords consumers with free, impartial, and simple to use mechanism for the resolution of consumer disputes.[61] It has been stated that the Ombudsman Service process of dispute resolution is basically 'quick, free, and simple alternative to court action.'[62]

One of the ADR schemes which is worth noting is the Consumer Dispute Resolution Limited (CDRL).[63] The CDRL like the other ADR schemes as noted earlier operate under the authority of the ADR Regulations 2015.[64] The CDRL has six ADR schemes which include a Retail ADR scheme.[65] The Retail ADR provides a forum for the resolution of disputes relating to faulty goods, product description, delivery, pricing, missing parts, customer service, and issues of misrepresentation.[66] The Retail ADR mainly resolves disputes between its registered members and consumers in respect of its core areas of operation. The crucial point that needs highlighting is that the service of the Retail ADR is free for consumers.[67] The decisions of the Retail ADR Scheme are independent and impartial and are binding on traders but not on consumers.[68]

Further guidance could be drawn from Dispute Resolution Limited ('the Ombudsman'). Essentially, 'the Ombudsman' is a non-profit ADR mechanism which activities encapsulate two distinct ombudsmen services. In particular, it runs the Furniture Ombudsman (TFO) and the Dispute Resolution Ombudsman (DRO). The activities of both the TFO and the DRO cover disputes relating to general goods and services in which its members are involved with customers. Both the TFO and the DRO provide reasonable, quick, and impartial out of court settlement of disputes between their registered traders and consumers and can make compensatory awards of up to £10,000 in a given dispute (excluding the cost of the goods or service that brought about the dispute).[69] The TFO and DRO contend that their principal goal is to 'inspire consumer confidence' by upholding independence, openness

---

[60] For details see, https://www.ombudsman-services.org/about-us/how-we-work.

[61] Ombudsman Services, What we do and how it works, available online at https://www.ombudsman-services.org/how-it-works accessed on the 25/12/2018; Dispute Resolution Ombudsman and The Furniture Ombudsman, 'Alternative Dispute Resolution Service: Consumer Guide' <https://www.disputeresolutionombudsman.org/wp-content/themes/responsive-Child/documents/consumer-guide.pdf> [7] accessed on 12/05/2025.

[62] Ombudsman Service Monitor, Good for consumers, good for business, March 2018, [9] available online at https://assets.ctfassets.net/46t2drav2f3e/8ml8D3B7VYogMKmAYOoM2/180a61f498f77a609d973d815bcbfb92/Consumer_action_monitor_report_2018.pdf access on the 26/12/2024.

[63] https://www.cdrl.org.uk/ accessed on 17/05/2025.

[64] Alternative Dispute Resolution for Consumer Disputes (Competent Authorities and Information).

[65] https://www.retailadr.org.uk/ 17/05/2025.

[66] https://www.retailadr.org.uk/about-retailadr/complaints-we-can-deal-with/ 17/05/2025.

[67] https://www.retailadr.org.uk/about-retailadr/complaints-we-can-deal-with/ accessed on 17/05/2019.

[68] https://www.retailadr.org.uk/about-retailadr/after-our-decision/ accessed on 17/05/2025; See also, https://www.retailadr.org.uk/about-retailadr/ accessed on 17/05/2025.

[69] Dispute Resolution Ombudsman and The Furniture Ombudsman (n 60) [7].

and transparency, fairness and accountability in their disputes settlement delivery.[70] To give effect to these underlining principles, the DRO and TFO investigate matters which are put before them by taking into consideration the facts of the dispute, the relevant laws, and the Ombudsman code of practice in arriving at a decision they consider to be fair and reasonable.[71] Both the DRO and TFO may award remedies such as; repair or replacement of the goods, full refund, partial refund, and compensation.[72]

Clearly, the ombudsmen ADR mechanisms largely act as an easy means through which consumers could seek redress in respect of faulty goods. Through the process of resolving the disputes, consumers are given clear explanations of what they need to satisfy before escalating the dispute to the ombudsman for determination.[73] It has been observed that Ombudsmen give consumers effectively clear explanations of the process to help complainants in formulating their claims without requiring legal representation and consequently make their decisions based on the principles of 'impartiality, transparency, effectiveness and fairness.'[74]

It can be seen that the ombudsmen ADR schemes play similar roles mainly to ensure that disputes between their registered members and consumers are amicably resolved without the need for the matter to progress to the courts. This is especially where the consumer is satisfied with the decision. It is clear from the illustrations that the decisions of the ombudsmen are only binding on traders but not on consumers. A consumer in any of the Ombudsmen services is always open to file a case before the court if unsatisfied with the outcome. Reifa and Willet particularly stress that the Ombudsmen ADR schemes are a well-structured free service with impartial decisions primarily based on the parties' recorded evidence with a binding effect on the trader but not on the consumer.[75]

Introducing a similar requirement in Ghana to require trade associations to establish Ombudsman ADR schemes through which arising disputes between their members and consumers could be addressed independently but on the merit of each case will be practically useful to aiding the cause of consumers in Ghana. It is important to note that most traders in Ghana are already constituted into sector associations and unions with district, regional and national leadership. It has been observed that whilst the trade associations operate in the various markets across the country, leaders of the association may often intervene in settling a dispute between their member and a customer in an informal manner.[76] It is worth pointing out that this is not

[70] Dispute Resolution Ombudsman and The Furniture Ombudsman, 'Dispute Resolution Ombudsman Limited Rules of Full Membership' <https://www.thefurnitureombudsman.org/_documents/Rules_of_Membership_mar19.pdf> [1]; see also, Dispute Resolution Ombudsman and The Furniture Ombudsman (n 59) [1].

[71] Dispute Resolution Ombudsman and The Furniture Ombudsman (n 60).

[72] Ibid.

[73] Dispute Resolution Ombudsman and The Furniture Ombudsman (n 60).

[74] Howells and Weatherill (2005), pp. 623–625.; Cortés (2017), p. 3.

[75] Reifa and Willett (2018), p. 673 [684].

[76] Nkansah et al. (2016), p. 305.

a regular practice and may only occur as a spur-of-the-moment event. Nevertheless, requiring the establishment of Ombudsman ADR redress platforms among these trade associations will enhance and better enrich the practical use of the associations of Ombudsmen services when established in resolving disputes between traders and consumers in Ghana.

In particular, giving a legislative force for the establishment of such Ombudsmen ADR services with a further demand for traders to refer consumers who have problems with defects which traders are unable to satisfactorily resolve will help afford consumers with a more affordable redress scheme. An ADR scheme of this kind in Ghana which does not impose extra cost on the consumer who is already battling with the problem of having paid for the faulty goods will be more attractive as an independent forum to fall on for a redress. A similar scheme in Ghana within the various trade sectors with the effect of requiring both the consumer and the trader to furnish the given ADR Ombudsman scheme with clear particulars of their respective claims in writing supported by their respective evidence will help ensure that disputes are dispassionately disposed of without the need to refer the matter to the courts.

The introduction of the Ombudsmen scheme that may only base its decision on the recorded evidence of both parties will eliminate the incidence of bias. It may further be helpful in the case of Ghana to require that before the claims of the trader and the consumer are sent to the neutral third party for adjudication, the names of both parties in the dispute are concealed from the reviewer of the case to further strengthen the complete independence of the decision. This will increase the confidence of consumers and further encourage their patronage of the ADR Ombudsmen services when introduced in Ghana. In conclusion, providing for the introduction of sector voluntary Ombudsmen ADR services will help resolve the present unsuitability of the court-connected ADR schemes.

7.3.2 Statutory Rights and Customary Dispute Settlements

As observed in Chap. 6, customary arbitration is an informal ADR mechanism in which parties voluntarily submit their dispute to a person, usually the traditional ruler of the community, for the purpose of having the matter determined impartially but, on its merit, was found to be a more accessible form of redress scheme that may be helpful in resolving most consumer claims. It was, however, observed that the majority of customary arbitrators are hardly aware of the existence of statutory rules in respect of matters that are placed before them for customary arbitration. Consequently, the extent to which the legislative remedies might offer guidance to the customary arbitrator(s) where necessary in reaching their decision for the good of consumers was left unresolved. Addressing this concern was therefore highlighted to be a crucial step in ensuring that consumers who resort to a customary arbitration scheme are guaranteed of obtaining remedies that may not be far from what they are provided by law in Ghana.

Under the English law, a consumer who refers a dispute to the ombudsman may obtain statutory remedies as they will be taken into account in reaching a decision. The DRO and TFO guidance to consumers particularly states that: '[w]hen administering disputes, we have regard to all of the relevant consumer legislation' and other non-legal factors that are relevant in giving an award which may be repair or replacement, refund or damages compensation.[77] The Ombudsman Services have also stated in their website in addressing a consumer complaint, the evidence submitted by both parties, and the Consumer Rights are weighed carefully against the relevant legislation and expected industry practice in arriving at a decision so as to put things right.[78] Riefa and Willet affirmed that a consumer who is successful in his complaint to the Ombudsman may be offered the traditional statutory remedies of repair, replacement, or refund of his money.[79]

In effect, the requirement for the quality of the goods and the remedies for breach will generally feed into determining the decision the ombudsman may eventually arrive at. It is, however, important to state that whilst ombudsmen take guidance from the available statutes on the subject to ensure that the decision they give is fair and reasonable taking into account all relevant circumstances in the given case, they 'are not necessarily bound by a strict interpretation of the law or precedent.'[80] The critical point is that the available legislation on the subject matter will provide some guidance to ensure that whatever outcome they arrive at is not oblivious of the law on the subject of the dispute.

Whilst the Ombudsman set up under the English law is completely different from the setting of customary arbitration in Ghana as earlier observed, they both offer informal redress in a form of mediation and adjudication of disputes that are laid before them. Some lessons from the Ombudsmen services may therefore be helpful in enhancing the interventions provided under the customary arbitration forum as popularly known in Ghana. In particular, considering the Ombudsmen practices as set out above, it will similarly be more helpful to have consumers being offered redress that are inspired by the statutory remedies although they are referring their dispute to the customary ADR scheme in Ghana. This is particularly important to ensure that the redress that is provided to a consumer who is resorting to the customary ADR obtains a comparable redress where appropriate. The critical question however remains as to how this might be achieved. Addressing this essential issue will be fundamental in ensuring that the legislative remedies are given the needed

[77] Dispute Resolution Ombudsman and The Furniture Ombudsman (n 60) [1].

[78] Ombudsman Services, How we work: How we make decisions, https://www.ombudsman-services.org/about-us/how-we-work accessed on 27/12/2024.

[79] Reifa and Willett (2018), p. 673 [692].

[80] British and Irish Ombudsman Association (BIOA), 'Ombudsman Schemes: Guidance for Departments, (April, 2010), para. 16.

attention (but not necessarily a strict interpretation) in the handling of a consumer disputes under the auspices of customary ADR.

To resolve the above concerns of how customary arbitrators might have appreciation of the requirements of the law in handling consumer disputes when such is referred to them, some lessons may further be drawn from the English law. The first critical point to note is that ombudsmen adjudicators are mostly made to undergo training to appreciate the various laws which generally border on consumers' rights and remedies. Lord Justice Briggs noted that whilst adjudicators are mostly legally unqualified, they are nevertheless 'given considerable training and a general understanding of the relevant law'.[81]

A further glance at the English law shows a varied publicity of the extent to which the law might be applied for the benefit of users of the law which the ombudsmen might also rely on for added guidance. For example, comprehensive Explanatory Notes of the entire provisions of the 2015 CRA and its schedules have been made freely accessible to the public and from which Ombudsmen adjudicators might draw guidance where appropriate in determining matters before them.[82] Moreover, guidance notes on how the law might be applied have equally been provided for businesses,[83] consumers,[84] and enforcers[85] which might as well be relied on by ombudsmen for the purposes of obtaining the relevant guidance in dealing with matters that relate to any particular provision of the CRA. It is important to stress that the overall essence of the respective publications on how the law might work is to ensure that stakeholders or users of the law properly apply the law which will consequently be to the benefit of consumers. Nevertheless, adjudicators and mediators under the sphere of the ombudsmen services may draw guidance regarding the expected requirements of the law from the publicised documents. As already submitted, this is not to give a strict interpretation of the law but only to better appreciate the basis of the contentions of the parties in making a final determination.

Whereas similar publications will be useful in Ghana in providing the needed education for the benefit of the public and from which customary arbitrators might

---

[81] Briggs (2015), para 7.21.

[82] This is available online at http://www.legislation.gov.uk/ukpga/2015/15/notes, accessed on 01/01/2025.

[83] The BIS (September, 2015) Consumer Rights Act: Goods, Guidance for Business, available online at https://www.businesscompanion.info/sites/default/files/CRA-Goods-Guidance-for-Business-Sep-2015.pdf accessed on the 01/01/2025; See also, Business Companion, Trading Standards Law explained: The sale & supply of goods, available online at, https://www.businesscompanion.info/printpdf/en/quick-guides/goods/the-sale-and-supply-of-goods accessed on the 01/01/2025.

[84] Citizens Advice, Examples of using the new consumer laws, available online at https://www.citizensadvice.org.uk/Global/Migrated_Documents/corporate/cra2015-practicalexamples.pdf accessed on the 01/01/2025.

[85] The CMA, Consumer Protection: Enforcement Guidance, (August, 2016), CMA58, available online at https://assets.publishing.service.gov.uk/government/uploads/system/uploads/attachment_data/file/546521/cma58-consumer-protection-enforcement-guidance.pdf, accessed on the 01/01/2025.

as well draw guidance from in dealing with matters, they will nevertheless be of less assistance to the many traditional rulers who have no English literacy, in whose jurisdictions the disputes are mostly referred to for arbitration. To ensure that traditional rulers who mostly act as customary arbitrators have in mind the requirement of the law in handling consumer matters requires that they are provided with some form of education. This could take different forms. First, there may be the need to afford them with formal training workshops on matters relating to consumer issues. Similarly, educational campaigns through electronic media especially radio and television on the principal requirements of the law may as well be very helpful in this direction.

Such educational campaigns may assist not only customary arbitrators in appreciating the law but it may as well afford traders and consumers the opportunity to better come to terms with the requirements of the law. The training workshops and educational campaigns will especially need to be conducted in the local languages of the various parts of the country in order to ensure that the desired result is achieved. The educational campaign could be championed by the proposed Consumer Protection Authority (CPA) and the National Commission for Civic Education (NCCE)[86] as was noted in Chap. 6. In particular, it is already part of the proposed CPP as was mentioned in Chap. 6 for the proposed consumer legislation to confer power upon the NCCE and the proposed CPA the role of affording the public with the needed consumer education when given legislative approval. It will therefore be more helpful to extend this educational mandate to include affording traditional rulers with formal training workshops as indicated above to help guide them in determining disputes relative to consumer matters.

In sum, affording customary arbitrators or adjudicators with capacity building training workshops will be helpful in empowering customary arbitrators in making determinations that may draw from the statutory remedies. Moreover, complementing the training with electronic (television and radio) campaigns about relevant consumer laws under the aegis of the proposed CPA and NCCE will be helpful in empowering customary arbitrators in respect of the law on consumer matters. This will have the effect of ensuring that when they are handling matters that are placed before them, they are able to draw guidance from the remedies for consumers under the proposed consumer law when implemented.

7.4 Resolving the Issue of Consumer Education and Awareness

In Chap. 6 as briefly mentioned earlier, it was highlighted that the adopted Consumer Protection Policy (CPP) 2014 requires the establishment of a Consumer Protection Authority (CPA) when eventually translated into law. The intended function of the

[86] Ministry of Trade and Industry (2014).

CPA when established was stated to include implementing policies and programmes for the benefit of consumers and traders. It was also found that the CPP envisages the legislation to be enacted to empower the National Commission for Civic Education (NCCE) to engage in public education and consumer awareness creation drives. It was however uncertain as to whether the educational function of the CPA/NCCE will cover individual tailored needs when the need arises. It was therefore argued that resolving this uncertainty is critical to ensure that the specific needs of consumers were met to better assist them to defend their rights when these rights are breached by traders.[87]

In a review of the English law, many consumer organisations may offer advice to consumers especially including the Citizens Advice Bureau, Which?, Law Centres and the Trading Standards Department.[88] The various consumer organisations largely provide 'free information, education, advice, campaigning in relation to law reform, research into law and policy' on current and future challenges.[89] Specifically, the Citizens Advice Bureau is the principal unit broadly responsible for providing individual consumers with personalised advice on matters that directly affect them.[90] *Benjamin's Sale of Goods* particularly stresses that Citizen Advice 'provide advice to individuals on consumer issues affecting them.'[91] The same can be said of the Law Centres in the various Law Schools in most of the Universities in the UK.[92]

It can be seen from the English law that consumers may be able to obtain legal advice regarding a matter of dispute regarding faulty goods. The advice has the tendency of empowering the individual consumer to be better able to assert his rights when confronted with faulty goods. A similar mechanism in Ghana that will offer free legal advice to consumers with individual tailored needs or problems will be helpful. In particular, such advice will better assist the consumer to take calculated decisions based on informed understanding of the requirements of the law and his potential chance of success or otherwise if he intends escalating the matter for redress.

Affording the consumer with such advice is especially important if he reaches a deadlock with the trader on the matter. This is particularly critical to better enhance consumer confidence in taking a decision to resort to either the ombudsman or the customary arbitration forum with leave to make a claim before the small claims track of the District Court if the proposals made before and in this book materialise. It will therefore be vital for the formulation of the actual consumer legislation to be clarified further so that the education and awareness envisaged extend to cover the provision of individual tailored advice when the needs arise. The clarification will ensure that when the law is eventually enacted, and the CPA is established alongside

[87] For details, see, para. 4.4.

[88] Bridge (2017), para. 14.249, p879; Reifa and Willett (2018), p. 673 [687–688].

[89] Reifa and Willett (2018), pp. 673–695, p. 688.

[90] For details see, https://www.gov.uk/citizens-advice-consumer-service accessed 02/01/2025.

[91] Bridge (2017) para. 14.249.

[92] For details see, http://www.lawcentres.org.uk, accessed on 02/01/2025.

the NCCE, consumers can be guaranteed of receiving reliable advice on the position of the law and on the claims they may be able to seek. The legislation should also encourage Law Faculties of the various Universities in Ghana to offer voluntary personalised legal advice to consumers with issues of their transactions. This will consequently boost the confidence level of consumers in seeking redress.

7.5 Conclusion

This chapter was meant to assist in resolving the various concerns about the mechanisms for the enforcement of consumer remedies for faulty goods in Ghana. The analysis was especially carried out drawing from the experiences of the English law in response to central research question regarding whether the shortfalls of the redress mechanisms in Ghana can be resolved taking lessons from the enforcement mechanisms of consumer remedies under the English law but viewed within the context of the domestic situation. This was especially noted to be critical to ensure that the existing remedies and the proposed amendments in this book are not just left on paper but capable of being enforced for the benefit of consumers who are supplied with faulty goods in breach of the required quality requirements under the laws in Ghana. The analysis showed that the English law mechanisms for the enforcement of consumer remedies for faulty goods hold a lot of promise in being able to effectively assist in resolving the concerns of the redress system in Ghana, but with some modifications to take account of the prevailing domestic circumstances.

The various lessons Ghana may learn from the English law particularly include the following: In the first place, the various measures under the English law that mitigate the cost of litigation for consumers will similarly be useful in encouraging consumers to seek redress when they are supplied with faulty goods for the present purpose. In particular, the authority afforded to the courts under the English law to rely on filed or recorded evidence in consumer disputes to give judgment where the matter in dispute is *prima facie* obvious will be helpful in mitigating the cost of litigation for consumers in Ghana. Another legislative measure that could cut down the cost of litigation to consumers in Ghana is the English law MCOL. Replicating a similar measure as shown in the analysis will eliminate the cost of travel, the cost of engaging the services of a lawyer and the unofficial payments to court officials which all culminate in discouraging consumers from seeking redress. The analysis further noted the consistency of the requirement for the claimant to pay a court filing fee prior to the determination of the matter but advocated for the payment modification in the introductions of the MCOL in Ghana. In particular, the analysis suggested that the requirement for the payment of the court filing fees for MCOL in respect of small claims should be modified to require the deferment of the average consumer payment of the filing fee to when the claim is successful. The analysis argued that this was necessary to help in boosting the confidence of the average consumer who cannot actually afford the legal cost, and those who are afraid of legal cost, and as a result, are deterred from contemplating legal actions.

Also, the power given to the English small claims track of the County Court to award remedies to the consumer claimant as the court thinks fit which the consumer did not contemplate will similarly be useful for consumers in Ghana. This will especially help in minimising the effect of the concern that a consumer without legal representation may be affected adversely. A similar benefit may also be made available to consumers if the English law allowance to the small claims track of the County Court to reject terms they found unfair even where the consumer did not raise in his claim as shown in the analysis is replicated in Ghana. Both the power to declare terms as unfair, and to award remedies the court thinks fit to the consumer will jointly address the issue regarding the court being restricted to the requested remedies of the consumer in his statement of particulars, which a lay consumer without legal representation may not properly state with the likely adverse effect of being deprived the remedies he would be entitled.

As further seen in the analysis, the ombudsmen services provided under the English law which offer a free, impartial, and speedy redress scheme for consumer disputes will equally be viable in affording redress to consumers in Ghana if the scheme is replicated in Ghana. This will particularly address the concern of the limited assistance presently associated with the court-connected ADR scheme in Ghana. In addition, the wide range of publications regarding the extent to which the law might be applied for the guidance of businesses, consumers and enforcers, which ombudsmen could rely on in appreciating the dispute between thc consumer and the trader are an important useful guidance for Ghana. However, in order to ensure that stakeholders such as customary arbitrators draw similar benefits from publications of a sort in Ghana will require that this is further modified to suit the circumstances in Ghana. In particular, many of the customary arbitrators to whom matters of consumer disputes may be referred have no English language literacy skills to be able to appreciate such publications. It will therefore be appropriate to ensure that this is modified to reflect the needs of the majority of customary arbitrators in Ghana. In the light of this, training workshops in the local dialects may therefore be helpful to ensure that customary arbitrators appreciate the requirements of the law. This may further be complemented with educational campaigns using the radio and television channels to highlight the principal requirements where faulty goods are supplied to a buyer. This will help address the question as to whether customary arbitrators have any idea of the requirements of the law for the purpose of guidance in deciding on the matters that are placed before them.

Moreover, the opportunity for consumers with problems regarding faulty goods to obtain free legal advice as it exists under the English law will similarly be very useful if replicated in Ghana. It will therefore be appropriate for the education and awareness proposed in the Consumer Protection Policy 2014, when translated into law, to cover the provision of advice to consumers. This will be important to give effect to consumers obtaining personalised advice when the proposal eventually receives legislative effect to become a law.

Clearly, adopting the above measures in Ghana will help provide consumers with a more dependable system of redress. This will prevent the possibility of the existing remedies and the proposals for reforms in this book remaining as 'tiger' on the statute books but without being applied for the benefit of consumers in Ghana. The next Chapter provides a conclusion to this entire book. It comprises a summary, findings, and recommendations for legislative and judicial actions and for future research.

References

Atuguba RA (2017) Reform of Civil Litigation in Ghana. Annual Conference of the Ghana Bar Association

Bridge MG (2017) Benjamin's sale of goods, 10th edn. Sweet & Maxwell

British and Irish Ombudsman Association (BIOA) (2010) Ombudsman Schemes: Guidance for Departments, para. 16

Business Companion, Trading Standards Law explained: The sale & supply of goods, Available online at, https://www.businesscompanion.info/printpdf/en/quick-guides/goods/the-sale-and-supply-of-goods. Accessed on the 1 Jan 2025.

Citizens Advice, Examples of using the new consumer laws, available online at https://www.citizensadvice.org.uk/Global/Migrated_Documents/corporate/cra2015-practicalexamples.pdf. Accessed on the 1 Jan 2025

Cortés P (2017) The law of consumer redress in an evolving digital market: upgrading from alternative to online dispute resolution. Cambridge University Press, p 3

Council Directive 2013/11/EU of the European Parliament and of the Council of 21 May 2013 on Alternative Dispute Resolution for Consumer Disputes and amending Regulation (EC) No 2006/2004 and Directive 2009/22/EC

CTSI, ADR approval, available online at <https://www.tradingstandards.uk/business-hub/adr-approval/adr-approval/>, Accessed 18 Aug 2025

Dispute Resolution Ombudsman and The Furniture Ombudsman., Alternative Dispute Resolution Service: Consumer Guide. <https://www.disputeresolutionombudsman.org/wp-content/themes/responsive-Child/documents/consumer-guide.pdf> [7] Accessed 12 May 2025

Dispute Resolution Ombudsman and The Furniture Ombudsman., Dispute Resolution Ombudsman Limited Rules of Full Membership. <https://www.thefurnitureombudsman.org/_documents/Rules_of_Membership_mar19.pdf>

Explanatory Notes to the Consumer Rights Act 2015

FOS, Our aims and values <https://www.financial-ombudsman.org.uk/about/aims.htm> Accessed 2 Apr 2025

Ghana Judiciary (2023) Practice Direction on Virtual Court Sessions, Practice Direction PD/CC/RCH/01/2023

Ghana Judiciary (undated) Links for Virtual Court Sittings, available online at https://judicial.gov.gh/index.php/virtualcourt Accessed on 05/03/2025.Alternative Dispute Resolution for Consumer Disputes (Competent Authorities and Information) Regulations 2015 S.I. 2015/542 implementing Directive 2013/11/EU on Alternative Dispute Resolution for Consumer Disputes

Hodges C (2009) Developing approaches to public and private enforcement in England and wales. In: Cafaggi F, Micklitz H-W (eds) New frontiers of consumer protection—the interplay between private and public enforcement. Intersentia, pp 151 [156]

Howells G (2009) Collective consumer redress reform - will it be a paper tiger? In: Cafaggi F, Micklitz H-W (eds) New frontiers of consumer protection—The interplay between private and public enforcement. Intersentia, p 329

Howells G, Weatherill S (2005) Consumer protection law, 2nd edn. Ashgate, p. 616
http://www.lawcentres.org.uk, accessed on 02 Jan 2025
http://www.legislation.gov.uk/ukpga/2015/15/notes, accessed on 01 Jan 2025
https://www.cdrl.org.uk/ accessed on 17 May 2025
https://www.gov.uk/citizens-advice-consumer-service accessed 02 Jan 2025
https://www.gov.uk/make-court-claim-for-money/court-fees accessed on 13 May 2025
https://www.ombudsman.org.uk/
https://www.ombudsman-services.org/about-us/how-we-work
https://www.retailadr.org.uk/ 17 May 2025
https://www.retailadr.org.uk/about-retailadr/ accessed on 17 May 2025
https://www.retailadr.org.uk/about-retailadr/after-our-decision/ accessed on 17 May 2025
https://www.retailadr.org.uk/about-retailadr/complaints-we-can-deal-with/ accessed on 17 May 2025
https://www.tpos.co.uk/ accessed on 16 May 2025
Kingham PR (n.d.) The Consumer Rights Act 2015: A Summary Of Key Changes. <https://goughsq.co.uk/wp-content/uploads/2015/04/Consumer-Rights-Act-2015-Summary.pdf> Accessed 12 Mar 2025
Lord Justice Briggs (2015) Civil Courts Structure Review: Interim Report. <https://www.judiciary.uk/wp-content/uploads/2016/01/ccsr-interim-report-dec-15-final1.pdf> Accessed 19 Mar 2025
Lord Justice Briggs (2016) Civil Courts Structure Review: Final Report available online at <https://www.judiciary.gov.uk/wp-content/uploads/2016/07/civil-courts-structure-review-final-report-jul-16-final-1.pdf> Accessed 19 Mar 2025
Ministry of Trade and Industry (2014) Draft Consumer Protection Policy. GOG
Nkansah et al (2016) Dispute resolution and consumer protection in Ghana. In: Oppong RF, Agyebeng K (eds) A commitment to law, development and public policy: a Festschrift in Honour of Nana Dr. Samuel Kwadwo Boaten Asante. Wildy Simmonds and Hill Publishing, p 305
Ombudsman Service Monitor, Good for consumers, good for business, March 2018, [9] available online at https://assets.ctfassets.net/46t2drav2f3e/8ml8D3B7VYogMKmAYOoM2/180a61f498f77a609d973d815bcbfb92/Consumer_action_monitor_report_2018.pdf. Accessed 26 Dec 2025
Ombudsman Services, How we work: How we make decisions, https://www.ombudsman-services.org/about-us/how-we-work. Accessed 27 Mar 2025
Ombudsman Services, https://www.ombudsman-services.org/ Accessed on 16 May 2025
Riefa C, Willett C (2018) Enforcement and effectiveness of consumer law in the UK. In Micklitz H-W, Saumier G (eds) Enforcement and effectiveness of consumer law. Springer International Publishing AG, p 673
Templars (2024) Dispute Resolution Digest available online at https://www.templars-law.com/app/uploads/2024/09/Dispute-Digest-Transcript-SEPT-24.pdf. Accessed 5 Mar 2025
The BIS (2015) Consumer Rights Act: Goods, Guidance for Business. Available online at https://www.businesscompanion.info/sites/default/files/CRA-Goods-Guidance-for-Business-Sep-2015.pdf. Accessed 1 Jan 2025
The CMA (August 2016) Consumer Protection: Enforcement Guidance, CMA58. Available online at https://assets.publishing.service.gov.uk/government/uploads/system/uploads/attachment_data/file/546521/cma58-consumer-protection-enforcement-guidance.pdf, Accessed 1 Jan 2025
Twigg-Flesner C (2017) Consumer sales law in the United Kingdom. In: Howells G et al. (eds) Comparative consumer sales law. Routledge, p. 128

Chapter 8
The Law on Faulty Goods, Consumer Remedies and Redress Mechanisms: Conclusions and Reform Proposals

8.1 Introduction

The object of this book was to ascertain the degree of protection available to consumers with respect to the requirements for the quality obligations of traders of goods, the remedies for consumers, and the mechanisms for the redress of consumer disputes in Ghana. The aim was to contribute towards addressing the potential deficiencies of the law in Ghana to ensure that consumers are afforded the needed protection when sold faulty goods. The book was explicitly grounded on the uncertainties about the quality of the growing technologically inspired range of goods alongside the widespread substandard goods in the market with the increasing potential of sellers supplying faulty goods to consumers.

uncertainties with technologically oriented goods The conduct of this book was found necessary on account of consumers' reluctance or unwillingness to seek redress when they are supplied with faulty goods and the fact that there are suggestions of the market being flooded with substandard goods meant to be sold to unsuspecting consumers. The book was, therefore, designed to address the following fundamental questions.

1. To what extent can the current requirements for the quality obligations of traders of goods afford consumers a sufficient degree of protection with respect to faulty goods in Ghana?
2. To what extent can English law and its EU experiences with respect to the requirements for the quality obligations of traders of goods assist in resolving any identified deficiencies in the law in Ghana within the domestic context?
3. Does the present law in Ghana provide sufficient remedies for consumers when they are supplied with faulty goods?

N. Yidana, *Consumer Law and Policy on Faulty Goods*, Ius Gentium: Comparative Perspectives on Law and Justice 134,
https://doi.org/10.1007/978-3-032-08700-3_8

4. Will the remedies for faulty goods under English law and its EU experience be useful in contributing towards resolving limitations of the law in Ghana, taking the local circumstances into account?
5. Are the prevailing mechanisms for the redress of disputes adequate and suitable for the enforcement of consumer rights in Ghana?
6. To what extent can the mechanisms for the settlement of consumer disputes under English law be helpful in addressing shortfalls of the means of redress in Ghana, taking into account the domestic circumstances?

8.2 Contribution of the Book

In addressing the above research questions, this book makes important original contributions by adding new insight to the growing body of literature on the field of consumer law in Ghana and beyond. As revealed in the analysis, the book brought to light the inherent deficiencies of the existing law in Ghana and proffered possible solutions that could enhance the frontiers of the law in Ghana for effective consumer protection.

This was done by first appraising the adequacy of the law in Ghana regarding the requirements for the quality obligations of traders, remedies for consumers, and mechanisms for the resolution of consumer disputes in Chaps. 2, 4 and 6 respectively. The identified deficiencies of the requirements for the quality obligations of traders, remedies for consumers and mechanisms for the redress of consumer disputes in Ghana were then subjected to a comparative discourse in the light of the English law and its EU experience in Chaps. 3, 5 and 7, respectively. The analysis was conducted taking into consideration the domestic circumstances in Ghana. Set out below is a summary of the findings in the various Chapters of this book.

8.2.1 Summary of the Quality Obligations of Traders and Proposal for Reform from the Comparative Analysis

Setting out to address the above research questions, the book began with a review of the law in Ghana, which spanned three Chapters (2, 4, and 6). The analysis commenced in Chap. 2 to address the primary key question regarding whether the requirements for the quality of goods obligations on traders were adequate to afford a sufficient degree of protection to consumers when they are supplied with faulty goods. The analysis identified a number of deficiencies that leave the law in a deficient state to afford adequate protection to consumers in matters of disputes over faulty goods in Ghana. In particular, the standard requirement as regards the quality obligations on traders of goods was identified as either where the goods are 'free from defects' or are of 'merchantable quality' depending on whether they are purchased under a contract of sale or hire-purchase, respectively. The operation of the different standard terms for the quality of goods was found not to be helpful to the average consumer who might get confused as to what to expect in the goods. The standards for the quality of goods were further found to lack definitions in terms of what they are meant to be in assessing the quality of goods in Ghana. It was similarly observed that the scope of assessing the quality of goods was confined to where the goods are free from latent defects—regarding the standard of the goods being free from defects, or where the goods are of a usable quality in respect of the merchantable quality standard of the goods. This was noted to create doubts as to whether the expectation consumers generally have about the quality of goods, such as the goods being safe, durable, and free from minor defects, among others, will be read into testing the quality of goods. This stated doubt was premised on the absence of their express clarification under the regime in Ghana.

It was further revealed that the requirements for traders to supply goods that fit the particular purpose of the consumer's declared idiosyncratic needs had not been addressed under the regime. The issue of how the law will apply where the consumer bought the goods for their multi-purpose functions was not addressed under the regime. Similarly, the issue of whether the fitness regime extends to cover where the consumer bought the goods on account of the seller's claims about the goods' fitness was found to be unclear. In addition, it was discovered that the quality obligations of traders do not cover a one-off transaction and thereby limit the protection for consumers. It was also found that whilst traders may be able to exclude their quality obligations by introducing exemption clauses, the regime lacks legislative control of unfair contract terms.

The identified deficiencies of the quality obligations of traders of goods in Ghana were examined in the light of the English law in Chap. 3 whilst taking into account the circumstances in the domestic setting in Ghana. The analysis found that the English regime offers very useful initiatives that are suitable for addressing the deficiencies of the regime in Ghana, subject to some modifications to contextually reflect the domestic problems in Ghana. On the issue of the different standard terms for the quality of goods, the analysis found that the term requiring the goods to be free from defects could be adopted as the main standard term for the quality requirements of goods traders sell to consumers in Ghana. Regarding the lack of a definition of the standard term for the quality of goods, it was discovered that the approach of English law's basic definition of satisfactory quality could similarly help resolve the limitations of the law in Ghana. In particular, it was established that the requirement under English law for the goods to satisfy the standard of a reasonable person taking into account the description of the goods, their price (if relevant) and other relevant surrounding circumstances, will similarly be helpful to resolving the lack of a definition for the standard of quality in Ghana, if adopted.

On the primary scope of quality assessment, it was found that latent defects, being the only criterion, will need to be expanded to include what have been termed as aspects of quality under English law. It was similarly found that the aspects of quality under the English law did not expressly include technical standard requirements. In the case of Ghana, it was shown that the quality criterion would be more helpful to consumers if the express quality factors were extended to cover technical regulatory standards in view of the heightened degree of substandard goods in the markets in Ghana. The modifications are necessary to give effect to tailored solutions to the problem with goods in the Ghanaian markets. So, in effect, the primary scope of quality in Ghana should reflect the goods being free from latent defects, free from minor defects, fit for all their common purposes, safe, durable, and conform to technical regulatory standards.

Moreover, it was discovered that the aspects of quality under the English law do not have automatic application to the test of quality of the goods but that any of the factors will only apply if the said factor is relevant in the particular case. In the case of Ghana, it was found that the approach of the English law on the application of the aspects of quality will need to be modified to meet the expectations of consumers in Ghana. It was particularly highlighted that consumers in Ghana will be better protected if free from defects or non-defective standard of quality of goods is expressed to connote that when the goods are supplied as new goods, they satisfy the various aspects of quality criterion. It was nevertheless noted that the application of the aspects of quality may be made to vary where the goods are bought as second-hand goods.

Chapter 3 also addressed the issue of the trader's obligation regarding the fitness of the goods for the idiosyncratic needs of the consumer. It was observed that traders should be required to deliver goods which are fit for the particular purpose of the consumer, whether or not that is the usual purpose of the goods along the lines of English law. It was however, noted that the clarification of traders' obligations to supply goods which are fit for the idiosyncratic needs of consumers should be subject to where the consumer had expressly or by implication made the particular purpose of buying the goods known to the trader. It was also found that the regime will be better enhanced for the protection of consumers if the quality obligations of traders expressly embraced claims of traders in respect of the particular purpose of the goods. This was found necessary to ensure that consumers are able to hold traders accountable when they relied on claims advanced by traders in respect of the particular purpose of the goods in making a purchase.

On the issue of the exclusion of one-off sales of an item from the quality obligations of traders, it was found that incorporating one-off transactions into the quality obligations of traders was useful to ensure consumers are given the needed protection when they buy the trader's used assets or second-hand goods. It was also revealed that statutory regulation of unfair contract terms was crucial to ensure that traders do not unfairly exclude their quality obligations in respect of goods they sell to consumers in Ghana. This was found necessary to ensure that the unbridled use of exclusionary statements by traders in Ghana are controlled and rendered incapable of depriving a consumer of the right to be supplied with the right quality of goods.

The adoption of the various highlighted measures, as argued in the analysis, has the potential of helping to resolve the uncertainties and limitations that were identified in Chap. 2 of this book with respect to the quality obligations of traders in Ghana. The introduction of the reforms, as indicated in the discussion, also has the prospective incentive of simplifying the quality obligations of traders of goods in Ghana to better serve the needs of consumers.

8.2.2 Summary of the Remedies for Faulty Goods and Proposal for Reform from the Comparative Analysis

Chapter 4 of this book analysed the adequacy of the remedies under the law in Ghana for consumers when they are supplied with faulty goods. The analysis discovered that the existing remedies are not adequate to provide consumers with the needed redress due to a range of uncertainties and limitations of the law. It was revealed that consumers may only be able to reject faulty goods or keep the goods and claim damages. It was found that the right to reject faulty goods under the law could only apply where the defects of the goods were not trivial but rather amounted to a breach of a condition of the contract. The analysis also discovered that there are no alternative remedies for consumers who reject faulty goods except to terminate the contract. This was found to be unsatisfactory when a consumer rejected faulty goods but wished to keep the contract alive if alternative remedies, such as repair or replacement with identical goods, could be provided. These were, however, found not to exist under the regime. It was also revealed that defects which are seen not to be in breach of a condition of the contract may also lead to the consumer obtaining damages, which may be unsatisfactory. The inadequacies of the remedies offered under the regime in Ghana were therefore found to need addressing in order to ensure that consumers are afforded the needed protection when they buy faulty goods in Ghana.

Chapter 5 proceeded to comparatively analyse the identified deficiencies of the remedies for consumers in Ghana through the lens of English law and its EU experience. The involvement of the EU law in the analysis was particularly confined to the laws of the EU that the UK implemented. Moreover, for pieces of EU-originated law in respect of which there are no UK case authorities, references were made to the decisions of the CJEU for guidance. It was revealed from the discourse that whilst the remedies under the English law and its EU experience provide useful guidance in fashioning out solutions to the concerns in Ghana, some aspects of the remedies, however, need to be modified to reflect the tailored circumstances in the domestic setting in Ghana. In particular, it was revealed that the law should clarify that the right to reject faulty goods includes minor defects in the goods except for defects which are so trivial to the extent of being *de minimis*. Unlike the English law, where rejecting goods with minor defects is subjected to the defects being a relevant factor, it was noted that the regime in Ghana will be simplified further if it is clarified that the right to reject goods with minor defects can be exercised where the goods are new goods. It was, however, noted further that where the goods are sold as second-hand goods, the application of the quality criterion could be subjected to the relevance of any of the factors as pertains under the English law.

Regarding the uncertainty of the time limit within which a consumer can reject faulty goods in Ghana, it was succinctly confirmed that the short-term period of thirty (30) days within which a consumer can reject faulty goods under the English law will similarly be suitable in resolving this uncertainty in Ghana if adopted. It was similarly found that the adoption of the 30-day short-term right of rejection will further ensure that consumers are afforded ample time to examine the quality conformity of the goods. This will, therefore, resolve the issue of the consumer losing the right to reject faulty goods when s/he is purported to have intimated acceptance without regard to whether or not he had examined the goods. In addition, it was noted that the final right to reject faulty goods under the English law, which retains the consumer right to reject the goods after the lapse of the 30-day short-term right, will similarly be helpful to consumers in Ghana if adopted. This was found to be necessary if the remedies of repair or replacement, as proposed in this book, failed to resolve the faults of the goods. It was further noted that the final right to reject faulty goods should similarly be subjected to the reduction of the amount to be refunded to be commensurate with the consumer use of the good if the rejection is exercised after six months as similarly provided under English law.

Moreover, it was discovered that the limited scheme of remedies for consumers in Ghana could be resolved if the remedies of repair and replacement under the English law were similarly introduced into the regime in Ghana. In considering introducing the remedies of repair and replacement to broaden the scope of consumer remedies in Ghana, it was found that effective integration of these remedies with the existing remedies of rejection and termination was crucial. In the light of this, it was noted that the regime will be more helpful if it is clarified that following the rejection of faulty goods, consumers are open to opt for termination of the contract or repair or replacement of the goods so as to ensure that an effective integration is achieved between the remedies of repair and replacement with the existing remedy of rejection and termination in Ghana as was shown in the analysis.

The analysis also demonstrated that the English law remedy of price reduction, which consumers could seek if repair or replacement is impossible, will similarly be useful to consumers in Ghana if given legislative approval. Another alternative remedy where repair or replacement was not possible was also found to be a replacement of the goods with close substitute goods. Although this was not an available remedy under English law, it was found to be an appropriate remedy which could benefit consumers in Ghana in view of the heavy dependence of Ghana on imports and the fact that it could take several months to get imported goods sold in the country replaced with the same kind of goods when they run out of stock.

8.2.3 Summary of the Mechanisms for the Resolution of Consumer Disputes and Proposal for Reform from the Comparative Analysis

Chapter 6 examined the mechanisms for the settlement of consumer disputes in Ghana. The analysis revealed that court proceedings, which provide a formal system of redress even in the lowest courts in Ghana, can be complex and unhealthy for the pursuit of consumer claims without the services of lawyers. The analysis also found the existence of proposals for the introduction of small claims courts to afford consumers informal hearing proceedings as a welcome recommendation. It was, however, realised that the proposal requiring the designated staff of the small claims court, when given effect, to only proceed to trial hearing after holding a pre-trial settlement negotiation and mediation with the parties could lead to role conflict and undermine the rules of natural justice.

The analysis also ascertained that the issue of the power of the courts to award remedies being limited to what the claimant states in his statement of particulars was not addressed in the proposed small claims court, which envisaged that consumers should be able to seek redress in person without the aid of lawyers. It was further found that the monetary jurisdiction of the District Court, which is the lowest court in Ghana, was inadequate to cover most consumer claims to enable consumers to benefit from the proposed informal rules, which this book supports.

In examining the means of redress, it was equally revealed that the court-connected ADR practice was not suitable for the handling of most consumer small claims. It was similarly found that the extent to which customary arbitrators may draw guidance from the relevant consumer laws to better inform their handling of disputes that are presented before them has not been addressed. In addition, the analysis revealed that whilst the Draft Consumer Protection Policy 2014 talked about consumer education and awareness, it was unclear as to whether there would be an opportunity for individual consumer advice when the need arose. Addressing the shortcomings of both the means of consumer redress currently in existence and the proposed reforms were therefore argued to be necessary to ensure that consumers are afforded a more enhanced system of redress.

As summarised above, the overall diagnosis of the state of the requirements for the quality obligations of traders, remedies for consumers, and means of enforcement of consumer remedies presently under the regime in Ghana are beset with a number of uncertainties and limitations which need to be resolved in order to ensure that consumers are better protected in Ghana. The above findings of the state of the regime in Ghana were further analysed through the lens of English law, taking into consideration the domestic situation in Ghana. The results are summarised below.

The concerns raised regarding the mechanisms for the resolution of consumer disputes were subsequently analysed in Chap. 7 of this book, drawing upon the experiences of English law. The discovery made from the analysis was that English law holds many promising mechanisms, but a number of modifications are necessary to take account of the prevailing peculiar domestic circumstances in Ghana.

First, it was found that the authority of the courts under English law to rely on filed or recorded evidence in consumer disputes to give judgment where the matter in dispute is prima facie plain and obvious will equally be helpful in mitigating the cost of litigation for consumers in Ghana. It was equally revealed that the practice of MCOL under the English law will equally be useful in cutting down on the cost of litigation for consumers in Ghana if adopted. In particular, the analysis found that the MCOL will eliminate the cost of travel, the cost of engaging the services of a lawyer and the unofficial payments to court officials which all culminate in increasing the litigation cost, which discourages consumers from seeking redress. It was, however, noted that whilst the requirement for the filing fee to be paid in a MCOL before the case can be processed is consistent with the current practice in Ghana, this will nevertheless need to be modified in introducing the MCOL in Ghana. It was particularly argued that the average Ghanaian consumer should be permitted to file small claims for free and only pay when his/her claim is successful. This was noted to be consistent with the practice in the Ghanaian society where a person will often pay something as a way of saying thank you, to a person who plays a helpful role in resolving his/her problem. This was further noted to be necessary to help in boosting the confidence of the average consumer who cannot actually afford the legal cost, and those who are afraid of legal cost, and as a result, are deterred from contemplating legal actions.

The discourse also revealed that the power accorded to the small claims track under the English law to award remedies the court thinks fit to the consumer, and to strike out unfair terms it thinks fit even if not raised by the consumer are similarly crucial in Ghana. This was found to be necessary in order to address the issue regarding the court being restricted to give its decision based on what the claimant prayed for in his statement of particulars which a lay consumer without legal representation may not properly state with the likely adverse effect of being deprived of the remedies to which he would be entitled.

Regarding the issue of the monetary jurisdiction of Ghc20,000.00 (about £3000) in the District Court, which will not be able cover many essential consumer goods, it was found to be appropriate for the monetary limit to be reviewed upwards so as to expand the jurisdiction of the District Court to enable it to entertain more consumer related matters.

The analysis further discovered that the ombudsmen services provided under the English law which offer free, impartial and speedy redress scheme for consumer disputes will equally be viable in affording redress to consumers in Ghana if replicated in the country. This will particularly address the concern of the limited assistance presently associated with the court-connected ADR scheme in Ghana.

It was also found that there was a need for the customary arbitrators, who are mostly the traditional rulers in most communities in Ghana, to be given capacity-building training in the various local dialects, as most of them are not literate in the English language. The training was found crucial to ensure that they have an idea about the laws so as to better position them to contribute to resolving disputes between consumers and traders within their communities. It was also highlighted that the training should be complemented with radio and television campaigns on the rights of consumers to keep arbitrators, consumers, and traders up-to-date with the requirements of the law on consumer matters.

The issue of consumer education and awareness creation was also discussed. It was revealed that the practice where individual consumers can seek free legal advice under the English regime will similarly be helpful in empowering consumers in Ghana if replicated in Ghana. It was therefore highlighted that the education and awareness proposed in the Consumer Protection Policy 2014 should give effect to consumer access to personalised advice when the proposal eventually receives legislative effect to become a law.

In sum, the overall comparative analysis revealed that whilst English law has important initiatives that might be useful in remedying the deficiencies of the law in Ghana, some modifications are necessary to effectively tailor the solutions to the domestic circumstances of Ghanaian consumers. The book specifically pointed out the reforms needed to the English law solutions that may be necessary to help ensure that the required protection is devised for more enhanced protection of consumers in Ghana.

8.3 Conclusion

As highlighted above, this book was carried out with the object of identifying and resolving deficiencies in the requirements for the quality obligations of traders, remedies for consumers and means of seeking redress for government action in affording consumers with the needed protection in respect of faulty goods in Ghana. In the light of these, this book confirmed that there are a number of deficiencies in the requirements for the quality obligations of traders, remedies for consumers and means of enforcement of consumer remedies in Ghana. This book further argued that the deficiencies which presently confront the regime will need to be resolved in order to afford the required protection to consumers in Ghana when they are sold faulty goods.

The book was also to ascertain the extent to which English law as influenced by EU law could be useful in resolving the defects of the law in Ghana taking into consideration the domestic circumstances in Ghana. The analysis revealed that while the English law and its continental EU experience offers very useful initiatives that are suitable to addressing many of the problems of consumers in Ghana, some modifications are needed to contextually tailor the solutions appropriately to the domestic problems of consumers in Ghana. Overall, this book has made recommendations regarding the extent to which the deficiencies could be addressed to ensure that the tailored needs of consumers in the local context in Ghana are properly met.

8.4 Significance of the Findings and Recommendations

Drawing from the conclusions reached in this book, the recommendations below are put forward for consideration in addressing the shortcomings of the regime in Ghana to better afford consumers the appropriate degree of protection. The recommendations will particularly be useful to the ongoing effort to formulate consumer-tailored legislation for the protection of consumers in Ghana. Moreover, the philosophical grounding of the various recommendations expressed in this book might act as reference material to the courts in determining matters that are put before them, especially if the various recommendations below are given a legislative endorsement. In addition, lawyers may also find the basis of the various recommendations, if implemented, practically helpful in seeking to guide their clients or defend them before a court of law. The recommendations are organised into the requirements for the quality obligations of traders, remedies for consumers, and means of enforcement of the rights of consumers respectively below.

8.4.1 Recommendations with Respect to the Requirements for the Quality Obligations of Traders in Ghana

1. Regarding the different standards for the quality of goods in Ghana, the requirements that goods should be non-defective or free from defects under section 13 (1) (a) of the Sale of Goods Act 1962, Act 137 is recommended for adoption as the standard term for the quality requirements of goods in both contract of sale and hire-purchase transactions in Ghana.
2. On the issue of resolving the problem of lack of a definition of what constitutes 'free from defects' or 'non-defective' as the standard term for the quality of goods, it is recommended that what amount to free from defects or non-defective should be what a reasonable person would consider as being free from defects bearing in mind the description of the goods, the price of the goods and other relevant circumstances including public statements about the goods.
3. In terms of addressing the limitation of the scope for the quality of goods, it is submitted that the criterion for the assessment of the quality of goods in Ghana should be extended from latent defects to cover the aspects of quality, including the state and condition[1] of the goods as similarly provided under English law.[2] Unlike English law, however, the criterion for the quality of goods in Ghana should be expressed to include the requirement that the goods meet the technical

[1] The 'state and condition' depicting the quality of the goods is presently provided under section 81 of the Sale of Goods Act, 1962, Act 137, Ghana. With this present proposed reform, state and condition should be classed as an aspect of quality to guide the determination of the quality of goods especially in future legislation.

[2] See Section 9(3), the UK CRA, 2015, See detail discussion in Chap. 3 of this book at para. 3.2.

standards of regulatory institutions in relation to the particular kind of product in question. In effect, the criterion for the assessment of the quality of goods should reflect the goods being free from latent defects, free from minor defects, fit for all their common purpose(s), appearance and finish, safe, and durable. Moreover, unlike the English law, which requires the application of any of the factors to be considered only in appropriate cases, it is recommended that in the case of Ghana, the aspects of quality should be constant requirements in the case of new goods and only vary in instances of second-hand goods.

4. The regime in Ghana was confirmed to be uncertain as regards whether or not the seller will be liable for claims he made about the particular purpose of the goods and that this needs to be resolved to bring clarity to the regime. This book recommends that sellers should be made explicitly liable for statements they make about the particular fitness of goods which induce consumers into buying the goods. This should particularly be given a statutory qualification to make the regime explicitly clear for the guidance of consumers and traders in Ghana. This will simplify the provision and eliminate any possible doubts as to whether the proposal for the introduction of public statement as a relevant factor for the test of quality above, if implemented, applies equally to the doctrine of fitness for the particular purpose the goods are meant to serve as disclosed by the seller. This is particularly useful where the pleading of the consumer is relative to a breach of the fitness requirements of the goods for the particular purpose indicated by the seller.
5. Uncertainties were also found to surround instances in which the consumer purchased the goods for a use that seems to depart from the usual purpose(s) of the goods. To address such idiosyncratic needs of consumers, it is suggested that there should be a clear provision that imposes liability on sellers when in breach for supplying goods which are fit for the consumer's disclosed purpose, whether or not that is the purpose of the goods similar as provided under the English law. This will ensure that consumers are protected when the goods are adapted for a particular purpose, which the seller is aware of, and the goods turn out not to be in conformity with the disclosed purpose(s) of the consumer.

8.4.2 Recommendations with Respect to the Remedies for Consumers in Ghana

1. The remedies available in the regime in Ghana were found to be limited and do not reflect the expectation of consumers particularly when taking into account the problems in the market in Ghana. In order to address this, this book recommends that cures such as repair, replacement, price reduction, and replacement with close substitute goods should be introduced as alternative remedies consumers could rely on for redress. In particular, consumers should be given the right to demand from the seller a repair or replacement of the goods where the

goods they buy are faulty. However, where repair or replacement is not possible or fails to resolve the problem, the consumer should be able to demand a reduction in the price of the goods commensurate to the value of the goods in their faulty state. On the other hand, the consumer should also be able to request the replacement of the faulty goods with close substitute goods, if any, where the other remedies are unavailable or those available are unsatisfactory in practically resolving the consumer problem.

2. The right of the consumer to reject faulty goods was observed to run with termination of the agreement due to lack of alternative remedies after exercising the right to reject. It was therefore submitted that this needed to be resolved to give the consumer the opportunity to continue with the contract if he wishes to do so. In the light of this, it is recommended that the right to reject faulty goods should be made to stand as the principal right with repair, replacement, replacement with a close substitute, price reduction and termination of the contract being the immediate range of options a consumer could resort to after rejection of the goods. Placement of termination of the contract as an alternative cure similar as repair, replacement and price reduction will essentially enable a consumer to make a choice among the cures to keep the contract alive while rejecting the faulty goods.
3. Although the consumer has a right to reject faulty goods under the law in Ghana, the exact time frame during which a buyer could exercise this right demonstrated a serious source of uncertainty. This book therefore contends that this confusion should be clarified with a provision clearly setting out the time period during which a consumer could reject faulty goods. The book specifically recommends that an initial thirty (30) day normal period should be stipulated during which consumers could reject faulty goods along the lines of the English law.[3] The time frame should, however, be made flexible in very limited instances in which the time could be reduced or extended. For example, where the life span of the goods is shorter than the thirty days, then the allowable time should be made the acceptable period for rejection. On the other hand, where the time required to effectively assess the conformity of the goods, which both the seller and the consumer are reasonably aware of, an extended time period could be agreed by the parties. This book suggests that the room for such variations should be given clear legislative attention.
4. Uncertainties may, however, emerge as a result of a repair or replacement being given on account of the goods being defective at first instance. To resolve the possible uncertainty under such instances, it is recommended that the 30-day short-term period should be suspended where a repair or a replacement is requested and then run for seven days or for the unexpired period, whichever is longer as similarly provided under the English law.
5. It was also discovered that there may be situations in which the proposed cures will prove futile. Similarly, it was also noted that in the instant case of 'credence'

[3] For detail discussion see Chap. 6 above at para. 3.1.

and 'experience' goods, defects in them may not easily manifest within the short time period of thirty days. To take care of consumers in such instances, it is submitted that it should be open to consumers to exercise the right of rejection of the goods beyond the initial thirty-day period subject to a reduction of the refund amount to take care of the consumer's use of the goods especially if this is to happen after the six months of the delivery of the goods along the lines of the requirement set out under the English law.[4] As was argued, this will ensure that consumers are not entrapped with faulty goods.

8.4.3 Recommendations on the Means of Enforcement of Consumer Remedies in Ghana

1. On the issue of the cost of litigation as a barrier to consumer redress, it is recommended that the lowest courts should be empowered to be able to make determination of matters based on filed or recorded evidence of the parties where the matter in dispute is *prima facie* obvious. In a further effort to help in mitigating the cost of litigation to consumers in Ghana, it is recommended that an online money claim system should be introduced within the lowest courts in Ghana with consumers being able to make claims online as similarly done under the English law. It is further recommended that the average Ghanaian consumers should be permitted to freely file for small claims but pay the filing fee when the claim is successful under the online claim when introduced.
2. Regarding the issue of the courts being restricted to give their decision based on what the claimant craved for in his statement of particulars, which a lay consumer without legal representation may not properly state, with the likely adverse effect of being deprived of the remedies he would be entitled, it is recommended that the courts should be empowered to award remedies to the consumer, and to strike out unfair terms even if both are not specifically put before the court as similarly contained under the English law.
3. In relation to the monetary jurisdiction of Ghc20,000.00 (about £3000) in the District Court being inadequate to cover essential consumer goods, it is recommended that the monetary limits should be reviewed upwards to ensure that a majority of consumer claims fall into the jurisdiction of the District Courts in Ghana.
4. With the financial burden associated with the court-connected ADR scheme in Ghana, which is of limited assistance to most small claims of consumers, this book recommends the introduction of the ombudsmen services to offer free, impartial and speedy redress services to trader-consumer disputes as similarly established under the English law.

---

[4] See section 24 (8) to (11) of the UK CRA, 2015; See the detail discussion in Chap. 6 of this book, para. 3.1.

5. Customary arbitration was found to be a more accessible alternative forum through which consumer disputes could be resolved. It was also found that the customary arbitrators who are mostly traditional rulers in the various communities in Ghana do not have English literacy and may not easily appreciate the laws on consumer matters. To ensure that they have an idea about the laws so as to better position them in their effort to contribute to resolving disputes between consumers and traders, this book recommends that they are given capacity-building training in the various local dialects about key fundamentals of the laws. It is further suggested that the training should be complemented with radio and television campaigns on the rights of consumers to keep arbitrators, consumers, and traders up-to-date on the requirements of the law on consumer matters.
6. Regarding the doubts about whether the proposed consumer education and awareness creation under the Consumer Protection Policy 2014 includes advice to consumers on their individual consumer issues, this book recommends that personalised advice to consumers on their daily encounters should be clearly incorporated into the forthcoming consumer protection regime to ensure that consumers are able to seek advice on their rights when the need arises as is the case under the English law.

8.5 Recommendation for Future Research

This book was mainly focused on the obligations of traders in supplying quality goods to consumers, remedies where traders are in breach and means of redress for consumers under the law in Ghana. In the course of the study, however, a number of closely related aspects were found to need further exploration to contribute to the advancement of the goals of consumer protection in Ghana. Time and space, however, did not permit their coverage in this book. Further studies in these areas will, therefore, be important to the projection of consumer rights in Ghana. In Chap. 1, in particular, the background outline of the problem of substandard goods in the markets may likely raise issues about product liability for damages or injuries caused to consumers. Whilst this is an important aspect that requires depth analysis, this was not covered in this book. Future studies directed at product liability for damages and injuries suffered by consumers will be helpful in contributing to better shaping the regime in Ghana. One aspect which similarly appears to need further study relates to situations where the seller's quality obligations will not apply in respect of his/her disclosure of known defects and where the buyer had examined the goods before purchase. Further studies that seek to answer questions regarding whether the seller's disclosure of defects and the consumer's examination of the goods could resolve the information imbalances between the trader and the consumer could be helpful. Another important aspect which this book has not addressed, but which is crucial to the cause of advancing the goals of consumers, is the mandate of regulatory institutions in respect of controlling the entry, distribution and sale of substandard goods in the markets in Ghana. Future studies on the obligations of regulatory institutions to fight the problems of substandard goods in the Ghanaian markets will be helpful in projecting consumers' interests in Ghana. Equally important, but which the scope of this book could not cover, is the issue of regulatory connected civil remedies for consumers in respect of goods they implicate which consumers have already bought. A future study will be helpful to contribute to the possibility of affording consumers with enhanced consumer civil remedies as an added advancement of the goals of consumer law in Ghana.

Table of Case Law

Ghana

Ababio and Another v. Adusei [2018] GHASC 19, CA, NO. J4/19/2014
AC International Ltd v Edlund Mining Ltd [2004] HI/176/2004/GHACA6
Adjetey Agbosu v Kotey [2003/04] 1 SCGLR 420
Agbedor and Another v Yeboa [1981] GLR 769
Akati v Nartey [1980] GLR 218
Akunor v Okan [19771 GLR 173
Ambrose Dotse Klah v Phoenix Insurance Co. [30th May 2012] CA, J4/19/2011
Andreas Bschor GMBH & Co. KG v Birim Wood Complex Ltd and Birim Timbers Ltd [2016] CA. No. J4/9/2015
Antwi and Another v Raman and Others [1992] 1 GLR 253
Asano v Taku & Another [1973] 2 GLR 312
Attorney General v Faroe Atlantic Co. Ltd [2005 – 2006] SCGLR 271
Bartholomiew & Co. Ltd. v Adu-Gyamfi, [1962] 2 GLR 62
Budu II v Caesar [1959] GLR 410
Continental Plastics Engineering Co. Ltd. v IMC Industries – Technik GMBH [2009] SCGLR 298
Cubagee v Asare and Others (2018) GHASC, C.A. J6/04/2017
De Simone Ltd v Olam Ghana Ltd (2018) NO. J4/03/2018
Dove v Wuta offei [1966] GLR 299
Frafra v Boakye [1976] 2 GLR 332
G. A. Sarpong & Co. v Silver Star Auto Ltd [2014] SCGLR; [2014] 4 GMJ
G. A. Sarpong& Co. v Silver Star Auto Ltd [2010] Suit OCC10/2009
Georgia Hotel Ltd v Silver Star [2012] 2 SCGLR
Ghana Muslim Representative Council v Salifu [1975] 2 GLR 246
Glencore A. G. v Volta Aluminium Co. Ltd [2015] CA, No. J4/40/2013
IFS Financial Services Limited v Jonathan Mensah & Stanley Owusu [unreported] Suit no GJ563/2017

N. Yidana, *Consumer Law and Policy on Faulty Goods*, Ius Gentium: Comparative Perspectives on Law and Justice 134,
https://doi.org/10.1007/978-3-032-08700-3

Japan Motors Co. Ltd. v Randolph Motors Ltd [1982-83] GLR 536
Kpeglo v SCOA Motors [1962] 2 GLR 82
Kwabena Ofori Addo v Hidalgo Energy & Julian Admoako Gymah [unreported] No.AC/198/2015
Madam Adwoa Frema v Abusuapanin Sarfo Boakye [2014] C.A. No. H1/59/2013
Mansa and Others v Adutwumwaa and Others [2012] CA No. J4/25/2012
Mante v Botwe [1989/90] 1 GLR 479
Manu v Kontre [1965] 375
Marian Awuni v West African Examination Council [21st July 2004], No. 9/2003
Mensah v Appiah and Another [1964] GLR 248
Nartey-Tokoli and Others v Volta Aluminium Co. Ltd [1989-90] 2 GLR 341
New Lucky Electrical Ltd. v Startrack Int. Ghana Ltd and Isaac Acquah [2010] Suit No. OCC 49/08
Osei Kwaku v Opanin Kofi Marfo and Another [2013] CA H1/34/2013
Pyne & Associates V African Motors [2017] GHSC CA. No. J4/38/2013
Republic v High Court (Comm Division, Accra) Exparte Chacem Ltd [2018] GHASC No. 34
Robin Hood Mills Ltd and Another v Farah [1963] 2 GLR 149
Rockson v Armah [1975] 2 GLR 116
Royal Ducth Airlines (KLM) and Another v Farmex Ltd [1989-90] 2 GLR 682
Sam Jonah v Richmond Aggrey and others [19th July 2013] C.A. No. J4/10/2013
Security Bank Ltd. v CBAM Services Inc [2007-2008] 2 SCGLR 894
West Africab Bakery v Mifzah [1972] 1 GLR 78
Yirenkyi v Tormekpey [1987-88] 1 GLR 533 CA
Yirenkyi v Tormekpey (1987-88) 1 GLR 533
Young Trading Agencies v Staveley and Co. Ltd [1977] 1GLR 123

English Case Law

Adam v Moneybarn No.1 Ltd[2025] SC DUM 6, [2025] 2 WLUK 206, [2025] G.W.D. 8-69
Armstrong v Jackson [1917] 2 K.B. 822
Ashington Piggeries Ltd and Another v Christopher Hill Ltd [1972] AC 441
Balmoral Group Ltd v Borealis (UK) Ltd [2006] EWHC 1900 (Comm) [2006] 2 Lloyd's Rep. 629
Bartlett v Sidney Marcus [1965] 1 WLR 1013
Bristol Tramsway v Fiat Motors Ltd [1910] 2 KB 831
Britvic Soft Drinks v Messer UK Ltd [2002] EWCA Civ 548; [2002] 2 All ER Comm 321 (CA)
BSS Group Plc v Makers (UK) Limited (t/a Allied Services) [2011] EWCA Civ 809; [2011] WL 2747641
Cammell Laird & Co. Ltd. v Manganese Bronze and Brass Co Ltd [1934] HL AC 402
Darren Egan v Motor Services (Bath) Ltd [2007] EWCA Civ 1002; [2008] 1 WLR 1589
Davies v Sumner [1984] 3 All ER 831
Griffiths v Peter Conway Ltd [1939] 1 AII ER 685

Henry Kendall & Sons (a firm) v William Lillico & Sons Ltd and Others [1969] 2 AC 31
Jewson Ltd v Kelly [2003] EWCA Civ 1030; [2004] 1 Lloyd's Rep. 505; [2004] 1 C.L.C. 87; [2004] B.L.R. 31
Jones v Bright [1829] 130 ER 1167
Jones v Just [1868] LR 3 QB 197
Kynaston-Mainwaring v GVE London Ltd, 2022 WL 10712475 (2022)
Kwei Tek Chao v British Traders and Shippers Ltd [1954] 2 Q.B. 459
Lamarra v Capital Bank plc [2006] CSIH 49; [2007] SC 95
Long v Lloyd [1958] 1 W.L.R. 753
Lowe v W Machell Joinery Ltd [2011] EWCA Civ 794; [2012] 1 All E.R. (Comm) 153; [2011] B.L.R. 591; 138 Con. L.R. 48; [2011] N.P.C. 72
Lutton v Saville Tractors (Belfast) Ltd. [1986] 12 NIJB 1
Macdonald v Pollock [2012] CSIH 12; [2012] 1 Lloyd's Rep. 425; [2013] S.C. 22; [2012] S.L.T. 462; [2012] G.W.D. 8-162
Medivance Instruments Ltd. v Gaslane Pipework Services Ltd (2) Vulcana Gas Appliances Ltd [2002] (unreported)
Peebles v Rembrand Builders Merchants Ltd [2017] SC DUN 28; [2017] WL 01831372
Preist v Last (1903) 2KB 148
R & B Customs Brokers Co Ltd v United Dominions Trust Ltd [1998] WLR 321
Richford v Parks of Hamilton (Townhead Garage) Ltd [2012] GWD 24
Slater v Finning (1997) Ac 473
Stevenson v Rogers [1999] QB 1028
Thain v Anniesland Trade Centre [1997] SLT [Sh Ct] 102
Thornett and Febr v Bears and Son [1919] 1KB 486
Ward v MGM Marine Ltd [2012] EWHC 4093 QB

CJEU
Case C-168/05 Mostaza Claro [2006] ECRI-10421
Joined Cases C-65/09 and C-87/09 *Gebr Weber GmbH v Wittmer Putz v Medianess Electronics GmbH* [2011] WLR (D) 210
Case C-404/06 *Quelle AG v Bundesverba'nd der Verbraucherzentralen und Verbraucherverbände* [2008] ECR 1-2685

Tables of Legislation/Regulations/Rules

Ghana

Alternative Dispute Resolution Act 2010 Act 798
Civil Proceedings (Fees and Allowances) (Amendment) Rules 2014
Constitution of the fourth Republic of Ghana 1992
District Court Rules 2009 C. I. 59
High Court and County Court Jurisdiction Order 1991
Intestate Succession Act, 1985
Legal Aid Scheme Act 1997
National Commission for Civic Education Act 1993 Act 452
Courts Act 1993 Act 459
High Court (Civil Procedure) Rules, 2004 C. I. 47
Sale of Goods Act 1962 Act 137
Hire-purchase Decree, NRCD 292
Court-connected Alternative Disputes Resolution (ADR) Manual 2010

UK

Alternative Dispute Resolution for Consumer Disputes (Competent Authorities and Information) Regulations 2015 S.I. 2015/542 implementing Directive 2013/11/EU on Alternative Dispute Resolution for Consumer Disputes
Alternative Dispute Resolution for Consumer Disputes (Competent Authorities) Regulations 2015 S.I. 2015/542
Civil Procedure Rules (as amended) - Rules and Directions 1998
Consumer Rights Act 2015 c15
CPR (amendments)- Small Claims Track
EU (Withdrawal) Act, 2018, Chapter 16
Sale and Supply of Goods Act 1994
Sale and Supply of Goods Act, 1994, c. 35
Sale of Goods Act 1979

N. Yidana, *Consumer Law and Policy on Faulty Goods*, Ius Gentium: Comparative Perspectives on Law and Justice 134,
https://doi.org/10.1007/978-3-032-08700-3

Sale of Goods Act, 1979, c. 54
Sale of Goods and Services Act 1982, c. 29
Supply of Goods (Implied Terms) Act 1973, c. 13
Sale and Supply of Goods to Consumers Regulation 2002 implementing the EC Directive 1999/44/EC on Certain Aspect of the Sale of Consumer Goods and Associated Guarantees, (25th May, 1999)
Sale and Supply of Goods to Consumers Regulations 2002 implementing DIRECTIVE 1999/44/EC OF THE EUROPEAN PARLIAMENT AND OF THE COUNCIL of 25 May 1999 on Certain Aspects of the Sale of Consumer Goods and Associated Guarantees
Unfair Contract Terms Act 1977 (UCTA)

Other Jurisdictions
Consumer Protection Act, No. 46, 2012 as revised, 2016, Kenya
Consumer Protection Act, No. 68, 2008, South Africa
Competition and Consumer Protection Act, No. 29, 2014, Irish
Trade Practice Amendment (Australian Consumer Law) Act (No. 2) 2010, Australia
Consumer Protection, CH 337C – 1

MIX
Papier aus verantwortungsvollen Quellen
Paper from responsible sources
FSC® C105338

If you have any concerns about our products,
you can contact us on
ProductSafety@springernature.com

In case Publisher is established outside the EU,
the EU authorized representative is:
Springer Nature Customer Service Center GmbH
Europaplatz 3, 69115 Heidelberg, Germany

Printed by Libri Plureos GmbH
in Hamburg, Germany